reader to review.

¶ The editors are John Lyons, Professor of
General Linguistics, and Roger Wales, Lec-
turer in the Department of Psychology, both
of the University of Edinburgh.

EDINBURGH UNIVERSITY PRESS
22 George Square, Edinburgh 8
North American Agent
ALDINE PUBLISHING COMPANY
320 West Adams Street, Chicago 60606

42s. net.

PSYCHOLINGUISTICS PAPERS

Psycholinguistics Papers

The Proceedings of
the 1966 Edinburgh Conference

edited by
J. Lyons
and R. J. Wales

Edinburgh
University Press

© 1966
EDINBURGH UNIVERSITY PRESS
22 George Square, Edinburgh 8
North America
Aldine Publishing Company
320 West Adams Street, Chicago 5
Australia and New Zealand
Hodder & Stoughton Ltd.
Africa, Oxford University Press
India, P.C.Manaktala & Sons
Far East, M.Graham Brash & Son

Printed in Great Britain
by Robert Cunningham & Sons Ltd.
Longbank Works, Alva

The Edinburgh University Conference on Psycholinguistics (18-20 March 1966) was one of a series of conferences and seminars in important inter-disciplinary fields being sponsored by the Research Board of the Faculty of Social Sciences, with Professor T. Burns as Chairman and Dr M. W. Flinn as Secretary.

The papers for the Psycholinguistics Conference were distributed to participants in advance of the meetings. Each session was devoted to one of the papers and began with formal, prepared comments by the invited discussants, followed by general discussion from the floor. The order in which the papers are printed here reflects the order in which they were discussed at the Conference. Each paper is followed by the comments of the discussants and a summary, edited version of the general discussion which took place. The following contributors were prevented by last-minute difficulties from attending the Conference: Mrs Ursula Bellugi, Dr A. L. Blumenthal, Dr J. J. Fodor and Dr E. J. Klima.

As editors of the proceedings of the Conference, our responsibility has been limited to the production of the present volume. The most difficult task, as always, has been the reporting of the general discussions. We were greatly helped in this work by Robin Campbell and Brian Young, who made notes throughout the sessions and subsequently transcribed the tape-recordings for us. A number of participants kindly supplied us with a written version of their comments immediately after the Conference ended. We are very grateful to them for assisting us in this way. Since we ourselves have arranged, condensed and, on occasion, paraphrased the record of the general discussion in order to achieve greater coherence and homogeneity of style, we alone are responsible for any inconsistencies or imperfections in these sections of the proceedings.

We must also express our gratitude to the authors and formal discussants who let us have their papers for publication within two weeks of the end of the Conference and authorized us to correct proofs on their behalf, collate references and produce a name index for the volume. We trust that we have not abused the confidence they placed in us.

We should also like to record our appreciation to Edinburgh University Press for the great assistance we received in the preparation of this volume for printing and to Robert Cunningham and Sons, the printers, for arrangements they made to ensure its rapid publication. Finally, we must thank Miss Sandra Morton, of the Department of General Linguistics, and the typists at the Social Sciences Research Centre for all the additional work they have done in connexion with the Conference and the publication of the proceedings.

J. L.   R. J. W.

CONTENTS

PARTICIPANTS AND VISITORS

Ursula Bellugi, Department of Social Relations, Harvard University
A. L. Blumenthal, Center for Cognitive Studies, Harvard University
L. Jonathan Cohen, Queens College, University of Oxford
Margaret Donaldson, Department of Psychology,
    University of Edinburgh
Professor J. A. Fodor, Department of Psychology,
    Massachusetts Institute of Technology
Colin Fraser, Department of Psychology, University of Birmingham
M. Garrett, Department of Psychology,
    Massachusetts Institute of Technology
Renira Huxley, Department of English Language,
    University of Edinburgh
A. R. Jonckheere, Department of Psychology,
    University College, London
Professor E. S. Klima, Department of Humanities,
    Massachusetts Institute of Technology
J. C. Marshall, M. R. C. Psycholinguistics Unit, Oxford
Professor D. G. McNeill, Center for Research in Language and
    Language Behavior, University of Michigan
J. Morton, M. R. C. Applied Psychology Research Unit, Cambridge
Professor R. C. Oldfield, Institute of Experimental Psychology,
    University of Oxford
Professor N. S. Sutherland, Department of Experimental Psychology,
    University of Sussex
J. P. Thorne, Department of English Language,
    University of Edinburgh
R. J. Wales, Department of Psychology, University of Edinburgh

Professor D. Abercrombie, Edinburgh ; B. Bett, Strathclyde ; Professor
T. Burns, Edinburgh ; R. M. Burstall, Edinburgh ; Ruth Clark,
Edinburgh ; D. J. Dakin, Edinburgh ; R. M. W. Dixon, London ;
D. Gerver, Oxford ; R. Goodwin, London ; Julie Greene, London ;
M. P. Haggard, Cambridge ; W. Huggins, London ; T. T. S. Ingram,
Edinburgh ; P. N. Johnson-Laird, London ; Sheila Jones, London ;
G. M. Kiss, London ; W. Lawrence, Edinburgh ; R. Levy, London ; Kate
Loewenthal, London ; Professor J. Lyons, Edinburgh ; Professor
A. McIntosh, Edinburgh ; J. Macnamara, Dublin ; Freda Newcombe,
Oxford ; Professor (Emeritus) J. Orr, Edinburgh ; Jess Reid, Edinburgh ;
B. Semeonoff, Edinburgh ; P. van Buren, Edinburgh ; Professor
W. H. Walsh, Edinburgh ; Y. Wilks, Cambridge ; A. Wingfield, Oxford.

First Session

J. P. Thorne
On hearing sentences

with prepared comments by
John Morton and
R. C. Oldfield

Chairman J. Lyons

Hearing a word in a particular sense.
How queer that there should be such a thing!
Wittgenstein
1953:144

J. P. Thorne

Suppose you and I are listening to someone speaking in a language which you understand but which I do not.[1] Obviously in one sense we hear exactly the same thing. Assuming that neither of us suffers from defects of the ear, nervous system, or brain, the processes of transmission of waves from the air to the fluids of the cochlea, the stimulation of the organ of Corti and subsequently of the neurons of the acoustic nerve will, presumably, be more or less identical. The situation is interesting because it is also possible to maintain that we hear something different. The use of the word 'hear', like the use of the word 'see', is systematically ambiguous.

'Hearing sentences' or 'hearing words' is an obvious way of describing what happens when we listen to someone speaking in a language we understand. It also provides a useful way of distinguishing between listening to someone speaking a language I understand and listening to someone speaking a language which I do not understand. Listening to someone speaking English I hear an utterance as a sentence or sentences. Listening to someone speaking almost any other language, I do not, or rather I cannot, hear it as a sentence or as a non-sentence. I cannot hear it as a well-formed sentence or a badly-formed sentence. In the absence of extra-linguistic clues I cannot hear that the speaker has come to the end of a sentence or that he has broken off in the middle.

The fact that 'hearing sentences' is an obvious description, even for people who are not linguists, of what happens when we listen to a language we understand is an interesting one (and of some relevance to the ensuing discussion) because 'sentence' and 'word' are abstract terms. They relate to statements of the structure of utterances. To understand an utterance is in some sense to know its structure. I cannot understand the utterance *The cat sat on the mat* and not know, for example, that *cat* is a structural element in a sense that *catsa* is not, that *the* occurs twice in it, and that *the* and *cat* go together in a way that *on* and *the* do not. In addition, the elements we call 'words' have an internal structure. This, too, I must know if I am to understand the utterance. I cannot understand the word *cat* and not know that part of its structure is the element 'animate'—something which distinguishes it from the word *mat* (for a

1. The first draft of this paper was written while the author was at the Center for Cognitive Studies, Harvard University, and was supported (in part) by a contract from the National Science Foundation, No. GS-192. The author wishes to acknowledge the benefit he has received from many discussions on this topic with Hamish Dewar.

3

discussion of these semantic categories, cf. Katz & Postal, 1964). I cannot understand utterances that are deficient in structure. I cannot understand *Up bicycle a the quickly* because it displays no structure above the word level. I cannot understand *I saw the thunk* because I do not know the structure of *thunk*.

It is a basic postulate of linguistics that the structural elements in language and the relationships between them are finite. On the other hand, since there is no limit on the number of utterances that can be produced in a natural language, these are exemplified in an infinite number of cases. The problem of formulating a description of the structure of a language therefore resolves itself into the problem of formulating a statement which is itself finite but which will cover an infinite number of cases. This is the problem which Chomsky solved by proposing that a grammar should take the form of an effectively computable set of rules for generating sentences. A statement of this kind— a generative grammar—will predict for any utterance in that language the structure the native speaker will perceive in it (cf. Katz, 1964). Such a statement, it can be claimed, will reflect the native speaker's knowledge of his language (his competence); a knowledge that goes far beyond a knowledge of the structure of all the utterances he has ever heard or will ever hear.

The description of hearing someone speaking in a language we understand as 'hearing sentences', therefore, seems not only natural but fairly illuminating. It emphasizes the point that understanding an utterance involves in some way a knowledge of linguistic structure. It also suggests an explanation of what happens when we listen together to a language which you understand but which I do not. Clearly you possess information which I do not. Equally clearly, it seems, you are able in some way to make use of this information. The difficulties start when we try to clarify this last statement. A possible account is that we receive the same acoustic data and that you (but not I) are able to employ your linguistic knowledge to interpret it—that is assign a structure to it. On consideration this account turns out to be misleading.

A recent experiment of Lieberman's shows this very clearly. Lieberman (1965) presented to linguists synthesized utterances from which all syntactic and semantic information had been removed (they were reduced to a series of uniform [a]'s) but which preserved the fundamental frequencies and envelope amplitudes of actual recorded utterances. The linguists produced transcriptions for these synthesized utterances containing pitch contours which followed accurately the contours of the fundamental frequency and which marked only two degrees of stress.

4

Listening to the actual utterances upon which the synthesized utterances were based, they produced transcriptions with pitch contours which bore little resemblance to the contours of the fundamental frequency and which marked four degrees of stress. Presumably one would achieve similar results by presenting utterances to two linguists in a language which one understood and the other did not.

It seems clear from the results of this experiment, therefore, that some of the features that we 'hear' when listening to speech are not present in the acoustic signal but are supplied by ourselves—the hearers—and that the controlling factor in this is awareness of structure. This finding runs quite contrary to the idea that understanding an utterance can be described as a two-stage process of interpreting what we hear. Instead of the recognition of structure being the result of applying an interpretation to what we hear, it seems that, in part at least, what we hear is a result of the recognition of structure.

Other, quite commonplace, observations also stand in the way of any simple equation of understanding with interpreting. Consider an ambiguous utterance: *I dislike playing cards*, for example. Encouraged to take it as an example of an ambiguous utterance (which means, in particular, not being given any context for it), you will hear it first as one sentence, then as another—suddenly. Did you interpret it one way and then in another? Did you decide to interpret it one way and then the other? Could you choose which way you interpreted it first? If I said to you *I don't mind playing chess. I dislike playing cards* would there be any doubt as to what you would hear?

The situation is analogous to that in which one looks at an ambiguous figure like the Necker cube or Wittgenstein's 'duck-rabbit'. First one sees it one way and then the other—suddenly. When the figure is placed in a context of objects seen from above, or rabbits, I see only a cube looked at from above, only a rabbit. 'Do I really see something different each time or do I only interpret what I see in a different way?' (Wittgenstein, 1953; 212; cf. Hanson, 1965: 4-30.)

Lashley (1951), in a well-known experiment, after priming his audience with the phrase *rapid writing*, read them the sentence *Rapid righting with his uninjured hand saved from loss the contents of the capsized canoe*. Is it reasonable to argue that the subjects of this experiment kept two sentences before them up to a certain point (perhaps until they heard *capsized*) and then abandoned one as a possible interpretation? Is it any more reasonable to argue that they began to organize the utterance one way and then abandoned this organization, reinterpreting what had already been heard?

5

I hold my hand over a drawing which you suppose to be a drawing of a duck. Slowly I move my hand away. At a certain point you see that I have added whiskers to it. Is it more accurate to say that you reinterpret the part you have already seen as part of a rabbit, or that you suddenly see that the drawing is a drawing of a rabbit?

In every natural language there are an infinite number of sentences which under normal circumstances cannot be heard. The sentence *The mat adores fish on Fridays* is an example in English. Spoken normally it will always be heard as *The matadors fish on Fridays*. (Notice that, on the other hand, I do not under normal circumstances hear the word *matadors* in *The cat on the mat adores fish on Fridays*.) If I can hear that an utterance is a well-formed sentence I simply cannot also hear it as another badly-formed sentence. I cannot, for example, hear *Snow fell* as an imperative or *Bring water* as a declarative.

Now it is part of the native speaker's knowledge of English that the verb *adore* takes an animate subject. A complete English grammar would have to contain a rule to this effect. Did you use that rule when you listened to the utterance *The mat adores fish on Fridays*? Were you at some point constructing an interpretation for this utterance beginning *the mat* which you abandoned when you got to *adores*? If hearing that an utterance is a sentence is the result of interpreting what we hear, that is of imposing an interpretation upon it by applying our knowledge of linguistic structure, how are we to explain that in circumstances like those just cited we always produce the 'right' interpretation? How do we explain this except by postulating a process which excludes the 'wrong' interpretations which arise from the application of information that is correct but irrelevant in the particular case? This then shifts the problem to finding an answer to the question 'How does such a process operate?'

Considerations of this kind underline the difficulties associated with analysis-by-synthesis models (Matthews, 1962; Halle & Stevens, 1964).[1] Analysis-by-synthesis undoubtedly provides the most interesting account of how we understand utterances so far proposed. Indeed, since it is the only performance model to take account of the fact that understanding an utterance involves knowledge of linguistic structure, it is perhaps the only model worthy of serious attention. Analysis-by-synthesis finds its place in one of the main traditions of perceptual theories, a tradition which includes the 'unconscious inference' theory

1. Matthews limits his discussion to analysis-by-synthesis as a model for an automatic syntactic analyser. As a model for human behaviour it is discussed by Katz & Postal (1964: 166-72).

of Helmholtz and the more recent 'hypothesis' theory of Bruner (1951) and Postman (1951). By incorporating the notion of a grammar (that is, a finite statement covering an infinite number of cases), it overcomes one of the main objections to these general theories: that by their account a human being has to accommodate an infinite amount of information. The basic postulate of analysis-by-synthesis is that understanding an utterance results from the hearer constructing an internal sentence to match it. The rules of the grammar that characterize our linguistic knowledge are here taken as instructions for forming utterances.

Matthews (1962) has calculated that a computer programme implementing the rules of a generative grammar of English set to run at random could take up to 10^{12} seconds (several million years) to produce a particular English sentence of 20 words or less. Clearly such a programme is of no practical value for the mechanical analysis of language until it has 'strategies' built into it to reduce the time it takes to produce a match for a particular input sentence. Equally clearly, without such strategies it is of little interest as a performance model. The interest of analysis-by-synthesis models depends entirely on the extent to which the strategies they employ provide an answer to the question 'How do we use our linguistic knowledge in understanding utterances?' So far the strategies that have been developed which make use of features such as the number of words in the utterance (hence assuming a pre-analysis of the utterance into words) provide no obvious answers to this question.

Perhaps the question is not being asked in the right way. Analysis-by-synthesis runs into the difficulties met by any approach that treats understanding as the application to what is heard of an interpretation formed from a knowledge of linguistic structure. It implies the existence of two processes where there seems to be only one. It separates elements which seem to be inseparable in linguistic perception—hearing from understanding, the acoustic data from its organization. The difference between listening to a language one knows and a language one does not know cannot be attributed to two operations taking place in the first instance and only one in the second.

The dichotomy is in part the result of an attempt to use both 'hear' and 'interpret' in their usual sense in a context where this is not appropriate. Berkeley (1843: §li) observed that when we listen to a language we understand it as if we are hardly aware of the sound of the utterances at all: 'No sooner do we hear the words of a familiar language pronounced in our ears, but the ideas corresponding thereto present themselves to our mind; in the very same instant the sound and the meaning enter the understanding; so closely are they united that it is not in our power to keep out the one, except we exclude the other also. We even act in all respects as if we heard the very thoughts themselves.' We are inclined to describe other languages and accents using terms like 'harsh' or 'melodious', but not our own. Distracted from what is being said to us we subsequently say 'I have only just heard what you said.' When we induce verbal satiation in ourselves, we say that the word we have been repeating over and over again has become a 'meaningless noise'. On the other hand (and more striking still) it seems an accurate account of the experience to say that we 'hear' what we 'say' in our heads. These considerations indicate that in describing the experience of listening to speech we cannot, in fact, use the word 'hear' in its ordinary sense.

One would not take seriously someone listening to sentences under noisy conditions who said 'I know it is a sentence but I don't know if it is an English sentence.' Asked to listen to utterances under noisy conditions, subjects will report hearing sentences other than those they were given, sometimes they will report hearing sentences where there were no utterances at all, but only very rarely will they report hearing ungrammatical sentences. On the other hand we frequently hear badly-formed sentences as well-formed. Asked to copy sentences containing grammatical errors, subjects will often quite unintentionally correct them. We say that we do not 'see' the typographical mistakes that we fail to correct when checking proofs. These considerations indicate that in describing what happens when we listen to speech we cannot in fact use the word 'interpret' in its usual sense.

Discussing visual experience, Wittgenstein (1953: 200) comments on the question 'But how is it possible to SEE an object according to an INTERPRETATION' that 'The question represents it as a queer fact; as if something were being forced into a form it did not really fit. But no squeezing, no forcing, took place here.' Wittgenstein's point is that there is in fact nothing strange at all in the account that we see an object according to an interpretation—that 'we interpret it and SEE it as we INTERPRET it' (1951: 193). Asking 'How do we hear that an utterance is a sentence?' also represents the process as queer. A gap is opened up between the utterance and the sentence.

It is not difficult to explain why the idea that understanding an utterance is the result of the hearer using his knowledge of linguistic structure to impose a structure upon what he hears should prove so attractive. The structure of linguistic perception is much more apparent than the structure of other forms of perception—presumably because we use utterances primarily for communication. The commonplace skills of reading and writing demand a fairly explicit application of a knowledge of linguistic structure. This often leads to serious distortion of the objective facts. For example, most people really believe that short silences invariably occur between each word in an utterance.

It is in linguistics that the very concept of structure is most clearly explicated. The tradition of analysing the structure of linguistic events in isolation from their occurrence is a very old one. People have been interested in concepts like 'word', 'sentence', 'noun phrase' and 'subject' for at least two thousand years. Even allowing for the great difference in the ages of the two subjects, it is still the case that there is incomparably more information about the structure of utterances in the average grammar book or dictionary than is to be found about the structure of the visual world in all the books of the Gestalt psychologists put together. Because we can produce such comprehensive and precise statements of our knowledge of linguistic structure it becomes difficult for us not to think of the process of understanding utterances as involving the use of this knowledge. Even more dangerous, it becomes difficult not to think of it actually involving the use of these statements. Hence the perceptual process appears an instantaneous intellectual process. Linguists, in particular, are apt to talk about understanding an utterance as if it were like running through the analysis of an example in a linguistics textbook at top speed. But the tendency to 'over-intellectualize' understanding has not been restricted to linguists. It has been the source of confusion in many philosophical discussions of meaning. Among other things, it has been responsible for the invention of a conscious, voluntary activity called 'meaning a word'.

'There is nothing here of a choice whereby, for example, we might at will think of one arrangement of parts rather than another. Instead the Gestalt laws observed by such phenomenon and the specific structure spontaneously and objectively assumed PRESCRIBE FOR US what we are to recognize "as one thing".' Köhler's (1938: 32) description of the process of visual perception applies equally well to linguistic perception. The psychological reality of linguistic units like WORD and PHRASE recently demonstrated by Fodor & Bever (1965) is not in question. What must be questioned is the psychological reality of linguistic rules. To say that linguistic rules abstractly characterize the native speaker's linguistic knowledge is not to say that he knows these linguistic rules. Linguistic rules specify WHAT we hear (in the same way as Gestalt laws, the factors of proximity, similarity, etc., specify what we see). It does not follow that they must enter into an account of HOW we hear what we hear. The aphasic's disability can be described as the result of a loss of

9

information; its manifestation, however, is not an intellectual failure but loss of mastery of a perceptual technique.[1]

A grammar will provide the most rigorous imaginable series of tests for a performance model; it will specify the results a performance model must give in every case. But the assumption underlying much recent work in psycholinguistics, that the study of the FORM of grammars is the right place to begin the study of performance models, is surely misleading. As long as this assumption is made we are in danger of asking questions to which there are no answers.

Discussion

JOHN MORTON

In discussing Thorne's paper, I find myself at a severe disadvantage. I do not, for example, unlike Wittgenstein, find it queer that there should be such a thing as 'hearing a word in a particular sense' (only that there should be such a sentence as *Hearing a word in a particular sense*), nor do I find it remarkable that our use of the word *hear* is systematically ambiguous (any more than I am surprised to discover that the word *table* is systematically ambiguous). Indeed I would claim that *hear* is no more ambiguous than the average everyday word. It is only when we try to use the word in a technical context that we may be troubled. I cannot tell what Thorne understands by 'the ordinary sense' of the word *hear*. Is it a descriptive word referring to the situation of a person whose ears and auditory cortex are being stimulated or does it refer to some internally-recognized, introspectible event which leads a person to say *I hear*.... If the latter, then we have no need to specify what operations have been performed upon the input in order to use the word, since the nature of the operation will be apparent (in principle) from the continuing phrase. Thus *I heard a sentence* implies that an internal event has occurred which was related (or was supposed by the system to be related) to auditory stimulation and concerning which I have responses available. *I heard a noise* implies exactly the same. In the former case the verbal responses (there may be other relevant responses available but these will not be considered) include a string of words, which a third person would consider to be the 'same' as the original string, and des-

---

1. It is interesting to speculate on the results of performing Fodor and Bever's experiment with aphasics—also with young children. One would guess that in each case the movement of the click would follow a quite different pattern from that observed in the case of normal adults.

criptions of various 'acoustic' parameters such as intonation, stress, voice, quality and the like. The experiment by Lieberman (1965) to which Thorne refers shows that, in some circumstances, such descriptions bear only a vague relationship to physical measures of the stimulus. When we say *I heard a noise* our description of the stimulus is likely to have a closer relation to the actual structure (with qualifications concerning the amount of information to be processed), but, none-the-less, the acoustic stimulus must have undergone complex processing for us to be able to say it was a *noise* and not a *train* or a *bird*. *Noise* is a label as much as *train*. I agree that *hearing a sentence* involves, if you like, monitoring one's own response, but this is incidental to the use of *hear*. St Joan *heard* her voices—the system made an error, though at a higher level.

I do not intend what I have said to be taken as a philosophical criticism of Thorne's paper. I have no philosophical training and, although I appreciate the complexity of the philosophical problems he raises, I cannot pretend to appreciate the problems themselves. My first point is rather that such problems are not relevant to the work of psycholinguists, or, rather, have not been shown to be relevant; and I would be surprised if a discussion of the logical inconsistencies of natural languages furthered our ends.

These ends, I take it, are to understand the mechanisms involved in language behaviour; and the method we use is to attempt to simulate this behaviour with models (of various degrees of specificity), computers, equations, or rules. If what Thorne is saying is that we cannot usefully talk about these mechanisms in natural language, then I agree. There are many psychologists who talk about 'perception' as if it were a single operation that produced some THING which was then reacted to—as if our behaviour was a series of 'double takes'. This leads to such statements as 'The word-frequency effect is all a response effect', or 'Perceptual defense is all in the stimulus', which, not surprisingly, are refuted in the following year by someone who holds the opposite viewpoint. This usage may be akin to Thorne's use of *hear* and *interpret*. However, I would criticize such theories by attempting to point out that the underlying mechanisms could not work. Thorne appears to criticize analysis-by-synthesis mechanisms by reference to linguistic anomaly. He described analysis-by-synthesis as an approach 'which treats UNDERSTANDING as the application to what is HEARD of an INTERPRETATION formed from a knowledge of linguistic structure (p. 7: my emphasis). But the words *understanding, interpretation* and *heard* are his own and do not describe the devices suggested either by Halle & Stevens

11

(1964) or by Matthews (1961). It seems paradoxical to point to Halle & Stevens' flow diagram and say that a particular part of it is (corresponds to, implies) 'hearing', or to say of Matthews' proposals that they constitute 'interpretation', or of either that their aim is 'understanding', and then criticize the models on the basis of these WORDS.

While I agree with Thorne's conclusion that analysis-by-synthesis is unlikely to provide us with a satisfactory performance model, it seems to me that the only valid way of criticizing such models, and the principles behind them, is in terms of the mechanisms: what they cannot do and whether they are necessary. This turns out to be a semantic trap in the end; for although analysis-by-synthesis is initially defined as matching some internally-derived signal or symbol string with an input string, both Halle & Stevens and Matthews (unlike the Haskins group with their 'motor' theory of perception: cf. Liberman, 1957; Liberman, Cooper, Harris & McNeilage, 1962) so modify their proposals in terms of 'preliminary analysis' that a strict 'matching procedure' becomes a very small part of the operation. Indeed, Halle & Stevens (1964) go so far as to say: 'A rough preliminary analysis at each of the stages...may often be all that is required—ambiguities as a result of imprecise analysis at these early stages can be resolved in later stages on the basis of the constraints at the morphological, syntactical, and semantic levels'.

Doubts as to the amount of synthesis in the system arise from considering how there can be a rough preliminary analysis in a system which produces an 'Output Phoneme Sequence' and which utilizes 'generative rules for transforming phoneme sequences into phonetic parameters'. Is the Output Phoneme Sequence likely to be incorrect? Is it likely to give positive but misleading information? It seems much more likely that it will give information of the form 'this phoneme is either /p/ or /b/ or /m/'. Such a statement could be made more economically by specifying, for example, the confirmed distinctive features, leaving the others unspecified. In this case we do not need 'trial phoneme sequences' from which to generate a match, indeed they would be inappropriate; for to produce a statement '/p/, /b/ or /m/' requires that the common features be confirmed in isolation. Thus their strategy system either has to produce for comparison all phonemes in all positions (if the analysis is imprecise, constraints will not be of much use at this stage) and select those with the best (preliminary) fit; or it merely has one attempt and passes information concerning the errors computed in the comparator on to the next stage. This error is supposed to control which phoneme sequence, or set of phonetic parameters, is next presented for comparison. It must therefore contain information about which parameters are

12

NOT satisfied. If the system can do this then we might expect it to be able to test for the presence of each feature (or other element) directly in a manner similar to a picture grammar (cf. Clowes, 1966). Do we make the kinds of recognition error which could be expected from such a system? Is this the nature of the 'rough preliminary analysis', and can this really be called 'analysis-by-synthesis'?

Lest it be thought that I am quibbling over terms, let us consider a later stage in the analysis—we will assume that the morphemes have been recognized (at least partially) and that the surface and deep structure analysis systems are ready to go into action (cf. Matthews, 1961; Thorne, Dewar, Whitfield & Bratley, 1965; Wales & Marshall, in the present volume). Thorne rightly states the basic postulate of analysis-by-synthesis: that 'understanding an utterance results from the hearer constructing a sentence to match it.' But is it any more necessary to match the sentence than it is to match a phoneme sequence which is a part of that sentence? If we consider the existence of constraint at the latter level, we must also consider it at the former level; and if we can show that certain elements of a sentence, without regard to syntactic structure, are sufficient to make it unambiguous, then why go to the trouble of fully matching it? Thus if I say, *Cat sat on mat—Fire spat—Fur flames—Cat withdrew—Quick—Ouch*, no one has any trouble in understanding what I am saying. Equally we can consider the example of the reversible passive given by Wales & Marshall (p. 71), of which, however, I offer a different account. Wales & Marshall suggest that since *The boy...hit...the girl* is semantically well formed, the implications of *was* and *by* are not explored. *The engine...repaired...the mechanic*, on the other hand, being semantically deviant requires, and so receives, a complete syntactic analysis. I would rather say that the string *engine, repaired, mechanic*, being non-ambiguous, will be acceptable to the supra-semantic system without further analysis, the LOGICAL structure of the original sentence (active or passive) being implicit in the string. Given *boy—hit—girl* on the other hand, we need further information in order to obtain a unique result, and so we take longer to process the sentence. Both accounts are compatible with Slobin's (1963) result. We might also note that *house build young* is not in this sense ambiguous, whereas *man —house—build—large* is. So we might expect to find differences of reaction to sentences of the form:

The young man built the house

and

The large man built the house.

13

The understanding of the latter sentence requires some registration of the word order (since the adjective could apply to either noun), whereas the understanding the former does not.

Does the system become an 'Analysis-by-Synthesis System' merely because it can utilize analysis-by-synthesis to iron out residual ambiguity, and is it necesssary to think of the system in any other way? Katz & Postal (1964: 168) go a stage further and say that in the light of their analysis 'the understanding of a sentence...is obtaining its semantic description' (my emphasis). If they wish merely to define the word *understand* in this way, then there is nothing more to be said, but such a definition is not useful. If they are using the word in its more usual (albeit imprecise) sense, then it is clear that 'understanding' is more than this, and 'understanding' is not necessarily all of this; and I am talking here in terms, not of the logic of the system, but in terms of the mechanisms (rules, processes) which operate. Thus when Thorne says 'to understand an utterance is IN SOME SENSE to know its structure' (my emphasis), this is only acceptable as a logical statement. It need not, and should not, be interpreted as saying 'to understand an utterance we always have to apply all the rules we would use in producing the sentence'. Given *house—build—man*, we do, in some sense, know the structure of the underlying sentence structure and can produce it.

If we wish to say that 'understanding' IS something, then it is necessary to go beyond the semantics of the immediate sentence and include some conceptual system which deals with objects, events, actions, and so on.

Compare:

1. 'The understanding of a sentence...IS obtaining its semantic description'.

2. ' "Pol...achi...lumn", he gasped with his last breath, but this was enough for Nigel to know that the Polish waitress who had served him that day with borscht and vodka was in real life the maiden aunt of the engineer who had invented the machine which would revolutionize potato farming and that his mysterious bill for 78 groats was in fact a secret message instructing him to meet them at the base of Nelson's Column in order to foil the plot of their natural enemy.'

That is understanding!

I wish to emphasize that I am not, at the moment, trying to claim that the brain never performs analysis-by-synthesis, merely that it is not necessary to assume it always, or even usually, does. I would accept the possibility of analysis-by-synthesis at the phonetic level under certain conditions (Morton & Broadbent, 1964), and I can see that there may

14

be good reasons for including a synthesis system in a syntax recognizer, though the algorithm for surface structure analysis developed by Thorne, Dewar, Whitfield & Bratley (1965) constitutes a very strong counter-argument.

Having suggested that in hearing sentences we do not necessarily use all the relevant structural rules, I would like to make what may turn out to be a similar suggestion for our production of sentences. In producing a sentence we do not usually start with S, and proceed to derive NP and VP, etc. Instead, some event occurs in what Wales & Marshall call the 'Conceptual Matrix'. Such an event may be of the form of a desire to express a relationship between *house, man,* and *build* (of course we need to develop a precise descriptive terminology for such events). We could express this relationship in either the active or the passive form. Since there is no received performance model of production, I am uncertain as to how deviant my viewpoint is; but part of what I think may happen is that whichever of *house* or *man* is first available as a response (in some speech motor code; cf. Morton, 1964*a, b*), this becomes the surface subject, and the decision as to whether the active or the passive form is used is determined by feedback from the phonological system to the Surface Structure Deriver (cf. Wales & Marshall, in the present volume: p. 55). My reason for suggesting this scheme is that we seem, where possible, to make the surface subject a word which has previously occurred. Thus we would say:

I saw the house. The house was built by the man.

or

I saw the man. The man built the house.

but not:

I saw the house. The man built the house.

or

I saw the man. The house was built by the man.

The situation seems analogous to the observation that when a word has been recognized or produced as a response, it is more likely to be available as a response in the near future (Morton, 1964*c*).

Finally, I would like to try and link together two problems which Thorne raises: ambiguity and the relation between sound and structure. Thorne examines what he calls 'the ambiguous utterance': *I dislike playing cards.* When I started to say this sentence, however, I discovered that

15

I could not say it ambiguously; that, when spoken rather than written, it did not seem ambiguous. I invited a few of my colleagues to try and utter the sentence ambiguously, and then had them judge each other's efforts. The result was that all the observers agreed in their judgments of the sentence. Now, assuming that this little experiment can be repeated, the result should not surprise anyone. If we use structural rules when we produce a sentence, we must use one or other of the two alternative sets of rules in uttering the sentence *I dislike playing cards*. If then certain aspects of structure are, under certain conditions, reflected in the acoustic pattern of the semantic utterance, the result found would follow. I do not mean to say that the structure of an utterance is labelled by a series of physical cues any more than I want to say that the phonological structure of an utterance is labelled by a series of physical cues. The two are merely correlated. Thus Lieberman (1965) showed that when a redundant word was gated out of its containing sentence and was presented in isolation, it was less intelligible than the same word gated out of a non-redundant context. Equally, in a one-subject experiment, people asked to make the *tránsport—transpórt* distinction by saying the word in isolation distinguished between the two very clearly by means of pitch, intensity and duration. When the words were embedded in a sentence, however, the distinction was not apparent in the isolated word.

These observations lead to the proposition that ambiguity, of certain kinds, only occurs within a section of an utterance when the rest of the utterance is sufficient to make that section unambiguous. This seems to imply the same order of feedback in the speech-production system as we have in the recognition system. For Thorne's other examples, these considerations do not seem to apply; and I share his interest and delight in ambiguity. I would like to present two further examples for your consideration. In the course of an experiment, I required subjects to complete sentences, one of which was *He asked the way to the....* I spoke the sentences conversationally, and typical completions for this example were *station, hospital, bus-stop*. One subject replied, and wrote, *time*. Even saying this apparently schizophrenic sentence aloud, most people take some time to make sense out of it, despite (or because of?) the fact that little or no phonological distortion is required. In contrast to this example, the four words *Whale oil bead hammed* are readily restructured, in spite of the fact that the change involves adopting a strong Irish accent.

To conclude, I agree with Thorne that structure must be involved in hearing (though not necessarily in 'hearing'); I agree with his assessment of the dangers of equating competence with performance models;

16

I agree with him that analysis-by-synthesis will not provide an adequate account of speech recognition (although not, on the surface, for the same reason); but I do not really understand the nature of many of his questions, nor what kinds of answers he requires. If I have answered any of his questions accidentally, I will be very happy; but in any event I hope I have been able to make clear the questions which interest me.

R. C. OLDFIELD

I must start by confessing that I find myself in something of a difficulty in commenting on Thorne's admirable and stimulating paper. To me, the ensemble of words like *hear, understand, recognize, interpret* presents so baffling and dimly appreciated a semantic web that any attempt to clear my mind about it would take all day, and would probably leave us all more confused than before. I do not suppose that the minds of other people here, in particular, Thorne's, are nearly as muddled as this, because in the course of discussion they will have sharpened the senses in which they are using these words and, at any rate implicitly or intuitively, will have got a grip on them. I would like first to give only one illustration of the kind of difficulty I find myself in before going on to offer a few comments on Thorne's views so far as I understand them.

Consider the word *interpret*. Thorne makes use of this word in confronting two views as to what happens when two identical physical stimuli provoke, in two different organisms, different internal states or responses: 'this [Lieberman's] finding runs quite contrary to the idea that understanding an utterance can be described as a two-stage process of INTERPRETING what we hear' (p. 5; my emphasis). When I try to think what I understand by the word *interpret*, what do I find? First, I turn to the usage suggested by the image of 'an interpreter', as it might be at a conference between two statesmen with no common tongue, or in a court of law when the defendant is a foreigner. This does not seem to help very much as his function is expressly that of recording as accurately as possible what has already been said in one language into another. He is a mere go-between or 'transducer'. Secondly, I think of the expression 'reading between the lines'. Here we have a situation in which a given stimulus already evokes, in accordance with existing experience or convention, one meaning which is, however, rejected in favour of another in consequence of the recipient being shrewder, more sceptical by nature, or taking into account particular features of the situation or particular special knowledge he possesses. Thus, I might say: 'He is going to the Paris Conference after all', which I INTERPRET to mean (or which, BEING INTERPRETED, means) 'we were right about

17

that blonde at UNESCO'. I don't think this sense of 'interpret' helps us either, for two reasons. The first is, that as in the previous sense, we start with a stimulus that already has a meaning at least for someone. The second is that, unlike the previous sense, the operation of interpreting is complex, and involves the importation of fresh information. This makes it not easily definable. It is, therefore, unsuited to its present role as a simple mechanical link in the definitive model.

A third thing I think of in connection with the meaning of the word 'interpret' is a phrase such as 'INTERPRETING this statute in the light of prevailing feeling as to the relation of the individual to the state...'. Here again something different is involved. The statute already has intention and a structure of definitely-stated, if general, principles. The art of framing good statutes consists, on the one hand, of getting something definite—some bite—into what is laid down and, on the other, of leaving them open to constructive implementation in keeping with future circumstances, which can be foreseen only to the extent that they are bound to be numerous and varied. In this context, I think the sense of 'interpret' is one quite different from that contemplated by Thorne as regards both what is interpreted and the operation itself.

This exhausts for me at the present moment the senses in which the word 'interpret' might be taken, but perhaps it brings us closer to the nature of the difficulty. Either 'interpretation' is an operation neutral as between input or output—a recoding, transducing or translation—or it requires some complex organism, armed with memory, judgment and so forth (in fact something like a human being) to carry it out. I conclude that Thorne's confrontation of the two views is not a realistic one inasmuch as one at least of the two alternatives is not acceptably formulated. Of course he might have used some other word in place of 'interpret', but I suspect he chose that one because many of the alternatives have already been explicated in ways detrimental to Aunt Sally's backbone.

The first comment I would like to make arises out of the following statement: 'A statement of this kind—a generative grammar—will predict for any utterance in that language the structure the native speaker will perceive in it. Such a statement, it can be claimed, will reflect the native speaker's knowledge of his language (his competence)...' (p. 4). Far be it from me to tell linguists their own business, but it seems to me that such a statement could be seriously misleading. Linguistics is an activity in which, by analysis of examples, the abstraction of elements and the formulation of rules or laws, an economical, consistent and rational description of the phenomena, is arrived at. In all this it resembles, and should presumably aspire to the status of, some kinds of natural science. But this by no means implies that it is THIS knowledge we must possess in order to produce and understand utterances. To claim this much would be on a par with claiming that the animal body must possess a textbook knowledge of thermodynamics and cybernetics in order to maintain a stable temperature. Only in the most remote and unprofitable sense can I be said to need a knowledge of statics and dynamics in order to ride a bicycle. Some people with far less knowledge of these subjects than I possess ride much better, and some with far more do not ride as well.

In order to find out how people produce and understand speech we have to set to work to find out all we can about the means by which in fact they do it: about the structure and functions of the mechanisms involved, the relations of these to other, non-linguistic capacities and so forth. One, perhaps not unhopeful, line is to take the results of linguistic science and use them to try and construct working models to simulate the behaviour of an actual living organism. But we must not suppose that what we achieve by this goes any further than what we do when we design a mechanical system to ape, let us say, the visual orientation behaviour of an insect. And we should bear in mind that natural gadgets often steal a march on human science and ingenuity. In saying this I am, perhaps, only re-emphasizing Thorne's own expressed distrust of the kind of view he attributes to linguists who 'in particular, are apt to talk about understanding an utterance as if it were like running through the analysis of an example in a linguistic textbook at top speed' (p. 9).

But what does he fall back on? He seems to be falling back on an appeal, based on introspection or intuition, to a particular, irreducible and unitary character of the experience of understanding an utterance. Thorne supports this with a number of examples, some of which (as he says) show obvious affinity to certain cases of visual perception. In all this I find a danger: once we start appealing to introspection it is very easy to select those instances of experience where the point at issue seems clear cut and irrefutable. We may, for instance, agree that there is some characteristic difference between the experience of hearing a clearly-articulated and sufficiently loud utterance in a language with which we are perfectly conversant and that of similarly hearing an utterance in a language of which we know absolutely nothing. But this is a black-and-white case, on which it is dangerous to base an argument. It is like discussing sensory mechanisms in terms of stimuli so chosen that each always either produces a sensation or does not. If we ARE going to introspect (and I am not sure whether it is wise of us), I will choose two

19

other cases to compare; that of hearing a sentence for the first time in a language I do not understand, and that of hearing the same sentence after having become so familiar with it by repetition that, whether orally or auditorily, I have 'got it by heart'. Once again I seem to detect something irreducibly different between the two cases. The latter experience has, by comparison with the former, something in common with the experience of hearing a sentence in my mother tongue. It is familiar and I perceive it as having a certain kind of structure, although this structure is not one deriving from, and an instance of, the phonology of the language's grammar and syntax. If, however, I hear in the same way, repeatedly, a number of sentences from this language, part of my appreciation of the structure of each will bear a relation to the inherent rules of that language. All this suggests to me that part at least of the peculiarity of hearing a sentence in our own tongue may be due, not only to the fact that we grasp it in a linguistic sense, but also the fact that by reason of knowing, at least partially, what is coming next, we are in a position to become aware of certain aspects of its structure which we could not otherwise experience. In both cases an important difference from the third—that in which we have knowledge neither of the sentence nor of the language in which it is spoken—is the relatively low information-content of the stimulus. In the case of the foreign utterance this arises from our having it by heart; in that of the utterance in our mother tongue from its linguistic redundancy.

Consider another case: hearing an utterance for the first time, in a foreign language with which I am partially familiar, I cannot understand it, although I know the meanings of all the individual words, or can guess from the context at the ones that I don't know. I then listen to that sentence over and over again. Eventually I understand it, in some sense, completely, and get much the same experience as I do in listening to an utterance in my mother tongue. This still applies equally if I have guessed wrongly at the meaning of one or another of the words—which may give me a surprise later on.

Thirdly, there is the case of the patient afflicted with a pure auditory verbal agnosia. Such cases are rare but well attested. A patient, while not suffering from any auditory defect except in respect of language stimuli, and while able to speak spontaneously and understand written material, cannot at all, or only with very great difficulty, understand speech. What is the nature of his experience? Does he discriminate between a meaningless utterance in his mother tongue and an equally meaningless one in a language he never understood at all? As he recovers (Dr Moyra Williams told me of a recent case, the result of a head injury, in which recovery was so rapid as to prevent adequate investigation) at what point can he be said to understand as he did before his illness? The point I have tried to make is that there is in general no clear-cut opposition between the state of mind of 'understanding' an utterance and that of 'not understanding' it and that it is dangerous to confine one's thoughts to rather special cases in which such an opposition may be seen to exist. The existence, in practice, of a rather fuzzy margin between 'understanding' and 'not understanding' an utterance suggests that a number of functional levels are involved in the process, and that, while within certain limits it might be possible to describe each of these separately, they are likely to modify each other's working. Any hope that we might, here and now, be able to give a convincing account in terms of a single jump in one direction from acoustic stimulus to structured meaningful percept is over-optimistic.

Thorne has, I think, hinted that all is not entirely well in the linguistic approach to the problem of how we understand utterances. Being incapable, by reason of my lack of skill in the use of linguistic techniques, of giving any direct help, I would like to try and further the discussion by taking up a different standpoint. This would be, roughly speaking, empirical and, I would like to think, biological—although I shall not try to press this latter pretension.

The linguist is naturally much in love with his subject matter, as I hope we all are, each with his own; and that subject matter shows certain discernible perfections of form and relationship. He tends, therefore, to accept as given, and as the basic norm for explanation of his problems, the most clear-cut, irreproachable exemplars of grammatical structure and relationship. It is rather as if the mid-nineteenth-century student of material systems, both living and inanimate, struck by the beauty and perfection of some naturally-occurring crystals, had decided to seek all his explanations of natural phenomena in terms of their manifest properties. As we now know, with the penetration of scientific advance to levels far below that presented directly to the senses, the crystal idea turned out to be an absolute winner. But not until it had become apparent that the crystals we normally see are the product of the working-out of more general laws in highly special circumstances, and that in other circumstances these same laws tend to produce organization in material systems far less striking from the point of view of simple definable form.

So I want to put the outrageously coarse question 'How far, IN PRACTICE, is grammatical correctness important, as opposed to scholastically commendable, in human communication?' If it turns out that it is really not always so very important after all, we might ask two further ques-

21

tions: 'What is special about the circumstances in which grammatical structure assumes practical importance?' and 'Is it not a *pis aller* to put heavy emphasis on structural features of this kind in devising theories about the hidden mechanisms which are basic to speech and language?'

So far as the first question is concerned, it seems to me that there are quite a few reasons for supposing that grammar is not as vital as all that for much effective verbal communication. In the first place, in inflecting languages, the inflexions are often redundant in the sense that gross mistakes do not for the most part lead to misunderstandings. Wrong genders and false conjugations may provoke smiles, but do not often result in the hearer understanding something specifically different from what the speaker intended to say. Indeed, it might be said that, just as speech is singularly resistant to a wide range of acoustic distortions (albeit that there are cases in which a slight change in the stimulus can provoke the perception of one phoneme in place of another), so also language in general is amazingly invulnerable to grammatical insult, if sometimes it shows an Achilles heel. This is the more so, the more we are concerned with speech as a two-way interaction between individuals —surely a more basic and original use of language than that in which one person alone makes a statement or declaration without the intervention of others. Where there is exchange, obscurities, ambiguities and potential misunderstandings are cleared up *ambulando*.

Again, consider ordinary conversation between linguistically equal people. As is well known, this often consists of an exchange of bits and pieces of verbal stimulus, deplorably deficient in syntactical structure. Just as in visual perception it seems that the eye's function is to sample the environment, in order to keep the brain's picture of the external world refreshed and up-to-date, so the function of these verbal scraps appears to be to keep two trains of thought in tune and in time with one another. I see little reason to suppose in such a case that these INNER trains are verbally encoded and that the verbal clues are shorthand paraphrases of such encoded versions.

To put the matter crudely, I suspect that syntax—at least in those higher flights of refinement which are invoked in much modern linguistic discussion—represents a kind of superstructure on language functions generally, and one as yet incompletely evolved. Elaborate grammatical structure tends to assume practical importance with the development of prolonged one-way communication in replacement of two-way interchange. I suggest that its use and the need of it, is tied up with the development of procedures of formal educational instruction, with the use of written language as an adjunct to, and replacement for, spoken

22

language, and with the speed of what Jackson and Head called propositional speech, of logic, of scientific knowledge and abstract thinking. Viewed in terms of the history of human language, these are relatively recent developments.

I hope you will not suppose me to be suggesting that the structural aspects of language, and the study of them, are not of the greatest importance. The possibility of monologue, which depends on them, has clearly been of vital significance to our social evolution. Without them, there could be no large scale refinement and articulation of the semantic aspect. What I am questioning is whether, in our attempts to find out what is involved in the basic process of understanding speech, too much concern with the elaborations of structure may not be misleading— rather like trying to find out the basic principles of the computer by study of the most sophisticated programming techniques.

I would like to ask our linguists how much progress has been made in analysing the evolution of the structural aspects of language, especially in relation to the different uses to which language has been put as a form of communication; and I would like to suggest to our psychologists that they go more fully into the structural requirements for effective speech communication in the different types of situation in which it is used.

General Discussion

M. Garrett, Sheila Jones, J. C. Marshall, J. Morton, R. C. Oldfield, J. Orr, N. S. Sutherland, J. P. Thorne, R. J. Wales, and Y. Wilks

The main points raised had to do with: (i) the notion of ambiguity and its implication for psycholinguistic research; (ii) the relevance of context and of stress and intonation in the understanding of utterances; (iii) what the linguist, on the one hand, and the Gestalt psychologist, on the other, means by 'structure'; (iv) the notion of redundancy; and (v) the possible parallels between the historical development of languages and the development of linguistic competence in the child.

Garrett pointed out that the latencies for providing an interpretation for ambiguous sentences are greater than for unambiguous sentences, even though the subjects in the experiment might report that they 'saw' only one interpretation; it was not obvious, therefore, that the same mechanisms are involved in the case of both ambiguous and unambiguous sentences. Under the impression that the sentences had been presented orally in the Bever & MacKay experiments referred to by Garrett

(Garrett subsequently corrected this impression: they were presented in written form), Morton suggested that greater latencies were only to be expected in the case of ambiguous sentences where additional information had to be 'processed'—in particular, information about intonational features, which might well be processed by a separate 'mechanism'. Marshall said that Morton's hypothesis presupposed that the sentences had always been given 'a canonical intonation' in the experiments. Sheila Jones raised the question of context in connection with allegedly ambiguous utterances; she also stressed the importance of taking into account the typical functions of different sentence-types, especially imperatives and interrogatives.

Thorne's use of the term 'structure' was challenged by Orr: how could one compare 'the STRUCTURE of utterances' and 'the STRUCTURE of visual experiences'? Thorne said that the term 'structure' was being used as it was used by Gestalt psychologists; and that, just as it was impossible not to believe in the psychological reality of the perceptual units postulated by Gestalt psychologists, so it was impossible not to believe in the psychological reality of linguistic units (cf. the 'click' experiments of Garrett, Bever & Fodor, 1966); what he could not believe in was the psychological reality of linguistic rules. The linguist's rules were statements made about the structure of the language he was describing; they were not instructions how to perform in that language. Wales drew attention to the difficulty encountered by Gestalt psychologists (a difficulty that Thorne might have overlooked): they were forced to postulate some kind of isomorphism between the environment being perceived and what takes place in the brain. Marshall took up this point, referring to Kohler's dualism and the philosophy of emergent properties into which he appeared to be forced at times, and suggested that the notion of 'structural description' developed by linguists might help to solve the Gestalt psychologists' difficulty—it would allow them to preserve their valuable insights about the nature of perception, without committing them to either the rejection of any mechanism at all or the acceptance of a very peculiar kind of mechanism. (Sutherland intervened to 'put the historical record straight': the Gestalt psychologists did not say that experience was isomorphic with the external world, but something quite different—namely, that experience, in particular perceptual experience, was isomorphic with the underlying brain processes.)

Wales thought that much of the discussion of Thorne's paper had been on too general a level: what was the point, for instance, of raising the question of the evolution of language, or of redundancy, unless one had some specific proposals? 'Redundancy' involved quantitative as-

24

sumptions; a description of what was being quantified was still required. Oldfield suggested that there might be some parallelism between the evolutionary development of language-structure and the development of language in the child, on the one hand, and its breakdown in people affected by brain-injuries. As for redundancy: he was not invoking it as an explanation, but merely pointing out that there was redundancy in the case of two different kinds of sentences—sentences in a foreign language learned by rote and predictable sentences in one's native language.

In conclusion, Wilks suggested that whether one referred to the single 'real' process as 'hearing' or 'interpreting' was a matter of taste and that, if Thorne gave no further hint of the quarry he was pursuing, he was doing no more than bringing Wittgenstein's worries before a wider audience.

Second Session

R. J. Wales and J. C. Marshall
The organization of linguistic performance

with prepared comments by
A. L. Blumenthal and
A. R. Jonckheere

Chairman David Abercrombie

R. J. Wales and J. C. Marshall

By way of introduction we must outline some of the theoretical preconceptions which are presupposed by our discussion of models for linguistic performance.

We take it that De Saussure's classic distinction between 'langue' and 'parole' is necessary if any sense is to be made of an area as complex as language functioning. A description of a language, in this sense, is a description of the KNOWLEDGE OF THE LANGUAGE which has been internalized by a mature, idealized 'speaker-listener'. (We place 'speaker-listener' in raised-eyebrow quotes to indicate that it is not necessary theoretically that this entity ever actually speaks or listens but merely that he possesses knowledge of the language which could be—and usually is—expressed by talking, and shown by listening).

The notion of an IDEALIZED 'speaker-listener' is necessary because all actual speakers clearly have limitations—they make mistakes, they become confused. Also their actual linguistic utterances clearly reflect much more than their linguistic knowledge. They reflect, for instance, whether or not the speaker is tired or angry. Also they reflect various constraints concerning non-linguistic knowledge. (No one needs to tell us that 'Black crows are black', except in introductory logic courses.) Linguistic knowledge is thus concerned with regularities in the sense that the ability to make intentional deviations and unintentional errors implies prior knowledge of the correct or standard form. A theory of linguistic knowledge is idealized in the sense that it MUST disregard psychological and pragmatic aspects of actual or potential utterances. The notion of a theory of competence such as we have described is, however, psychological in one sense—in the sense that it purports to be a principled account of the linguistic knowledge of human beings rather than a totally *ad hoc* description of the language. This is necessary, for clearly one could give any number of descriptions of a language. The enterprise only becomes interesting when one attempts to specify why one description should be better than another. A theory of linguistic knowledge attempts to account for our 'intuitions' concerning the language and to 'project' a finite corpus of utterances to a set of rules which describes the infinite range (not merely number) of sentences—most of which never have and never will be uttered. The success, or otherwise, which is attained in pursuing these goals thus enables theories of language (and the descriptions of particular sentences which they imply) to be judged in terms of their descriptive and explanatory adequacy.

29

This discussion then serves to elucidate our notion of theories of linguistic competence.

What, then, is a theory of linguistic performance? It is a theory of how, given a certain linguistic competence, we actually put it to use—realize it, express it. It is also a theory of the limitations of the mechanisms, which enable us to express our linguistic competence. It is not merely the theory of competence with the idealization removed, as has been suggested by Chomsky. For we want to be able to explain NORMAL performance—when the translation from competence to performance is proceeding smoothly—just as much as we want to explain errors and deviations. We would expect a further subdivision of a theory of performance into two aspects: a functional, formal theory expressing the general type of system which subsumes linguistic performance (this theory will be phrased in psychological mentalistic-terminology) and an account of the specific mechanisms which realize the system described by the first component (this theory will be phrased in physiological terminology).

We note that the more careful theoretical psychologists have used distinctions which are roughly analogous to those described above. Thus Lashley states that rats which have learned the STRUCTURE of a maze by running through it can (without further training) also express their knowledge by swimming or rolling through it. Tolman (in like fashion) distinguishes between LEARNING and PERFORMANCE and Hull between HABIT STRENGTH and REACTION POTENTIAL. The further distinction between the functional and the mechanistic aspect of the performance theory is also acknowledged by these authors in the same way as their functional theories are distinguished from the specific physiological mechanism which 'realizes' the function. (Lashley, of course, investigated aspects of the physiology.) Later workers, unfortunately, have often been vaguer about the 'level' of theory they were working in.

One of the central considerations in the study of language has been, and continues to be, the order and relation of items within sequences of intelligible utterances. To put this plainly, in the form Lashley (1951) stated it, the central problem language raises for potential psychological explanation is that of serial order. The problem is that an utterance is not composed simply of a sequence of responses strung together (perhaps under the hypothetical control of a stimulus condition and intraverbal association). The organization which linguistics has typically invoked to account for this state of affairs is that of grammar. In particular this syntactic organization is not something directly represented in any simple way in the physical properties of the utterance (cf. Chomsky,

30

1959), that is we reject the claim of Joos (1954) that 'text signals its own structure'. Our purpose in this part of the paper will be (i) to show the need for an independent specification of the structure; (ii) to illustrate the forms of specification that have been either advanced or assumed, and some of the psychological uses to which these have been put; (iii) to present an attempt at preliminary model building, which might wed the most powerful syntactic description available to a psychological model which might utilize this in behaviour.

The need for independent specification of syntactic structure will become particularly obvious in the discussion and review of various approaches that have characteristically been taken. However, two points may be made at the outset: first, the specification must be INDEPEN-DENT OF REALIZED BEHAVIOUR. Without a stated (or assumed) structural characterization, the argument from temporally contiguous associations between stimuli and responses is invariably circular, and will remain so until stimuli and responses are independently specified— a point tacitly accepted by Meehl (1951). The tautology is perhaps best seen in the typical use of such terms as 'similar' in relation to stimuli and responses (cf. Osgood, 1949). The strongest exponent of the S-R operational approach (cf. Peters, 1951) is Skinner (1938, 1951, 1957). Keller & Schoenfeld (1950), writing in the master's thumbprints, define two stimuli to be similar 'when we made the same sort of response' (p. 124). But as Chomsky (1959) reasonably asks, 'When are responses of the same sort?' Short of an independent structural description of a given state of affairs—of however simple a form—a definition of behavioural relations, when made explicit, reveals tautology of a theoretically un-interesting kind. (Verplanck (1954) in a detailed discussion of the diffi-culties of adequately defining 'stimulus' and 'response' concludes that in Skinner's use of 'stimulus' it is not identifiable independently of the resulting behaviour.) It might be objected, by those who invoke inter-vening variables within some mediational framework, that this form of model would escape the above strictures. However, the only models known to us use, within the mediational network (of whatever kind), terms with the same formal properties as the terminal points, and again tend to invoke realized behaviour as a component in explicit definition (Rozeboom, 1960). This is not of course to deny the intuitive appropri-ateness of such notions as 'similarity'; but it is one thing to assume this as given, and quite another to attempt to characterize the nature of the 'similarity'. Perhaps one of the most important aspects of a structural description is to perform the latter function.

The grammatical structure needs to be specified independently, not only of realized behaviour, but also INDEPENDENTLY OF MEANING; this is the second point. Since language is properly conceived as a system requiring unified description, it will not be claimed that the distinction between syntax and semantics is absolute. Rather it will be evident that there are likely to be strong relations between these components. For this reason, without making the distinction, it might be tempting to ignore the set of problems of one in favour of the other. This approach is inadequate for at least two reasons. First, the problems of syntax and semantics, being at many points different in kind, require to be specified independently BEFORE reference to one another; otherwise one runs the risk of proposing 'solutions' which are artifacts, because one has missed the significance of other aspects of the total linguistic system. (Also as Chomsky, 1957, extensively argued, not to make the distinction results in an inability to specify the relations and distinctions apparent in *Healthy young babies sleep soundly, Colourless green ideas sleep furiously*, and *Ideas green sleep furiously colourless*.) Secondly, the relative independence of initial specifications is required to avoid *post hoc* argument—an unprincipled appeal to semantics to determine some particular problems in syntax, or the converse.

SYNTACTIC COMPETENCE AND PERFORMANCE

This section, for convenience of exposition, will take its primary orientation from the competence models that have been stated or assumed in the process of psychological explanations of aspects of serial order in language. The subdivisions are not meant to be hard and fast, as clearly there will be considerable overlap involved in some of the classifications of material. Our discussion will be as follows:

1. The questions raised for a performance model
2. Associationist models and finite-state languages
3. Phrase structure models
4. Transformational models.

1. *Introductory questions*

It is being assumed here, and has been argued in more or less detail elsewhere (e.g. Chomsky, 1964, 1965; Miller & Chomsky, 1963; Katz, 1964), that no performance model which provides interesting answers to any relevant questions about language will be developed unless it is based upon an appropriate matching competence model. Lashley (1951: 509, 512) concluded that syntactic structure 'is a generalized pattern imposed on specific acts as they occur' and 'that a consideration of the structure of the sentence and other motor sequences will show...that there are behind the overtly expressed sequences, a multiplicity of integrative processes which can only be inferred from the final results of their activity'. The usefulness of a competence model for performance considerations is stated by Chomsky (1959: 56) thus: 'it should be possible to derive from a properly formulated grammar a statement of the integrative processes and generalized patterns imposed on the specific acts that constitute an utterance'. Several of the more important questions about performance explanations are raised and illustrated by an experiment of Miller & Isard (1963). In essence, they studied 'the perceptual consequences of linguistic rules'; that is, with white noise masking, the intelligibility of various strings of words were tested, ranging from (*a*) fully grammatical strings, through (*b*) anomalous (i.e. 'grammatical but semantically deviant' after the pattern of *colourless green ideas sleep furiously*), to (*c*) random ordering of words in strings of (*a*). Rank order for intelligibility of the strings and words within the strings were (*a*), then (*b*), then (*c*). (These findings have much in common with those of Oldfield & Zangwill, 1938.) Some of the general questions raised or implied by Miller & Isard's study are:

1. How do the competence and performance notions 'match'? In particular, does the introduction of the notion of a 'linguistic rule' do violence to the possibility of a 'scientific' explanation? Presumably a great deal of the potential problem here is undercut if it can be shown in principle that competence and performance can be usefully and adequately integrated in the explanation of linguistic behaviour—although we recognize now that perhaps the weasel words are 'adequately integrated'.

2. What are the formal relations between syntactic and semantic considerations? How far, and when, do semantic specifications need to be invoked for explanatory purposes—that is how much of the 'semantics' is in fact in the 'grammar' and vice versa?

3. With the apparent impossibility of obtaining a strong operational definition of 'grammaticalness' (cf. MacClay & Sleator, 1960), how much information is being lost when the student of performance is forced to concern himself with what Chomsky (1965) calls 'acceptability'?

4. What kinds of psychological mechanism and conceptual theorizing are going to be helpful (or misleading) when it comes to explaining performance? What constraints will be needed in order to attain the equivalents of 'descriptive' and 'explanatory' levels of adequacy (Chomsky, 1964)?

33

5. In what ways may competence models be turned into sources of useful performance hypotheses; and what are the appropriate experimental procedures for addressing ourselves to these problems? (Saporta, Blumenthal, Lackowski & Reiff, 1965, show the ease with which experiments may in DESIGN use procedures which do not appropriately distinguish between the alternatives being tested.)

6. The kind of mechanism which could, and perhaps does, instantiate the description provided by the performance model, is yet another question.

We do not have—and believe no one to have—any firm formal answers on any of these issues. However, implicit in our review, discussion, and summary, we hope there will be indications of the directions of possible answers, in greater or lesser detail, to all these points.

2. *Association models*

Association theories have been typically motivated by the problem of reference, rather than that of serial order. In so far as this is of prior relevance to semantics, the associationist contribution is discussed in the appropriate section below. However, in that associationism has generally failed to distinguish and specify grammar and meaning, the form of the argument has to be stated initially, since so much experimentation has utilised the notion of serial order in an associative context, if only to randomize or measure it. Association theories are characterized by a number of notions, notably that mental functions are to be reduced to elementary (neural) events that are co-ordinated (or concatenated) in a typically linear form. Further, the theories utilizing these notions gained, and continue to gain, much of their motivation from an attempt to produce monistic, empirical alternatives to the Cartesian use of 'mind' as an accepted theoretical construct, distinguishing that level of discourse from the physiological mechanism that enshrined it. Within the context of twentieth-century experimental psychology—with the notable exception of Gestalt psychology—associationism has had its historical empirical background translated into operational behaviourism. Behaviourists have repeatedly argued that 'mentalism' and 'vitalism' are scientifically 'soft' and in an attempt to circumvent this conceptually, the head, when hit, has made a noise for one of two reasons: (i) because of the reverberation of passive mediating networks of connections (i.e. various mediation theorists such as Hull, 1939; Jenkins, 1963; Osgood, 1951); (ii) because the head is hollow (Skinner, 1938). In short, associationism is an appeal to the explanatory adequacy of the combination of elementary (mental or behavioural) events through experience. If we can

34

specify sufficiently adequately the conditions of experience, and postulate the mechanism of their combination, the expectancy is that we should be able to explain the changes that will occur in the resulting behaviour. Since the primary requirements are the elements and their combination, and the conditions of experiencing them, and since these are sufficient for descriptive explanation, the argument runs that we are being 'dualistic' and 'unscientific' if we demand also a structured description of the experience itself; to speak of 'experience' is 'mentalistic'. Since the argument against the need to specify the structure of experience has been countered on many sides (e.g. Chomsky, 1964, 1965; Ausubel, 1964; Scheffler, 1864; etc.) and since much of our own argument is aimed to show the inadequacy of simple monistic formulations, let William James (1890) argue the point in his own pungent style:

The 'experience-philosophy' has from time immemorial been the opponent of theological modes of thought. The word experience has a halo of anti-supernaturalism about it; so that if anyone express dis-satisfaction with any function claimed for it, he is liable to be treated as if he could only be animated by loyalty to the catechism, or in some way have the interests of obscurantism at heart. I am entirely certain that, on this ground alone, what I have erelong to say will make this a sealed chapter to many of my readers. 'He denies experience!' they will exclaim, 'denies science; believes the mind created by miracle; is a regular old partisan of innate ideas! That is enough! we'll listen to such antediluvian twaddle no more.' Regrettable as is the loss of readers capable of such wholesale discipleship, I feel that a definite meaning for the word experience is even more important than their company. 'Experience' does not mean every natural, as opposed to every supernatural, cause. It means a particular sort of natural agency, alongside of which other more recondite natural agencies may perfectly well exist.

As a gross over-simplification we might argue that the associationism of Aristotle was concerned with the description of the classifications and relations of natural events, and that the British empiricists were concerned to utilize this approach to description as an explanatory alternative to Cartesian dualism. As probably the best formally explicit account of what an associationist theory might postulate we cite Hartley's (1749) five cases, Hartley being particularly appropriate for the additional reason that his theorizing antedates most of the notions implicit in s-r theory (Fodor, 1964):

Case 1. Let the Sensation A be often associated with each of the Sensations B, C, D, &c. i.e. at certain times with B, at certain other

35

times with C, &c. it is evident...that A, impressed alone, will, at
last, raise b, c, d, &c. all together, i.e. associate them with one
another, provided they belong to different regions of the medullary
Substance; for if any Two, or more, belong to the same Region,
since they cannot exist together in their distinct Forms, A will
raise something intermediate between them.

Case 2. If the Sensations A, B, C, D, &c. be associated together,
according to various Combinations of Twos, or even Threes,
Fours, &c. then will A raise b, c, d &c. also B raise a, c, d, &c....
It may happen indeed,...that A may raise a particular Miniature,
as b, preferably to any of the rest, from its being more associated
with B, from the Novelty of the Impression of B, from a Tendency in the medullary Substance to favour b, &c. and, in like
manner, that b may raise c or d preferably to the rest. However,
all this will be over-ruled, at last by the Recurrency of the Associations; so that any one of the Sensations will excite the Ideas of
the rest, at the same Instant, i.e. associate them together.

Case 3. Let A, B, C, D, &c. represent successive Impressions, it
follows...that A will raise b, c, d, &c. B raise c, d, &c. And though
the Ideas do not, in this Case, rise precisely at the same Instant,
yet they come nearer together than the Sensations themselves did in
their original Impression; so that these Ideas are associated almost
synchronically at last, and successively from the first. The Ideas
come nearer to one another than the Sensations on account of their
diminutive nature, by which all that appertains to them is contracted.
And this seems to be as agreeable to Observation as to Theory.

Case 4. All compound Impressions $A + B + C + D$, &c. after sufficient Repetition leave compound Miniatures $a + b + c + d$, &c.
which recur every now and then from slight Causes, as well such
as depend on Association, as some which are different from it. Now,
in these Recurrencies of compound Miniatures, the Parts are
farther associated, and approach perpetually nearer to each other,
agreeably to what was just now observed; i.e. the Association
becomes perpetually more close and intimate.

Case 5. When the Ideas a, b, c, d, &c. have been sufficiently
associated in any one or more of the foregoing Ways, if we suppose
any single Idea of these, a for Instance, to be raised by the Tendency of the medullary Substance that Way, by the Association
of A with a foreign Sensation or Idea X or x, &c. this idea a, thus
raised, will frequently bring in all the rest, b, c, d, &c. and so
associate all of them together still farther.

36

And, upon the Whole, it may appear to the Reader, that the simple Ideas of Sensation must run into Clusters and Combinations, by Association; and that each of these will, at last, coalesce into one complex Idea, by the Approach and Commixture of the several compounding Parts.

Hartley's formalism makes quite clear how closely related to associationism are finite-state language characterizations (e.g. information theory of the form proposed by Shannon, 1949). As formal theoretical systems for our present purpose, they may be treated together. Their major contributions to theorizing are threefold: (i) they stressed the importance of looking for a mechanism; (ii) they stress the importance of description; (iii) they highlight the need for explanation.

We are clearly a long way towards specifying the mechanism if we can (*a*) fully distinguish all actual or possible regularities in behaviour from all non-regularities, and (*b*) explain how the behaviour is or might be produced in such a way that the descriptive distinctions are maintained. Put simply, the main problem here is that, as native language users, we understand and produce a potentially infinite range of sentences; and at the same time, recognize relationships between some of these. What is needed, therefore, is at least a descriptive procedure which will explicitly distinguish between all sentences and non-sentences within the language, and make formally explicit what are the relationships we recognize (without recourse to subjective introspections, that is, without characterizing one's behaviour and intuitions). Unfortunately association theory (and by the same token, finite-state language descriptions) is inadequate on both points.

(*a*) Chomsky (1955, 1956) has shown that explicit association connections, that is finite-state languages, used as competence models, fail to describe and distinguish all the infinite range of possible sentences available to the native language user. There are three main points here: (i) whilst finite-state grammars may alternate between right- and left-branching to produce nested constructions, they cannot produce co-ordinated ones; (ii) they fail to correctly describe continuously self-embedded sentences as possible within languages; (iii) that whilst any finite but unbounded set of terminal strings may be described, this involves both a large, complex set of *ad hoc* rules and an almost total loss of structural description that correctly describe intuitive relations.

(*b*) Chomsky & Miller (1959) and Miller, Galanter & Pribram (1960) have shown that even as performance models, finite-state descriptions are dramatically inadequate as the basis of a mechanism for learning to use English sentences (to speak, read and recognize) by differential reinforcement, partial or otherwise, of serial associations. Each word in an English sentence carries on average about five bits of information, thus the number of different meaningful sentences twenty words long must be $(2^5)^{20}$ or approximately 10^{30}. Hence it would require in a century a rate of learning of around 10^{10} sentences per second to acquire this repertoire. (It is interesting to note in this regard that much has been made of experimental psychology's claim to be a science in terms of its methods of measurement. It would seem that this was one attraction of information theory and its (continued) use with language materials.)

A further problem for explanation using association as a base, is what Rock (1961) has called the Hoffding function (1897). Essentially it breaks down into two aspects, both of which have to do with the learning of an association between A – B. To ascertain whether the association is formed we have to present A to see if it elicits the appropriate response B. Having presented A_1 in the context of B_1, what properties of A_2 are recognized as being similar to A_1 when presented subsequently, which enable the possible associative link to be utilized? Secondly, rather than one link there must of necessity be at least three in the formation of the SIMPLEST association.

$$A - B$$
$$| \quad |$$
$$a - b$$

Thus, if the response B is not elicited, it is never clear which of the bonds has not been brought above threshold. A similar argument is proposed by Hebb (1949).

Jenkins & Palermo (1964: 145), in a review which recognizes the structural aspect of language, address themselves to explaining this in mediational terms. They summarize the problem as follows: 'Higher order regularities make it all the more necessary that psychologists deal with phrase-structure grammar seriously and attempt to explicate two problems: (a) how do verbal utterances become members of classes such as 'noun-phrase' and 'verb-phrase' (especially when the speaker may not be able to tell the investigator that there are such things as nouns and verbs) and (b) how can sequences be formed of materials in classes?'

Unfortunately, despite its intrinsic interest, in Jenkins & Palermo (1964) and Jenkins (1965), there is a general failure even to approach a mediational account of phrase structure; their reviews largely concern themselves with pairs and classes whose general definition seems of identical form to the procedure used by Fries (1952)—namely sentence frames. Since it should be possible (in principle) always to express

38

associative strength in terms of probabilities of response, Jenkins' form of argument is closely akin to arguing from the notion of 'statistical approximations'. As Chomsky (1957: 16-17) has made clear, it is impossible in these terms to explain the recognition of structure in anomalous strings such as *colourless green ideas sleep furiously* and distinguish them from *furiously sleep ideas green colourless*. Again, in the context frame *I saw the weak—*, it is clear that *mountain* and *of* are equivalently improbable as associations. Yet *mountain* is here structurally more acceptable. There is no way, short of an appeal to the grammar, to decide between these. It might be argued that this associative decision is made because the sentence would probably be assumed to end after one further word. So let us consider *I saw the weak Lolabumbu*. With this frame *Lolabumbu* is probably taken as a noun. The mountain's name is thus *Lolabumbu*. It is not clear why one or other of the mediating possibilities should be chosen for *weak*. Thus we might have *I saw the weak(ness) of Lolabumbu*, or (fully non-deviant) *I saw the weak people of Lolabumbu*. Associative explanations fail to give anything other than *ad hoc* explanations here, and fail entirely to reveal structural relations without falling back on the grammar. Further, the sentence frame fails to distinguish the structures of such sentences as:

$$\text{The child is} \begin{cases} \textit{interesting} \\ \textit{expecting} \quad \textit{to watch} \\ \textit{willing} \end{cases}$$

and if these were acquired merely by association through position they would have to be unlearned to allow the possibility of understanding. There is nothing in the surface structure of the sentence to indicate what would be a viable slot, and selecting the possibilities strictly according to associative principles would more often than not give the wrong answer (cf. Lees, 1964). The typical shift from syntagmatic to paradigmatic associations that occurs as children's language develops (Ervin, 1961, and Brown & Berko, 1960), especially between the years of six and ten, appeared from McNeill (1963) to be explicable in terms of frequency of occurrence in particular word positions. However, McNeill (1965) now suggests that a more coherent explanation consists in assuming this to be primarily a semantic rather than a syntactic issue. Since, for most practical purposes, the child's syntax is well developed by the age of four to five, while the semantic system is developing markedly from six to eight, the latter age-range fits most closely the period of the associative shift. The suggestion is that the associative matching is done in terms of the semantic markers shared by two items. Initially, therefore, the fact that there are few markers may well cause the matching to extend beyond the boundaries of particular syntactic classes. (For discussion of semantic markers, see the relevant section below.)

Speaking of Miller, Galanter & Pribram (1960), Jenkins & Palermo comment (1964: 143): 'They take the grammatical model advanced by Chomsky and, approving of it, install it. Unfortunately they do not tell us how Plans are acquired or how they are executed, with the result that an independent explanation of grammar in terms of traditional psychological constructs is little advanced'. Unfortunately, it would seem that traditional psychological constructs avail us little without having an appropriate grammatical model installed.

Quite apart from the fact that mediation theory (cf. also the discussion of Osgood's model below) is insufficient even as far as it goes, there is a further consideration to be mentioned here. The assumption is often made that so long as some explanation fits a limited subset of problems, so it may be maintained regardless of knowledge of further relevant sets it does not cover. Clearly, limited generalizations (even bad ones) are better than none at all; but when the problems requiring explanatory generalizations have been made as clear as they have recently in the area of language, and more fruitful attempts have been made to extend psychological toeholds to these areas, it is distressing to see 'traditional psychological constructs' being maintained regardless of the power of the generalizations they make possible. The mention of a few experiments may serve to clarify the need for more than associative links as explanations—even mediated links. Glanzer (1963) distinguished 'content' words from 'function' words according to Fries' (1952) terminology and used classes of these words together with nonsense syllables in rote-learning experiments. Using a paired associate paradigm of word +nonsense syllable (and, nonsense+word), he found the recall scores significantly higher for content than function words. Glanzer argued that this was probably a result of the typical role of content and function words—that of the latter being more usually to function in a relational category between content words. Consequently, in a further experiment using the content or function words bounded on both sides by nonsense syllables (NS-W-NS), he found the relative ease of recall of the classes of words reversed. This shows that here the condition facilitating learning is not a left-right association nor a right-left association, but a higher order node which must be rewritten as its full grammatical expansion. Epstein (1961) used nonsense syllable strings with grammatical features allocated in a structured manner (i.e. similar to Jabberwocky). In an experiment using total presentation of the string on each learning trial,

40

he found that such grammatical strings when compared with their random ordered equivalent were significantly easier to recall. Epstein (1962) repeated and confirmed this result, together with anomalous strings. When, however, he used the same sets of material in a serial anticipation experiment, with memory drum presentation of 2 sec/item, the difference disappeared between the structured and unstructured materials. Miller (1962a) has shown in a speech perception task, using strictly defined sets of material, that grammatical constraints produced significant effects only when the rate of presentation in the task was speeded up. Miller argues this is probably because at the slower rate sufficient interrelationships between the words can be established to eliminate differences in performance. Wales (1964) operating from Miller's results repeated Epstein's experiment, using both meaningful grammatical and anomalous strings, and two rates of presentation—o·8 sec/item and 2 sec/item—with a memory drum. Significant differences were found between grammatical and ungrammatical strings for both normal and anomalous strings at the faster rate of presentation. At the slower rate this difference was reduced for the normal sentences and lost for the anomalous strings. Thus it is the grammatical structure itself which seems no longer to be utilized. This result with rate of presentation may serve to also explain Slamenca's (1959, 1961) inability to find any differences between retroactive interference effects using nonsense syllables and with 'connected discourse'—together with the fact that the latter attains an unusually complex level of anomaly.

Lambert & Paivo (1956), in studying the relative recall rates for adjectives followed by nouns and nouns followed by adjectives, found the latter condition to facilitate learning. This was attributed to associative clustering. Gonzales & Cofer (1959) extended this study and showed that the likelihood of this clustering occurring in members of one form class influenced total recall and clustering tendencies in the other. They also reported that mismatches between adjectives and the nouns they modified reduced clustering and total recall. Associative clustering may adequately describe these results, but it does not explain them. One explanation which suggests itself is that adjective-noun relations are derived in the surface-structure of a 'sentence' from the deep-structure order noun-adjective (e.g. *old man* from *the man is old*). This explanation suggests further hypotheses about children's acquisition of adjective-noun relations. The general point that associative strategies in paired-associate learning show a positive correlation with their relatedness to syntactic organization has been demonstrated by Martin, Boersima & Cox (1965).

41

Information theory as formulated by Shannon (1948, 1951) has of course produced experimental and theoretical evidence relevant to linguistic performance. Garner (1962), Miller (1951), and Miller & Chomsky (1963) review most of the general issues and findings; and Broadbent (1955) and Treisman (1964) have discussed those considerations relevant to selective attention. The general trend in most of these results is well illustrated by Miller, Heise & Lichten (1951), where they report a study of the intelligibility of words which improved as a function of their predictability from the contexts in which they were heard; that is, intelligibility decreased with the rise in number of alternatives and the number of alternatives was restricted by the context in which the word appears (also Bruce, 1958). After the inability of such finite-state notions to handle competence considerations adequately, the main objection to applying these to performance is that they would involve an enormously large set of parameters (cf. Miller & Chomsky, 1963: 422-30).

There are, however, two aspects of the application of information theory notions which have often escaped critical notice. Both concern the use of the Shannon Guessing Game technique as a measure of the predictability of letters or words in particular contexts. The first has to do with the immediate application of findings from the method to intelligibility in white noise masking. Since the states generated by a k-limited Markov source have the property of being probabilistic but unconditional, there are no grounds for assuming that the guessing-game has, theoretically, prior validity as a measure of predictability, owing to contextual constraints. Therefore, there seems no reason why we should not use intelligibility measures to 'predict' guessing-game results. This empirical circularity suggests we need other explanations for predictability of words in context (cf. Miller & Selfridge, 1951, who explain the results of recall by the relation to English of a particular order of approximation).

The second problem in guessing-game results has been reported in Treisman (1961) and Goldman-Eisler (1964). Put very simply it is that neither left-to-right guessing, nor right-to-left, correlates with intelligibility as well as bi-directional prediction. This strongly indicates that the predictability of words is derived optionally from operating on syntactic information about the structure of the sentence on either side of the position to be predicted. Morton (1964) has shown that syntactic considerations are necessary to account for errors made in reading statistical approximations. Treisman (1964) illustrates the potential usefulness of some selective attention studies. She reports an experiment measuring the temporal lags, both forwards and backwards, which constrain recognition (in the dichotic listening situation) that the message in the other ear is the same as in that attended to. The particularly interesting feature of Treisman's results is that the lags for bilinguals recognizing that the message to the other ear is the same are little less when that message is in the other language. Unfortunately it seems impossible from this experiment to see whether it is the syntactic or semantic features which mediate recognition.

3. Phrase-structure models

As Chomsky generates the base component of a transformational grammar by using a Phrase Structure Grammar (PSG), some psychologists (e.g. Jenkins & Palermo, 1964; Osgood, 1965) seem to have the slightly odd notion that a performance model which successfully utilizes a PSG may conveniently ignore transformational complexity as an inconvenient option provided by linguists who are best ignored. However there is much of interest and importance in the psychological studies of PSG. PSGs are a formally explicit (i.e. generative) system of rewrite rules performing a linguistic function analogous in many respects to traditional parsing. By the use of a native speaker's intuition, the sentence may be subdivided into progressively smaller immediate constituents which mark the natural internal relations of the sentence. PSGs take this a stage further with the application of formal rewriting rules, which introduce labelling to the procedure. This may now be expressed by labelled bracketing or labelled tree diagrams which are formally identical in the information carried. Here is an over-simple example of a set of PSG rules: a sentence S consists of a noun phrase NP and a verb phrase VP; then our first rule is:

1. S → NP + VP. Where → indicates that we can rewrite S as NP + VP.

Further rules might be:

2. NP → D + NP
3. VP → Verb + NP
4. D → *The,*
5. N → *man, boy, ball,* etc.
6. Verb → *hit, took,* etc.

By applying rules we could derive such sentences as *The ball hit the boy, The boy took the ball, The boy hit the man.* Other rules of formation are concerned with subcategorizations of nouns and verbs. PSGs are importantly distinguished as to whether they are context sensitive or not.

43

The labelled description expressed as a tree structure obtained through the application of PSG rules in known as a P-marker.

As a link with the last section let us start by citing the hypothesis of Johnson (1965). He proposed that sentences are processed from top to bottom, and left to right of a tree representation of the P-marker of the S. This, Johnson argues, is shown by the transitional probabilities of errors (a questionable notion in this context) correlating with the height of the appropriate node in the tree diagram. Even such an apparently simple hypothesis simply cannot hold, since it involves a number of assumptions which are not empirically substantiated. The two main objections are, first, that it assumes that one cannot start to process a sentence until that sentence has been heard or seen in its entirety; and secondly, following from this, that the hypothesis appears to imply that sentences are processed from right to left. Marshall & Wales (in preparation) have repeated and extended Johnson's experiment and their data cannot be accounted for in simple terms but necessitate distinctions only made possible by introducing the notions of deep structure and transformations. Osgood (1963) has attempted to integrate PSG structural information with certain Markovian properties. The model is hierarchically organized into levels determined by PSG considerations with probabilistic generation within levels. Production is served by moving progressively down through levels; understanding by processing up through levels. Osgood assumes that Johnson's results give reasonable cause for arguing for probabilistic properties within levels.

There are a number of important objections to this superficially plausible model:

1. There is no principled way of deciding when and how the movement between levels is made, whether up or down.

2. There is no indication how Osgood's model can introduce transformational complexity without further (infinitely) *ad hoc* complexity.

3. It is difficult to see how the possibility of infinitely long sentences can be incorporated. There would need to be recursion on all levels; but if this must be the case, what sense is there in further talk of probabilities?

4. It is perfectly possible that there would be a mismatch in probabilities between levels. Thus in the extreme example of anomalous sentences the lexical items have low transitional probabilities, but may have high probability higher level relations, for example NP + VP. (cf. also Stolz, 1965, where predictability of

words in a given corpus was not significantly correlated with the constituent analysis).

5. Yngve (1960), basing his hypothesis on Miller's (1956) summary of results on information processing limitations, suggested that these would restrict generation as production 'from top to bottom'. One important implication of this hypothesis is that there are finite memory restrictions on 'depth', thus left-branching contributes equally to unacceptability as nesting and self-embedding. All the empirical evidence on this latter aspect suggests the contrary is true. Both Johnson's and Osgood's formulations are open to the objection that they are not substantiated empirically and are theoretically implausible (cf. Chomsky, 1965: 197-8).

6. Osgood's introduction of probabilities into his model in order to avoid talking of 'choice' and 'decision' (while finding a sympathetic reception in the light of wilder 'activist' hypothesis-testing notions) is nevertheless vacuous as it stands. Osgood asserts (1963: 741) that '"decision" in behaviour is simply selection of the momentarily most probable alternative within any divergent hierarchy'. If this means anything, it presumably means that a response which is more or less probable is more or less probable because it is more or less probable. Prediction is not identical with explanation, and Osgood does not give appropriate regard to the level on which the terms 'choice' and 'decision' are being used (cf. MacKay, 1960; Scheffler, 1964).

7. There seems no way in which such a model may show the syntactic constraints which hold between discontinuous constituents, for example *the* MEN...*held on to the point* and *the man...holds on to the point*. The gap may be filled by an indefinitely long grammatical string thereby making probabilistic constraints meaningless.

An alternative approach in applying psychological constraints to phrase structure formulations has been proposed by Braine (1963a, 1965a). His position is that grammatical structure is utilized by contextual generalization: (i) What is learned are the locations of expressions within utterances. (ii) Units (i.e. expressions whose position is learned) can form a hierarchy in which longer units contain shorter units as parts, the location of what is learned being the location of a unit within the next-larger containing unit, up to a sentence. (iii) The learning is a case of perceptual learning—a process of becoming familiar with the sounds of expressions in the positions in which they occur and recur. All this says is that, when someone has experienced sentences in which a segment occurs in a certain position and context, he later tends to place this segment in the same position in other contexts. Thus the context of the segment will be said to have generalized and the subject to have shown contextual generalization. This, therefore, falls under the general heading of stimulus response generalization. Braine tested his hypothesis by using simple artificial languages (e.g. A + P Q) with children as subjects. The assumption that there would be a difference between children's and adults' performance in the same situation and the same material is not upheld by Wales & Grant (1966). This suggests that Braine's experimental method does not distinguish the method of learning grammatical structures in children. Bever, Fodor & Weksel (1966*a*, *b*) have argued that Braine's approach is inappropriate because he does not distinguish between surface and base linguistic structure, and because he seems to assume that linguistics is simply empirical. Braine (1965*b*) answers ably many of the detailed arguments put forward by Bever *et al.*, but seems to miss their particular thrust. He fails to defend his (1963) notion of transfer between sub-languages as a device for accommodating transformational complexity, yet argues strenuously that there is no great theoretical necessity to distinguish between surface and deep structures at the 'kernel sentence' level. At the same time it is not clear how Braine would distinguish and handle (in psychological and linguistic models) the complexity of labelling demanded by subcategorization within a 'phrase structure component' which is neither clearly psychological nor linguistic—that is, there is no way of indicating the knowledge that would, for example, enable the contextual generalizer to recognize a mistake.

None of this is to deny the psychological reality of phrase-structure. Thus Wales (1966) presented sentences in three parts which were cut either (i) at the end of a syntactic constituent, or (ii) elsewhere in the sentence. It was significantly easier to learn the sentences when presented as (i) than when presented as (ii). Thus it is easier to decode a sentence in its natural syntactic constituents, which form the parts presented in (i). It should be noted that the transitional probabilities are exactly the same for both conditions, the sentences being the same.

An important extension of the psychological application of PS constituents is the series of studies by Schlesinger (1966), using as a basic experimental tool the eye-voice span (EVS)—that is, how far ahead of the voice the eye scans the text during reading. Schlesinger illustrates his hypothesis with the sentence *The woman teacher, who had taught him Latin, was very pleased*. He argues that the EVS will be determined not so much by the actual syntactic constituent of the complete sentence but by what may be taken to be the end of a possible constituent chain, given that the subject is ignorant of the subsequent words. With various experimental designs and materials, he found the EVS to be predictable on this basis.

When PSGs are fully formed, they will nevertheless enumerate only a fraction of English sentences in a principled fashion. Even then they only allow of a form of description such that each sentence must be associated with at least one P-marker; and this raises the problem of how a finite mechanism needed for a performance model can be integrated with the infinite number of descriptions needed to account for the infinity of potential sentences. Many of the limitations of PSGs have been shown by Chomsky (1963), Postal (1964a, b). Stockwell (1963) summarizes a number of these. PSGs are weak in the following ways, which have special force in performance models: (i) Discontinuous constituents cannot be derived in a principled manner, with the rewriting restrictions of not allowing symbols on the left to appear on the right of the same rule. If this restriction does not obtain, class membership between higher and lower nodes in a tree cannot be maintained. (ii) PSGs employ very complex and duplicate sets of rules and labelling in generating any but the simplest strings. (iii) They cannot generate co-ordinated structures of infinite length without enormous and counterintuitive bracketing. (iv) They fail both to distinguish the deviations of ambiguities and to show relatedness in sentences where a native speaker knows it exists.

4. Transformational models

Many of the weaknesses of PSG derive from the frequently recurring requirement that the tree as a whole be made available to a rewrite rule. This is precisely what is made available to transformational rules, and this was one of the main reasons why Chomsky distinguished between deep and surface structure (1955, 1957). The PSG was now used to generate a base structure (whereas previously there had been solely surface structure) of essentially simple base components on which operated transformational rules to derive the surface structure. These rules may operate on base strings to delete, add, permute, or substitute symbols. This is to say that transformational rules operate not only on terminal symbols in the base string but on the whole of the base P-marker. Thus within linguistic theory—*pace* Braine—there is no such thing as 'kernel sentence' without a transformational derivation. (The form of the rules before the recent revisions is discussed in Chomsky, 1961.)

Stemming from suggestions originally in Miller *et al.* (1960), psychological experiments were typically designed to indicate how the psycho-

47

logical difficulty of processing was correlated with the discrepancy between surface and deep structures. Thus Miller (1962) reported results from a sentence-matching task involving relations between sentences marked by transformational relations—that is, active to passive (Pas.), negative (Neg.); interrogative (Int.), to (Pas.Neg.); (Pas.Int.) and (Neg.Int.): to (Pas.Neg.Int.). Miller found a fair relation between the time taken to perform the matching and the number of transformations involved in the relation between the sentences concerned. Marshall (1964) using an anagram task obtained essentially similar results, with an additional gross difference attributed to the differences produced in having transformations of the same base P-marker or different ones— that is, an effect of 'set' perhaps due to semantic differences in the two situations.

Underlying both of these sets of experiments there was a common set of assumptions. Before the recent revisions introduced into T-G, the linguistic theory postulated a precise deep structure and a related T-marker as optional. Therefore more than one surface-structure could be derived from the same deep-structure. Hence the deep form of (Neg.), (Int.), and so on, might be the same. Therefore differences were a function of the base form plus the T-marker with the T-marker being the measure of difficulty. Miller and Marshall and others, whilst recognizing that the linguistic theory itself was neutral with respect to psychological performance, assumed it a reasonable hypothesis that the latter might correlate with competence notions. They thus attempted to quantify transformational complexity in psychological terms as the increment in processing time over a constant base—a hypothesis in general substantiated. Miller & McKean (1964), in a chronometric study, which broke the sentence matching task down into its component parts and using greater precision of measurement, found that certain qualifications were needed, especially in respect of the assumption that transformations are uniformly difficult within a given level.

Attempting to replicate this pattern of findings, Mehler (1963), using similarly constructed sets of sentences in a free recall task found that the results did not wholly confirm expectations, but subjects recall could typically be described as a base (kernel) form + a transformational footnote. The interference produced by presenting sets of sentences together might account for the lack of specific additive effects correlating with transformational complexity. Coleman (1964) has found that readability measured by multiple-choice comprehension tests relates to transformational complexity. Thus in two versions of a text, the first containing nominalizations, passives and adjectivalizations, and the

48

second containing corresponding active declarative forms, the latter was better understood. Wales (in preparation) compared the learning of sentences derived from embedding or conjoining transformations operating on a distinction of Fillmore (1961) concerning the 'traffic rules' for the order of application of rules within a grammar (Lees, 1960). It was assumed that, if sentences were memorized by a process of distinguishing the kernel and the transformations which operate on it, the embedded sentences derived from single kernels would be easier to learn than conjoined sentences based on two or more kernels. Although both types of sentence were equated for length, the number of trials for learning were in the expected direction. This result can be interpreted in terms of performance only if we assume that there is some ordered priority in the application of the available analytic procedures. It leaves quite unclear precisely what it is that serves to determine the differences observed. Miller & Isard (1964), in discussing the free-recall of self-embedded and other kinds of nested constructions, suggest that to explain the relative unacceptability of the former, a store of analytic procedures must be postulated, each procedure relating to the possible kinds of phrase and the store being so organized that a given procedure cannot be utilized while it is being executed.

Thus the initial attempts to produce performance correlates of transformations were encouraging and seemed to fit fairly well rule-governed hypothesis-testing mechanisms such as the Tote proposed by Miller *et al.* (1960). Perhaps they were too encouraging. Some seem to assume that the active comparator hypothesis (the principle of 'analysis by synthesis' proposed by Matthews, 1962, and by Halle & Stevens, 1964) with the mechanism generating multiple possible synthesized 'sentences' to match the input and thus analyse its structure, could actually work, although obviously it is far too long to operate efficiently and appropriately as a performance model.

Within the linguistic theory there seemed to be problems associated with the optional character of the T-markers. Recent revisions of transformational theory have made possible the elimination of the T-marker. We shall briefly illustrate the argument for the revision (for fuller exposition, cf. Lees & Klima, 1963; Katz & Postal, 1964; Chomsky, 1965; Postal, 1964c.) Let us consider the passive transformation. Previously the theory needed to introduce an *ad hoc* restriction to prevent the passivization of middle verbs (e.g. *weigh, fit*). These raised problems which are simply illustrated. Thus of the two sentences *He weighed ten pounds* and *He weighed the girl*, only the latter may take the passive form. To get around this *ad hoc* restriction, the theory is now formulated in such

49

a way that the passive is regarded as a possible realization of a manner adverbial and the co-occurrence restrictions are handled by stating that any sentence which freely takes all manner adverbials has a passive form. Thus passives are now generated in the deep structure by labelling '*by* + passive' with manner adverbials, and thus the transformation is made obligatory in the base structure.

A further motivation for this change was that it allows the semantic component to operate with maximum generality. Previously some transformations preserved, and other transformations changed, meaning. This obviously presented problems for generalization (although not necessarily insuperable ones; cf. Staal, 1965), but it is now possible to operate by stating the generalization that no transformation changes meaning. This does now require that the analysis has to be syntactically motivated or it becomes unnecessarily arbitrary. However, this provides stronger correlative motivation within a psychological model for arguing that the syntactic processing has priority over the semantic.

It must be stated immediately that despite all appearances to the contrary, under the new formalization all the previous psychological results stand. This is because the discrepancy between deep and surface structure is as before, and, in fact, the previous results can be accounted for more systematically on the grounds that some deep structures are more 'difficult' to generate (in some psychologically interpretable sense of 'difficult').

Few experiments have been performed in the light of the revised form of the transformational competence model.

Two most interesting experiments of Savin & Perchonok (1965, 1966) use an assumption about short-term memory analogous to Archimedes' principle. A sentence is presented to a subject together with a string of unrelated words and the subject is instructed to remember the sentence and the additional words. Savin suggests that the number of unrelated words recalled would be fewer as a function of the amount of 'storage space' taken up by the sentence. They found that fewer unrelated words were recalled in the case of sentences such as passive, negative, emphatic or 'Wh-' questions, than with the active declarative forms; and that fewer still were recalled with (Neg.Pas.) or (Pas.Int.) sentences. The particularly important aspect of Savin & Perchonok's results is that sentences such as the 'Wh-' questions were in fact shorter than the active declarative, and thus sentence length itself cannot be used as an explanation of the memory effect. In an extension of this experiment, Savin compared surface structures derived by self-embedding or right-branching from essentially the same base form. When the sentences preceded the unrelated words the number of latter was equivalent for the two conditions; when they followed the words, the self-embedded form interfered much more with memory. This suggests very strongly that sentences are initially processed and stored primarily in terms of their deep structures, and that the relative unavailability of self-embedding is a result of surface structure constraints.

Further evidence showing the importance of deep structure for performance is provided by an experiment of Blumenthal (1966). Subjects were presented with sentence lists and then prompt-words for each of which the subjects attempted to recall a sentence. The prompt-words were chosen for their grammatical function, with the intention of observing how this function related to their facilitatory effect in prompting recall. First of all, simple active sentences were used, and it was found that the words functioning as 'subjects' increased recall more than words functioning as 'objects'. This technique was then applied to transformational hypotheses comparing the recall of (a) normal passive sentences where by-phrases contain the logical subjects, and (b) passives with non-agent by-phrases substituted for the normal by-phrases. Here (a) and (b) have identical surface structure forms but different deep structures. Blumenthal found that the effectiveness of the prompt word varied according to relations determined by the underlying structure. Thus by-phrase nouns were more effective for normal passives than those with non-agent.

One result which appears to run counter to the trend indicated by these experiments is that reported by Clark (1965). Using active and passive frames, he found that the substitutions for lexical items were totally dissimilar. However with the new form of the grammar we would not necessarily expect that the patterning would be the same in performance, since the competence model now generates the actives and passives as related to different strings derived by obligatory transformations.

Marshall (1965) reported that 'set' produced by presenting ambiguous sentences, after a number of unambiguous sentences with the same surface structure, resulted in paraphrases of the ambiguous sentences in the same direction as those given for the unambiguous. There was also some suggestion that reaction-times of judgements of 'grammatical' or 'ungrammatical' were longer when the response was made to a sentence which was not included in the set of the preceding sentences, than when it was included.

As a more analytic experimental procedure, Fodor & Bever (1965) have operated with a technique first used by Broadbent & Ladefoged

51

(1960). In a dichotic listening situation the objective position of a click in one ear, relative to a sentence in the other ear, is subjectively displaced. Fodor & Bever suggest that this subjective displacement is the result of a perceptual unit resisting interference, and they suggest that the unit is determined by the primary constituent break in the derived surface structure of the sentence. Their results do in fact show a tendency for the click's subjective position to migrate towards these constituent boundaries. That these results are not simply the result of intonation and pauses is shown by Garrett, Fodor & Bever (1966), where the same kind of results are obtained in the case of ambiguous constituents which are joined with one or other of two disambiguating contexts. When the same recording is used for each of the ambiguous examples, the subjective displacement is determined by the grammatical structure imposed by the disambiguating contexts. Thorne & Wales (in preparation) have suggested that Fodor & Bever's results are an artifact stemming from the fact that, in the particular sentences they use, surface structure constituents frequently coincide with deep structure relations. They argue that the perceptual units are determined by a correlation between deep and surface structure. Thus in the sentence *He came yesterday*, both surface and deep structures mark the primary constituent boundary between *he* and *came*; whereas in *Probably he came yesterday*, while the surface structure retains the same primary break, the deep structure now marks it being between *Probably* and *he*. Thorne & Wales further suggest the possibility that the click is subjectively displaced according to the first encountered sentential unit in deep and surface structure to which it relates (e.g. *The boy hit the girl* in the sentence *The boy hit the girl who had the ball*, if the click occurs objectively before the end of *girl*).

PERFORMANCE PROBLEMS

After a necessarily brief review, with the distortion usually attendant on such brevity, what general questions emerge as especially thorny and relevant to performance models? While it is obvious that hearing and speaking are in certain respects different functions, yet it is equally obvious that there is some direct central relationship which must be taken account of in any model. The obviousness of this point sometimes results in linguists and psychologists forgetting it in their theoretical writings (cf. Marshall & Wales 1966, for a discussion of this danger). It is this relatedness which gives the notion of competence some of its special force in psycholinguistics.

52

Stemming from the explicit specification of a competence grammar there are two available temptations: (i) to assume that the rules of competence are incorporated and applied directly in the analysis of sentences (one example being the approach of 'analysis by synthesis' of Matthews, 1961); or (ii) to label the competence grammar as 'linguistics' and assume that psychological performance explanation will be distinct from competence (e.g. the approaches of Jenkins, 1965, on the one hand, and Thorne—this volume—on the other). These temptations raise the whole issue of the relationship between a model and that which is modelled.

Much of the impetus for research and discussion in this area comes from automata theory and computer simulation. The essence of this approach was expressed by Craik as follows (1952: 57): 'My hypothesis then is that thought models, or parallels reality—that its essential feature is not "the mind", "the self", "sense-data", not propositions but symbolism, and that this symbolism is largely of the same kind as that which is familiar to us in mechanical devices which aid thought and calculation.' That is, the essential feature is information processing (in its most general sense) and this may, if appropriately stated, be mechanically simulated. This gives operational significance to what otherwise might be vague 'mentalist' concepts, and increases assurance that no false assumptions have crept into the system. An instance of the value of simulation in revealing inexplicit assumptions in verbal theories is provided by the inability of Feigenbaum's programme—the Elementary Perceiver and Memorizer (1959, 1962)—with associationist assumptions to distinguish and mark two different occurrences of the same item in a list. This is because a distinction between 'type' and 'token' is not available. The general context of developments in this field—as they relate to psychology—are surveyed by Miller, Galanter & Pribram (1960), and by Newell & Simon (1963). For more detailed discussions of the relevance and implications of automata theory for linguistic performance see Chomsky (1963), Chomsky & Miller (1963), and Miller & Chomsky (1963).

Some of the different kinds of problems in this area are: (i) What kind of finite automaton (cf. the human brain) would accept as input an infinite set of grammatical strings in natural languages, and also reflect the limitations of immediate memory? (ii) What heuristic devices are most appropriate as models of human behaviour? (iii) Is it necessary to assume that analysis must proceed from left to right in a single pass? (iv) How may the real time of simulated processing be related to the rate of human processing of language? (v) With many formal and substantive issues of transformational grammars still undecided, the form of algebraic models which might incorporate these grammars remains unclear. A competence grammar may be expressed as an abstract system of rules and a performance model will be expressed (ideally) as an algorithm. It is tempting to assume that the difference between the two is to be found in the form of expression. However, some competence grammars may (in principle) be expressed as structure assignment algorithms; and the performance model incorporates further heuristic information about the way in which the organization of this knowledge is limited in the search for solutions which are accepted as being good enough most of the time.

Following Craik (1952) and Minsky (1965) we may express the problem of relating competence and performance in this way: For *US*—the observers—*C* is a model of language *L* to the extent that *US* can use *C* to answer questions that interest them about *L*. When *US* answer questions about how men *M* process *L* we attribute this ability to some internal mechanism *P*, inside *M*. It would be convenient if we could discern physically within *M* two separate regions *C** and *P**, such that *C** really contains the knowledge and *P** contains only general-purpose machinery for coding inputs, decoding outputs, and general administrative work. 'However one cannot really expect to find in an intelligent machine a clear separation between coding and knowledge structures, either anatomically or functionally because (for example) some *knowledge* is like to be used in the encoding and interpretive processes.' (Minsky, 1965: 45.) It seems to us, therefore, that until fully explicit models of competence and performance are available, such that formal properties may be studied and (perhaps) compared, the technical ability to delineate the model's boundaries will not be available in ANY absolute sense. Since it is already clear that competence is neutral with reference to many performance problems, and that it is in some sense true that performance incorporates competence, it seems perfectly appropriate to pursue the goal of a performance model by making explicit use of competence notions, without being wholly committed to homunculi manning internal generators and comparators.

A SCHEMA

In the light of the studies reviewed thus far, together with those referred to below, we suggest that we are now in a position to attempt to schematize the processes of linguistic performance. The diagram of this schema in Figure 1 is in NO SENSE to be understood as a model. For it to be a model we would expect to specify the form of the inputs, the decisions

54

made on them (i.e. the set of analytic procedures and their order of application), and the outputs at each stage. Such a schema does serve, however, in the following ways: first, it indicates the hypothesized order of processing linguistic information and suggests the most fruitful points of study; secondly, by comparison with alternative formulations (e.g. Miller, 1962; Halle & Stevens, 1964; Morton, 1964*b*) empirical grounds for substantive claims can perhaps be tested; thirdly, it helps to keep as a central aim that linguistic performance is best considered as a system,

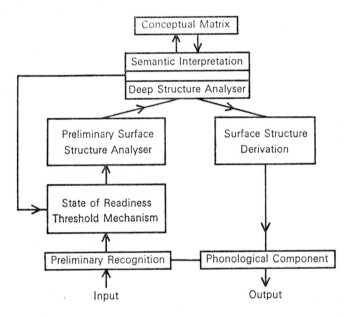

Figure 1. A Schema of Linguistic Performance

and avoids the proliferation of unrelated models which account merely for particular instances; lastly, it highlights the tentative nature of all current performance considerations.

The following notes on the schema make a few basic assumptions: (i) that it is a functional characterization; (ii) that the basic unit of performance is the sentence—in comparison with most psychological models based on single words; (iii) that the analysis of sentences is continuous, rather than operating on input strings in temporary stores; (iv) the aim is to produce the simplest stage analysis of the kind required by

P E

the evidence to date; (v) at any given time, the process operates only uni-directionally—that is, recognition and production procedures cannot be simultaneous.

Preliminary recognition. Space does not allow us to reveal in detail our incompetence here. For reviews of different approaches to how the performer converts the physical input into 'symbolic' information cf. Miller (1951, 1956*b*); Libermann (1957); Malmberg (1963); Halle & Stevens (1964). We might be bold and make a few brief points. Many studies do not take into account the redundancy available in language structures; consequently absolute accuracy of initial discrimination is very rarely necessary. Usually, syntactic and semantic information—and perhaps situational expectancies—may be used to 'reconstruct' the form of the input. By an analogy from mechanical pattern recognition, Clowes (personal communication) has suggested that the input might be operated on rapidly in this way: initially and approximately 'from the bottom up', taking the input information with the constructed tree. The analysis is then checked by producing a context-free P-marker 'from the top down'. By such a back-tracking method perhaps sufficiently accurate initial recognition could be implemented to allow the analysis to proceed. Temporal factors seem to be relevant to the recognition of structural properties in the input (cf. Lenneberg, in preparation).

State of readiness. This threshold mechanism is presumably regulated by situational expectancies and feedback instructions on the basis of sentential constraints and semantic coding. This is placed after the preliminary recognition of the input to allow for some of the results from dichotic listening experiments (Treisman, 1964*b*): for instance, some contextual constraints can cause a shift of attention to what must be at least a partially processed input though initially not attended to. Also, Sperling (1963) summarizes some results which suggest that most (visual) input information is stored and available, if only for a very short time. There are some interesting and relevant questions about the significance of 'short term memory' to language processing (cf. Broadbent, 1958; Peterson, 1963). Perhaps the development of performance—especially in production—can be expressed as a function of an interaction between short term memory and competence. But most comments at this stage—like these—consist in hand-waving.

Preliminary analysis of surface structure. This stage is labelled 'preliminary analysis' in order to emphasize the point that in recognition not all the surface structure information is processed. Rather, following Thorne Dewar, Whitfield & Bratley (1965), this stage of analysis proceeds with a view to providing an input for deep structure analysis as quickly as

56

possible. This is not to deny that in a complete model many features would be shared between this stage and the derivation of surface structure in speech production. Thorne *et al.* propose an algorithm which operates on a written input, and on the basis of immediate prediction, assigns continuously to it all possible surface structure analyses which might serve as input to a deep structure analyser. It is impossible to summarize verbally the algorithm here. There are however three features of particular interest:

1. the programme assigns structural descriptions to the input predictively—as compared to synthesizing matching comparisons;

2. it operates with a very small dictionary of closed class items and a handful of other ad hoc items (cf. Krule, Kuck, Landi & Manelski, 1964; whose programme includes every item in the dictionary);

3. the time taken approaches possible comparison with human processing times.

Deep structure. We would expect that as in the other stages, so the deep structure would operate on the input just as soon as it was available. One reason for distinguishing this stage from that which precedes it is that, with the algorithm proposed by Thorne *et al.* as a basis, there are explicit hypotheses available of a form not yet possible in terms of the deep structure. Although we cannot yet offer any suggestion as to the nature of this component we can still produce some tentative hypotheses from the competence model. Thus we expect it to assign relational notions over a phrase-structure component such as that given as output by the model in Thorne *et al.* These relational notions should suggest some, perhaps arbitrary, indices of complexity of the differences between the surface and deep structures when hearing and producing sentences.

Semantic component (this is discussed in more detail below). It is directly associated with the deep structure component. In hearing sentences the semantic component interprets the base structure. Thus it is only when 'words' are input to the deep structure analyser that we would expect them to be 'looked up' in the semantic dictionary. With the syntactic processing preceding the semantic in hearing (the converse in production) we have a rudimentary hypothesis about one major factor which would eliminate much needless search time. We also have an opposite notion to Morton (1964) who implies that both when sentences are heard, and when they are produced, the input string is 'looked up' in the semantic—logogen—store, before syntactic processing.

In PRODUCTION most of the above holds in the reverse direction, though the schema is so presented as to express the existence of important differences and expectations between the two. Thus it is only in production that ALL surface structure information is produced. The phonological rules, in production, will have articulatory information, that is, will be of 'distinctive feature' form (Jakobson, Halle & Fant, 1952; Jakobson & Halle, 1956; Chomsky & Halle, 1965). Of considerable interest are the results of Leiberman (1965) implying the apparent subjective reconstruction of intonational judgements when trained observers have sentential information.

It seems quite likely that much of the nonsense-syllable literature in the tradition of Ebbinghaus (e.g. Underwood, 1965), and that of 'acoustic-confusions' (Conrad, 1962; Wickelgren, 1965) could be explained by reference to the articulatory stage. We would also expect that a performance model developed on the basis of this scheme would be able to explain some further general findings. How the selections in production from the semantic component relate to the base structure which is implemented to translate this into sentential forms, should help to explain results on the significance of hesitation phenomena reported by Maclay & Osgood, (1959); Goldman-Eisler, (1958); Boomer, (1965). In shadowing, the distinction found by Chistovich (1960)—between subjects who could shadow very closely but could not report the content of the message, and subjects who shadowed with a much greater lag and reported understanding—would suggest the possibility, in certain circumstances of performance, of moving between related stages of hearing and production rather than continuing to process the input automatically through every stage.

SEMANTIC COMPETENCE AND PERFORMANCE

It is clear that a full account of the grammatical competence of a native speaker does not exhaust the speaker's linguistic knowledge. Syntactic theory must be supplemented by an account of the semantic rules which enable the speaker to distinguish between English and Jabberwocky. Part of this problem is to provide a formal statement of the conceptual structure of a word or morpheme dictionary, the 'physical' outputs of which may be represented (phonologically) by a distinctive-feature matrix (Halle & Chomsky, 1966) or (graphemically) by a picture-grammar (Clowes, 1965).

It is possible to formulate a simple model in which words are the atomic elements of the system and their inter-relationships are overtly marked by 'associative' connections between words, as indivisible entities. (By 'words' in this and following passages we refer not to a phonological or graphemic representation but to the concept (thought, idea) represented by the word.) Elementary markovian models of this nature have been proposed by such theorists as Hobbes (1651), Hartley (1749) and Mill (1869). Hobbes' accounts reads as follows:

from St Andrew the mind runneth to St Peter; from St Peter to a stone; from stone to foundation; from foundation to church; from church to people, and from people to tumult; and according to this example the mind may run almost from anything to anything.

What is being proposed, then, is a single-level system (all symbols are terminal symbols of the semantic component) but with no further constraint upon the rules allowable.

Thus both

A → B   (Table → Chair)

and

B → A   (Chair → Table)

are theoretically possible rules. Divergent connections

$$A \rightarrow \begin{bmatrix} B \\ C \\ D \\ \cdot \\ \cdot \\ \cdot \end{bmatrix}$$

are possible, as are convergent connections

$$\begin{bmatrix} B \\ C \\ D \\ \cdot \\ \cdot \\ \cdot \end{bmatrix} \rightarrow A$$

The total 'dictionary in the head' can therefore be represented as a vast interconnected net, with the direction of the connection marked but no further labelling. Figure 2 illustrates the point (Kiss, 1964, contains a detailed account of such a net and its properties).

We shall, for the moment, ignore the question whether or not our semantic competence (or part of it) could be represented in such a form, and review some of the psychological literature which assumes a representation in this form.

If we assume that we can collect pertinent and reliable data concerning such networks by the simple expedient of giving people a word and saying to them 'Tell me the first different word which comes into your head after I have shown you this word', it becomes possible to define various notions of 'strength of association or relatedness' over such networks. We can then examine how the network (or selected sub-parts of it) is put to use in typical psychological situations (e.g. in learning and recall experiments). Various early investigators (Kent & Rosanoff, 1910;

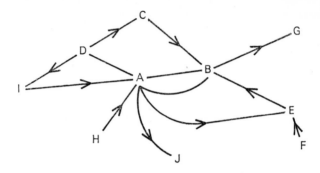

Figure 2

Russell & Jenkins, 1954) proposed quantifying 'strength of relationship' in terms of the percentage of subjects who produced a particular response to a given stimulus word. Experimentation (Jenkins & Russell, 1952; Jenkins, Mink & Russell, 1958) revealed that when lists of words, containing Kent-Rosanoff associatively-paired items, were presented to subjects in a random order, associated pairs tended to appear together in free-recall (so-called 'associative clustering'), and that the frequency with which this clustering occurred was directly related to the associative strength of the connection. A more complex measure, the number of associations which two words have in common, was also shown to be positively correlated with clustering in recall (Bousefield, Whitmarsh & Berkowitz, 1960). A measure of total associative communality for a list (the mean percentage of times that the members of a list elicit each other as primary responses) was also shown (Deese, 1959, 1962) to predict the number of items recalled for a list (after one presentation) and to predict the kind of extra-list intrusions which occurred. Finally we note that considerable success has been obtained in predicting facilitation and interference effects in 'mediated' paired-associate learning

60

paradigms from associative data. Representative experiments show that if a subject learns the (nonsense-syllable:word) pair

zug — table

this facilitates the later learning of the pair

zug — chair

It is assumed that the associative connection between 'table' and 'chair' is responsible for this effect. It has also been shown that learning the pair

zug — soldier

facilitates the later learning of

zug — navy

In this case the associative norms do not show a direct connection between *soldier* and *navy*. They do, however, show a connection between *soldier* and *sailor* and between *sailor* and *navy*. It is therefore hypothesized that the link via *sailor* mediates the obtained facilitation. Representative experiments and theorizing will be found in Russell & Storms, 1955; Jenkins, 1963; Higa, 1963. The results we have briefly described are congruent, then, with the notion that some aspects of our semantic competence can be represented as a simple associative net. However, rather than attempt to present a detailed retrieval system which operates upon such a net, we shall next discuss certain facts of competence which cannot be expressed within such a theory and which therefore constitute a refutation in principle of the original hypothesis.

The speaker of a language knows not merely that certain words of that language are related to each other, but also knows what is the nature of the relationship in each case. He knows that certain words are synonymous—*ill* and *sick*—whilst others are antonymous—*ill* and *healthy*. He knows that the set of words *man, carpet, lorry, fish* are conceptually related by virtue of their referents being physical objects, and that they thereby differ from *idea, truth, happiness*, and *theory*. The speaker further knows how lexical information operates in conjunction with syntactic information. He thus knows that some sentences are paraphrases of each other: *The man hit the woman* and *The woman was hit by the man*. He knows that some sentences are vacuous: *My aunt is a woman*, and that others are contradictory: *My aunt is a man*. He knows that some sentence tokens are ambiguous: *He wore a light suit*, and that others, containing perhaps the same ambiguous word, are not: *He painted the wall a light colour* and *The parcel was light enough to carry*. He knows that certain sentences are semantically deviant: *Golf plays John* (although perfectly good uses can be found for many such sentences).

In principle, any native speaker has available to him a sufficient amount of such 'intuitive' data concerning his language to enable the theorist to proceed with the formal explication of semantic structure without, in the present state of the art, having to collect data under rigorously defined experimental conditions. For those who bemoan the absence of 'operational definitions' for such notions as synonymity and paraphrase, we merely point out that any operational procedure must be tested (for its validity as opposed to its reliability) against the original intuitions it is supposed to 'measure', and is also tested by the congruence of its results with the most highly-valued theory of the domain to which it purportedly refers; these points have been extensively argued in the literature (cf. Katz 1964; Chomsky, 1965). A meta-theory for semantic descriptions must then make available hypothetical constructs which are capable of representing the types of knowledge we have outlined (cf. Katz & Fodor, 1963). We shall next describe one plausible approach to the representation of the conceptual structure of lexical items.

In the course of their investigations into the semantic component of a full linguistic theory, Katz & Fodor (1963) proposed a standard form for representing lexical information. This work was extended in Katz & Postal (1964) and in Katz (1964c). In brief, what is suggested is that a lexical entry be characterized as a set of syntactic markers, followed by a set of semantic markers (discrete conceptual elements) and a selection restriction, which excludes semantically deviant concatenations of words. An example should clarify what is intended. Katz (1964c) proposes the following putative entry for *Knife*:

KNIFE Noun, Common noun,...Count noun; (Physical object), (Non-living), (Artifact), (Blade), (Handle), (Eval$_{use}$: (Ease of dividing substance softer than its blade)); $<$SR$>$.

The entry thus represents the following facts:

'Noun' indicates that *Knife* is equivalent (in this respect) to *Woman* and different from *Go*.

'Common Noun', that *Knife* is equivalent to *Woman* and different from *Jane*.

'Count Noun', that *Knife* is equivalent to *Woman* and different from *Rice*.

('Physical Object'), that *Knife* is equivalent to *Woman* and different from *Idea*.

('Non-living'), that *Knife* is equivalent to *Stone* and different from *Woman*.

('Artifact'), that *Knife* is equivalent to *Telephone* and different from *Stone*.

('Blade'), that *Knife* is equivalent to *Razor Blade* and different from *Telephone*.

('Handle'), that *Knife* is equivalent to *Spoon* and different from *Razor Blade*.

('Eval$_{use}$'), indicates that the referents of those words obtaining the marker (Artifact) may (optionally) be evaluated in terms of the uses to which they are put (*The knife is good/bad*). They thus differ from words containing the marker (Role), for example *Teacher*, whose referents are evaluated in terms of the performance of duties appertaining to this role, and from words such as *Liquid* which cannot be evaluated without producing expanded forms which specify particular circumstances—*The liquid is good for washing in/drinking*.

('Ease of dividing substances softer than its blade') specifies the standard use to which knives are put.

Placing this marker within the (Eval$_{use}$) marker indicates that knives are evaluated in terms of this particular marker and are not evaluated by virtue of being, for example, physical objects or of having blades.

Finally, a selection restriction, <SR>, is required in order to show for instance that words containing the marker (Non-living) cannot be concatenated with predicate adjectives such as *tired* (*The knife is tired*), whose subject nouns must contain the markers (Living) and (Animal).

Little is known about the ordering of semantic markers although it is clear that there are category inclusion relations such that the category represented by one semantic marker is a subcategory of another marker. We would want to say that the category represented by the marker (Human) is included in the category (Animate) which is in turn included in the category (Physical object). Where such relations hold, the dictionary is obviously simplified if the rule is stated once for the whole dictionary rather than the information being included in each individual lexical entry. In summary, the complex conceptual structure of a word is represented by a partially-ordered list of syntactic markers, semantic markers, and a selection restriction. All these elements are non-terminal symbols. Once more space demands that our account of this work be ludicrously over-simplified and

63

we refer the reader to the original sources previously mentioned. In reply to the kind of argument which we have outlined in the previous section the association theorist could presumably reply 'I entirely agree—but we never said we were interested in semantics. We are studying ASSOCIATIVE processes'. This is, in effect, Deese's (1962) answer, where he argues that it is wrong or pointless to classify the structural nature of associations because Associations are Associations are Associations. Our answer to this strategy is fourfold. We shall argue:

1. that a competence theory of semantics is necessary;

2. that this same competence theory can serve as a principled basis for explaining results obtained by associationist experimenters and described by associationist theories;

3. that the competence theory can adequately characterize results obtained by associationist experimenters which run counter to associationist theory; and

4. that many psychologists who believe they are associationists in fact PRESUPPOSE a structured semantic theory.

The combination of these arguments leads us to suppose that there is no such thing as association if association theory is interpreted as embodying a substantive hypothesis rather than as being a vague way of talking.

Earlier in this paper we illustrated the kind of data which necessitated the development of a semantic theory. It would seem that many 'associative' relationships can be easily characterized as conceptual relationships specified within this semantic theory. For instance, Jarret & Scheibe (1962) included the word pairs

A   *command* : *order*
       wish : *want*
B   *command* : *cabbage*
       wish : *table*

in a paired-associate learning experiment. It is clear that any results which show the A pairs to be easier to learn by virtue of their 'associative' relationship lend equal support to the notion that the obtained greater ease of learning is due to the conceptual similarity (in this case, synonymity) between the members of the A pairs. We note, indeed, that Cofer (1957) reported a study showing a high correlation between judged synonymity ratings for word-pairs and the extent of overlap between the associations to each of the judged word-pairs. Jenkins, Mink & Russell (1958) included

man : *woman*
king : *queen*

64

as instances of pairs having a high associative strength. In this experiment also the obtained clustering in free-recall can be equally well explained conceptually. The words in each pair differ by virtue of sex-antonymy, and nothing more. Where the dictionary entry for one word of each pair contains the marker (Male) the other contains the marker (Female). The various kinds of specific antonymy relationships which hold for certain word-pairs would seem to be particularly powerful psychological variables. One conclusion reached by Carroll, Kjerdergaard, & Carton (1962), in an especially pertinent and precise experimental study, reads as follows: 'A large component of what is referred to as communality of response to the K-R stimulus list is based upon the responses to a relatively small sub-set of stimuli which can be identified behaviourally and which are here called opposite-evoking stimuli.' Moran, Mefferd, & Kimble (1964) also report that subjects tend to come to 'free'-association testing situations with strong 'sets' to give synonyms, antonyms, and superordinates. Those subjects with antonym sets tend to produce especially fast responses.

Various directionality of generalization effects would also seem to be accounted for in terms of the hierarchical structure of some lexical entries. Thus Mink (1957) and Maltzman & Belloni (1964) note that a response learned to the word *eagle* generalizes to *bird*. However, a response learned to *bird* does not generalize to *eagle*. This is not unduly surprising as clearly the word *eagle* contains the semantic marker (Bird) whereas the reverse is not true.

It is true, of course, that there will be 'associative' connections between words which are not marked at all in a semantic theory. For instance, the relationship between

$$
\left.\begin{array}{l} milk \\ snow \\ lint \end{array}\right\} : white
$$

or between

$$
\left.\begin{array}{l} skunk \\ cabbage \\ goat \end{array}\right\} : smelly
$$

The relationships here are not semantic but rest upon possible stimulus-properties of the referents of *milk, snow* etc. It is, however, precisely in this kind of situation that experimental results have been somewhat equivocal. It would seem that when such material has been presented in what might be called a concept-specification situation, that is, when more than one example of the relationship has been presented simultaneously,

65

positive results (e.g. ease of learning as a function of the strength of the connections between the list-members) have been obtained (Underwood & Richardson, 1956; Kaplan, 1959); but negative results have obtained when the material was presented sequentially in a learning situation (Richardson, 1962). This, however, is exactly what one would expect if people used their common semantic knowledge of word-relationships as a matter of course in order to structure learning situations, but if they had to learn, almost from scratch, which specific referential property (out of a rather large number of possibilities) had been used by the experimenter in constructing his material. The ability, then, of unlabelled associative networks to incorporate such relationships does not mean that associative theories express more generalizations than semantic theories; rather, they express pseudo-generalizations between concepts which are better kept apart. It would seem that early experimenters, from Thumb & Marbe (1901) to Esper (1918) and Jung (1919), were well aware of these points. (Woodworth, 1938, contains an excellent summary of this work.) Monolithic association theories merely obscure important qualitative differences.

One way of looking at work in this area then is to ask, first, what kinds of structure exist in typical lists used in experiments, and, secondly, what strategies will people adopt in order to discover this structure—specifically, are the strategies biased in certain directions? We would expect that a list, randomly selected, of highly-associated word-pairs would contain examples of different types of semantic relationship—for example full or partial synonymy, antonymy, category inclusion—and also of different types of relationship concerning the actual referents of the words (e.g. their physical characteristics, places where they are typically found and so on). No GENERAL principle of conceptual similarity will inform such a list, although the general principle of associative relationship by definition will. This statement seems to be true of most of the published experimental lists. On the other hand, a list containing word pairs selected according to a single conceptual variable (synonym, antonym, etc.) has, by definition, a general semantic principle of organization, although the associative strengths of the pairs may be quite low. Whenever tests have been made of the relative psychological potency of associative (but nonconceptual or inconsistently conceptual) versus conceptual (semantic) variables it would seem that the conceptual variables are more powerful. Thus Higa (1962), studying interference effects in paired-associate learning (word: nonsense-syllable), showed that lists which contain pairs of synonyms and lists which contain pairs of antonyms produced greater interference effects (i.e. retarded learning) than lists containing highly associated, but inconsistently structured, word-pairs. Equivalently, Marshall & Cofer (1961), studying clustering effects in free recall, showed that word-pairs which were semantically related, but only slightly related associatively, clustered to a significantly greater extent than word-pairs of greater associative relatedness but where the nature of the relationship was in terms of real-world knowledge. It would seem, then, that whilst people can and do use non-semantic knowledge in order to structure learning tasks, semantic skills and strategies are dominant. This is only reasonable, as semantic theory explicates what people must know if they are speakers of the language, and further explicates it in a highly systematic form. Knowledge of the real word, however, will be probabilistic and is unlikely to admit of fully general description (Bar-Hillel, 1960).

Finally we note that many investigators who have studied psychological concomitants of so-called 'taxonomic associations', such as

eagle
crow → *bird*
pigeon

must presuppose internally-structured dictionary entries if their account of the relationships obtaining in their material is to be more than an *ad hoc* operational procedure. The demonstration by Bousefield (1953) of 'associative' clustering in free-recall on the basis of such taxonomic relationships is a typical experiment.

It is of interest that the dominance of semantic categories can sometimes be demonstrated in exceptionally crude ways. Thus many investigators have reported greater semantic than phonological generalization using classical conditioning paradigms (see Razran, 1961; Riess, 1940; Lacey & Smith, 1954). It is, however, unclear why experimenters should want to study human conceptual organization via such measures as salivatory responses, GSRs and dilation of blood vessels in the head. We must refer in this connection to the accumulating evidence that the successful demonstration of conditioning and generalization effects, both classical and operant, in human subjects appears to depend upon the subject's awareness of the intended relationship between stimulus and punishment or reward (see Branca, 1957; Chatterjee & Eriksen, 1960; Feather, 1965; Spielberger, 1965). This implies that cognitive theories are necessary to explain conditioned salivation. It might be simpler, then, to dispense with rolls of cotton wool in the mouth and to study cognition more directly (but, for a defence of such peripheral techniques, see Luria & Vinogradova, 1959, especially the sections on brain-damaged children).

Evidence of a different nature concerning the effect of awareness of semantic relationships comes from an experiment by Bruce (1956). Bruce investigated the intelligibility of semantically random and constrained word lists (parts of the body, things to eat) at different signal-to-noise levels. The lists containing related words were, predictably, easier to hear, but only when subjects realized that a semantic constraint had been imposed upon these lists. Analysis of the individual data revealed a sudden increase in intelligibility when the subject notices the principle which informed the material.

The general question of 'availability' and 'awareness' of semantic information is also raised by studies of 'semantic satiation'. It has long been known (Bassette & Warne, 1919) that prolonged massed repetition of word seems to produce feelings of 'loss of meaning'. This effect is known as semantic satiation. More recent studies have tried to index and quantify such meaning loss by showing that massed repetition leads to atypical free-associations being produced (Smith & Raygor, 1956), and to neutralization of judgements on the evaluation, potency and activity scales of Osgood's semantic differential (Lambert & Jakobovits, 1960). In our terms, however, such measures are non-conceptual (i.e. they do not provide an account of semantic relationships concerning meaning and reference in the traditional sense). Fillenbaum (1964), on the other hand, studied the effect of massed repetition upon semantic decision-making. Subjects were required to judge, as quickly as they could, whether or not two words were synonymous. Before performing this task they repeated words which were either identical with, unrelated to, or synonymous with one of the words of the judgement task. The results indicated that prior semantic satiation of the words used in the later synonymity decision task produced significantly faster judgements than when an unrelated word had been satiated. This would seem to indicate that whatever is satiated in semantic satiation it is not knowledge of word-meaning. It seems probable, then, that the term semantic satiation refers to a loss of affective vividness. There is some evidence, however (Yelen & Schulz, 1963) that, on some of the semantic differential scales, massed repetition leads to more extreme rating being produced. No systematic explanation of this finding was offered by Yelen & Schulz.

SOME RELATIONS BETWEEN GRAMMAR AND SEMANTICS

We may reasonably demand that a semantic theory should do considerably more than provide an account of word-meaning. Most notably, it should provide an account of the meaning of sentences. It is in this area

68

that traditional learning theories have been even more unhelpful than usual. Representative accounts (Skinner, 1957; Mowrer, 1954, 1960) tend to assert that the sentence is a 'conditioning device' which allows the meaning of, for example, *is a thief* to be conditioned to the meaning of *Tom*. We presume that this strange device would also condition the meaning of *ate twelve bananas* to the meaning of *Tom* (under the appropriate conditions and after the appropriate number of reinforcements). It might be thought that two-stage (i.e. 'mediational') associative theories are capable, in principle, of accounting for the data, which we have argued require explication by a semantic theory. Fodor (1965) has, however, shown that single- and two-stage associative theories are formally indistinguishable in terms of their substantive claims. They differ only in that some of the processes and entities postulated in the two-stage account are unobservable. In the absense of a formal account of QUALITATIVELY different semantic relations the question of whether we write our conditioning diagrams as S → R or as S → s → r → R is of interest solely to type-setters.

Rather than attempt to unravel the 'pseudo-scientific gobbledegook' (Fodor, 1965) of these theories we will describe very briefly some recent linguistic attempts to specify the syntactic structures which are relevant to semantic interpretation. Some aspects of these have already been mentioned. To repeat them from a different viewpoint may serve to clarify some of the interrelationships involved.

The essential insight of transformational grammar (Chomsky, 1955) was that sentences must be characterized by two structural descriptions, not one, as would be the case with PSG. This insight is clarified and generalized in Chomsky (1965). The necessity for two structural descriptions can be clearly seen from such forms as imperatives. The surface-structure *Go away* is understood, by ordinary speakers and traditional grammarians, as a realization of the underlying form:

IMP + *You* + *will* + *go* + *away*

One of the sources of evidence for such a statement is that fact that 'tag questions' of the form

Go away, will you?

are fully grammatical, whilst there are no sentences of the form, for example,

*Go away, did he?

Syntactic theory must therefore provide, first, a description of the underlying or deep-structure of sentences and, secondly, a description of the surface- or derived-structure. The function of transformational rules is to map deep into surface representations. The strong (and hence, if incorrect, easy to falsify) hypothesis advanced by Katz & Postal (1964) and Chomsky (1965) is that only the deep-structure receives a semantic interpretation (or, to put it another way, no transformational rule changes meaning). In the course of this work some preliminary attempts have been made to characterise such notions as 'subject', 'direct object', 'main verb', 'modifier of head noun', in terms of unique sub-configurations of symbols in underlying phrase-markers. These relational concepts are clearly essential to semantic interpretation. Consider the sentences:

The Apache are eager to kill
The Apache are easy to kill.

The sentences, whilst appearing superficially to have the same structure, clearly entail quite different subject-object relationships (Chomsky, 1964). The attitude of the US cavalry would thus be more determined by the deep-structure of the sentences than by the surface-structure. Katz & Fodor (1963) and Katz & Postal (1964) provide an outline of a finite set of 'projection rules', which are applied from the 'bottom' to the 'top' of underlying phrase-markers in order to amalgamate the semantic readings of lower-order constituents (down to the individual lexical items, of course) to form readings for higher-order constituents (right up to the initial 'S' symbol). Formal definitions can then be stated, in terms of the projection rules and derived readings, for such notions as a sentence that is 'semantically well-formed', 'semantically anomalous', 'semantically ambiguous', 'analytic', 'synthetic' (see Katz, 1964*b*; Staal, 1965).

We would expect speech-recognition (sentence-recognition) to involve, then, the extraction of the deep-structure of an utterance from the surface-structure which, at most, constitutes the overt input. We would further expect that representations in memory will be in the form of deep- rather than surface-structures (or perhaps even more accurately, in the form of the semantic reading of the deep-structure). The fact that memory for the 'gist' of a sentence (or paragraph or book) is more accurate than verbatim recall may be blatantly obvious but none-the-less requires an explanation.

Little is yet known concerning the psychological aspects of deep-structure but the results which have been obtained are encouraging. Blumenthal (1965) studied the recall of ordinary full passives as compared to passives with deleted agents and non-agent *by*-phrases inserted (e.g. *The gloves were made by tailors* and *The gloves were made by hand*). The effectiveness of the agent and the non-agent *by*-phrase as an aid in prompted recall was studied. As expected, the logical subject was a more efficient prompt than the non-agent phrase. Slobin (1963) has reported that children appear to have especial difficulty with 'reversible' passives (compare *The boy was hit by the girl* and *The engine was repaired by the mechanic*). The task used was deciding whether a sentence was true or false of a given picture. Confusion between the logical subject and the logical object is possible in one case, but not in the other, and is reflected in the errors made. This variable would also appear to be an important determinant of performance in short-term memory tasks using adult aphasics (Newcombe & Marshall, 1966). The problem may arise when (especially under time-pressure?) an attempt is made to interpret the surface-structure directly. *The boy...hit...the girl* is semantically well-formed (the implications of *was* and *by* are accordingly not explored). *The engine...repaired...the mechanic* is semantically deviant and hence force consideration of *was* and *by* in order to extract a non-deviant reading for the sentence node. The above analysis suggests that the greater psychological difficulty of reversible passives may be due not so much to confusions in memory but rather to erroneous (incomplete) analysis of the input. Thorne's (1966) perceptual analysis model should throw some light on this problem. (The reader may recall a partially analogous argument arising from Gomulicki's, 1952, re-evaluation of Bartlett's, 1932, data on the recall of culturally unfamiliar material.) Marshall (1965) reported experiments in which it was shown that subjects' semantic interpretation of ambiguous sentences (e.g. *The man looked over the girl*; *Visiting relatives can be boring*) could be biased in the direction of the deep-structure of the sentences which preceded them in a paraphrase production task (e.g. *The man stared across the street* or *The man switched on the radio*; *Collecting antiques can be rewarding* or *Amusing films can be exhausting*). Mehler (1965) has performed white noise experiments on the intelligibility of similar material. Subjects heard, and had to repeat back, ten partially masked sentences of a particular syntactic type and an eleventh 'set-incongruous' sentence (with the same surface-structure as the preceding ones but a different deep-structure). In general, the results indicated that the deep-structure incongruous sentence was more difficult to perceive. A particularly neat experiment by Savin (1966) emphasizes the fact that memory-representations are coded and stored in terms of deep-structure. It is well-known that self-embedded sentences (*The man—that the woman saw—left the office*) are, in some sense, more difficult to remember than their right-branching equivalents (*The woman saw the man—who left the office*). Miller & Isard (1964) is a representative experiment. Yet the deep-structure of such sentences is either identical or closely similar. The results obtained by Miller & Isard could, however, arise from at least two causes: (i) because they have an especially complex representation in memory; (ii) because their deep-structure is difficult to compute—and so in effect was not learnt in the first place. Savin tested these explanations in the following manner. Self-embedded and right-branching sentences either followed or preceded by strings of nouns were presented for recall. The results showed that when the sentences were FOLLOWED by the word-strings just as many words could be recalled correctly after self-embedded sentences as after right-branching ones. When the sentences were PRECEDED by the word-lists, however, fewer self-embedded than right-branching sentences could be recalled (after correctly remembered word-lists). These results, then, show that, as predicted by deep-structure theory, self-embedded and right-branching sentences take up equivalent amounts of 'memory-space'. Psychological differences between such sentences are due to the difficulty of obtaining their deep-structure. (It is known that for any given finite automaton there will always be a degree of self-embedding which is uncomputable by that automaton; Chomsky, 1956, 1959.) It would also appear, as we have mentioned before, that most of the early psychological results on the relative difficulty of learning, remembering, and unscrambling different sentence-types can be interpreted in terms of the discrepancy between surface- and deep-structures for these types. In most of the relevant cases, Miller's (1962b) 'kernel form + syntactic footnotes' memory-storage hypothesis can be successfully reinterpreted within the later developments of linguistic theory. Further psychological support for the notion that semantic relations are expressed by the deep-structure and that transformational complexity will therefore impair comprehensibility (or at least require more computation in order to discover the meaning) comes from experiments by Coleman (1964). Coleman had matched groups of subjects read, once, passages containing many passives and nominalized forms of verbs and adjectives, and the same passages converted (wherever possible) into the more underlying active main verb forms. The results of a multiple-choice questionnaire given afterwards revealed that significantly more was recalled from the active verb passage than from the original highly transformed one. This result was found on all the measures of performance used, including scoring synonyms as correct.

As indicated above, some suggestive results on the representation and coding of adjective + noun phrases are provided by Gonzales & Cofer (1959), using the technique of clustering in free-recall (previously described for single word studies, e.g. Jenkins & Russell, 1952). In one condition, they presented subjects with a list of nouns containing the marker (Higher Animal) modified by adjectives denoting strength or power, and a list of nouns containing the marker (Article of clothing) modified by colour adjectives. Pairs from the two lists were presented in random order. In the other condition, the adj + noun pairs were cross-classified with respect to these semantic markers (e.g. *brown horse, powerful lion; blue dress, strong shirt*). Subjects were then asked to recall only the nouns. It was observed that, in free-recall, the nouns initially presented in the first condition showed a significantly greater tendency to cluster into the (Higher animal) and (Article of clothing) groups than they did in the second (adjectives cross-classified) condition. In further experiments Gonzalez & Cofer showed that noun-lists which show no tendency to show clustering in free-recall could be made to do so by presenting them initially in adj + noun phrases where the adjectives (alone) are known to cluster. (Again in the free-recall task, only the nouns were asked for.) Equivalent results were obtained for the reverse condition, that is, for presentation of adj + noun phrases, where the adjectives, singly, do not cluster but the nouns do.

Gonzalez & Cofer interpret their results in terms of mediated associations, but Cofer (1965) admits that this does not give an especially sensible or explanatory account of the findings. Here we will just point out that the technique might be a useful one for studying predictions derived from semantic theory. The necessity for structural (i.e., syntactic and semantic rule-governed) models for perceptual tasks using language-material can even be demonstrated when the material consists of statistical approximations. Thus Morton (1964a), studying the fast reading aloud of zero- to eighth-order approximations (and text), found that the majority of errors were made when attempting to preserve grammatical and semantic continuity in highly abnormal material. Verbs and pronouns were altered, or invented, to agree with preceding noun phrases; further errors were then made in order to agree with previous errors; synonyms and alternative members of antonym-sets were frequently substituted for the stimulus words. It is of interest that this last type of error bears a striking relationship to the reading errors, with no time pressure, made by certain dyslexic patients; cf. Marshall & Newcombe (1966) for a representative case-study.

A potentially rewarding area for testing theories of performance is the study of 'semi-sentences' (in the sense of Katz, 1964*b*). Experiments by Miller & Isard (1963) and by Marks & Miller (1964) show that sentences which break the selectional rules of the grammar, such as *Colourless green ideas sleep furiously*, are less intelligible in noise and more difficult to learn than fully well-formed sentences. Roberts & Marshall (1966) studied the effect of breaking either subcategorizational or selectional rules in NP + V + Adj constructions—*The man found sad* or *The chair seems sad*. Two tasks were used: solving sentence-anagrams and correcting the sentences. Time and error scores for both tasks indicated that sentences which broke subcategorization rules were more difficult to handle than sentences which broke selectional rules. This is to be expected as the grammar (Chomsky, 1965) is ordered so that subcategorization rules are applied in a base-structure derivation before selectional rules. Hemming (1966) studied a constructional semantic task based on the observation of Katz (1964) that English nouns may be partitioned on the basis of whether or not they contain an evaluation marker (compare *The knife is good* with *The planet is good*). Subjects were given pairs of evaluative adjectives and nouns whose lexical entries either include or do not include an evaluation marker. Their task was to produce, as quickly as they could, a well-formed sentence containing the given pair of words. Significantly longer was taken to produce sentences which included the evaluative adjective and non-evaluative noun pairs.

Coleman (1965) has reported experiments concerned with the rating, for grammaticality, of word-strings, which apparently break the rules of the Chomsky (1957) and Lees (1960) grammars on various levels, and with the learning of these strings. Coleman interprets his results as confirmation for a linguistically defined 'scale of grammaticality'. The paper, however, produced more confusion than it resolves. Coleman appears to treat the hierarchical levels of derived constituent structure as if they were no more than a Markovian 'substitution in frames' schema with the classes more or less narrowly defined. This ignores the fact that rewrite rules operate on the basis of preceding choices, and plays havoc with the morphophonemic rules of these grammars. The general point here is that grammars have many different types of rules, all of which can be broken. But breaking a rule of one type must not be regarded as equivalent in any psychological or linguistic sense to breaking a rule of a different type. Note that the attempt to specify degrees of grammaticality described in Miller & Chomsky (1963), which appears superficially to be related to Coleman's procedure, is stated only in terms of sub-classes of nouns and verbs.

Marks (1965) contains a fuller account of psychological aspects of 'semi-sentences', including some interesting results on the interaction of serial order, of final production, upon judgements of grammaticality. It would appear that ungrammaticality, or rather unacceptability, is greatest when similar distortions appear early in sequence, on any level. For an important discussion of the problems involved when studying the learning of syntactically structured strings, without either phonological or semantic information, see Miller & Stein (1963).

We hope that the scope of investigations of 'semi-sentences' will eventually be broadened to include formal studies of such rule-breakers as poets and schizophrenics. It is clear that the ability to produce and understand various kinds of 'semi-sentence' is a part of normal competence (for discussion cf. Katz, 1964*b*; Cohen, 1965). Many examples of this fact have become cliches—*Misery loves company*. Various standard works of literary explication (e.g. Empson, 1955; Richards, 1929; Wellek & Warren, 1949) contain extensive discussion—sometimes on a fairly rigorous level—of the type of data which must eventually be accounted for in any theory of cognitive skills. We do not believe it an accident that finite dictionaries of rhetorical devices exist, although the danger for theories of, for example, metaphor is that the number of different kinds of 'similarity' that human beings can recognize may be impossibly large (cf. Koen, 1965, for a preliminary psychological investigation of metaphor; and Levin, 1962; Thorne, 1965, for suggestions concerning various kinds of syntactic explication of poetic discourse).

We are not competent to discuss schizophrenia in any detail but will just indicate some of the more pertinent problems with reference to our present topic. Lorenz (1961) writes: 'We are faced with the paradox that while we recognize schizophrenic language when we see it, we cannot define it.' Some examples will illustrate the point: *I find all the things that are Thursday ; The colours of tradesmen are mostly dry as when the grass withers—red as when it burns away*; *I started with a sense that justice was next to the nebulous thing which no one can describe*. We do not, of course, claim that all schizophrenics talk like this, or even those who do, do so always. Many, however, sometimes do and would be described, for obvious reasons, as 'thought-disordered'. This fact may take us out of the realm of language studies as such; for, if the schizophrenic has disordered feelings, thoughts, beliefs, and so on, or is unwilling to disclose his thoughts except in code, then we would expect no more than that this would be reflected in his language. The paranoid patient who complains that 'the prime minister and the archbishop are poisoning me with x-rays' may have a pathological belief system, but nothing is wrong with his language. However, when the patient's speech seems similar to certain types of poetic or mystical discourse we might expect that rigorous linguistic studies of 'semi-sentences' may give some insight into the underlying 'thought-disorder' or 'communication-barrier'. A theory of 'semi-sentences' should help us to discover the 'source' sentences which underlie the overt behaviour. Any general theory will again probably depend upon our being able to provide finite and non-trivial accounts of such notions as 'possible metaphor'. Whitehorn (1958) gives examples of cases where the physician has 'spotted' the metaphor and been able to conduct sensible discussion with the patient on this basis. Lorenz (1963) and Forrest (1965) provide useful discussions of the role of 'style' and 'poetics' in schizophrenic language. Bateson, Jackson, Haley & Weakland's (1956) 'double-bind' account of schizophrenia may throw light on the sense in which the patient both does and does not want to communicate. Laffal, Lenkoski, & Ameen's study (1956) of a patient who regularly exchanged *yes* for *no*, *right* for *wrong*, and *do* for *don't* is interesting in this connection. One point at least is clear: if language studies are to be of any use in this area we must go well beyond counts of the relative frequency of *I* and *you*, abstract and concrete nouns, and so on. We must describe when and how specific rules of the semantic component are broken by individual patients.

Complete performance theories will need to go beyond semantic studies and will have to systematize various 'pragmatic' rules that select utterances which are not merely well formed but also 'appropriate to the situation'. It is known both from comparative grammatical studies (McMahon, 1963), and from studies of problem-solving and concept-formation (Hovland & Weiss, 1953; Bruner, Goodnow & Austin, 1956; Donaldson, 1959) that negative information is more difficult to process than positive information. Experiments by Wason (1961) use tasks concerned with odd and even numbers. Subjects were required to determine whether a statement about a number is true or false and to produce a number that will make a given sentence either true or false. Even at the end of practice it was found that negative statements (e.g. *Seven is not an even number*) required longer to evaluate, and the numbers longer to produce, than their corresponding affirmatives (*Seven is an odd number*). This, however, raises the question why we have negative statements at all. In a later paper, Wason (1965) hypothesizes that 'In assertive discourse the function of such statements is generally to emphasize that a fact is contrary to an expectation'. Consider the sentence *A pig is not a bird*; this is true but ridiculous. No one would have supposed that a pig was a bird. But *A spider is not an insect* is quite reasonable. Many people believe that spiders are insects. Equivalently, a statement such as *The train was not late this morning* seems to presuppose that it normally does arrive late (cf. *The man did not beat his wife last night*). Wason's experiments used material which was overtly described by such sentences as (*a*) *Circle No. 4 is blue and the rest are red* (the 'exceptionality group') or (*b*) *Seven circles are red and one is blue* (the 'ratio group'). Subjects were then presented with specific stimulus items and had to complete sentences such as, for the (*a*) group, *Circle No. 7 is* (*is not*) —— or, for the (*b*) group, *Exactly one* (*seven*) *circle*(*s*) *is* (*are*) (*not*) ——. The results indicated that 'When the stimuli are described in terms of an exceptional item and a residual class, the response to negative statements is facilitated, if these statements deny that the exceptional item possesses the property of the residual class.' No such facilitation of negatives was found when the stimuli had previously been described in terms of a larger and a smaller class. The influence of the affective connotations of negative statements is studied in Wason & Jones (1963) and in Eifermann (1961). Eifermann's experiments use Hebrew, which possesses two negative terms, one used in all contexts, the other in all contexts except prohibitive ones.

We may also inquire into the pragmatic function of the passive (another form which is difficult to handle psychologically and seems at first glance to have no purpose). Laird (1966) has reported experiments in which subjects were required to draw such 'situations' as *Red follows blue* and *Blue is followed by red*. It was shown that the area of the drawing given over to the surface subject of both actives and passives was greater than the area given to the surface objects of both types. Furthermore, the area given to the surface subject of passives was greater than that given to the surface subject of actives. We might therefore hypothesize that the function of the passive is to emphasize the importance of the logical object by placing it in the position of the surface subject (in actives, of course, surface and logical subjects occupy the same position). Evidence for this notion is also provided by Anderson (1963) who showed that recall is better for the surface subject than for the surface object in both active and passive sentences. Clark's (1965) results are also interesting in this connection. Subjects were asked to fill in the content words of active and passive sentence frames. An informational metric was calculated of the constraint imposed by the choice of 'actor' upon 'verb' and 'logical object', of 'logical object' upon 'verb' and 'actor', and so on. The pattern of these constraints differed between the active and passive frames. (For a general discussion of, and experiments on, the notion of 'reasonable verbal encoding of a given situation', see Carey, 1964.)

Finally, we invite the reader to consider what has gone wrong with the following communications (Parsons, 1965):

1. *Mr — was elected and has accepted the office of People's Church-warden. We could not get a better man!* (Parish magazine)

2. *The Prime Minister said it was a loose classification by the Board of Trade. 'Locomotives, ships, and aircraft' should have read 'Wire mattresses, tacks, nails, and manhole-covers'.* (Daily Mail)

3. *A farmer's wife is best shot.* (Glasgow Evening Citizen)

Our ability to explain these jokes (for English speakers) would be a good informal test of our understanding of linguistic performance.

ON EVALUATION PROCEDURES

In conclusion, a brief note on implicit theoretical issues, may be in order. Some of the distinctions to which we have referred above stem from the discussion of grammatical theory by Chomsky and his associates. We assume these distinctions to have relevance to discussion of theory in social science, and psychological theory in particular. A clear distinction is drawn by Chomsky (1965) between the ways grammars may be justified. One way is to compare them with respect to their descriptive adequacy, which in turn may be on two levels. They may be compared as to (i) their WEAK descriptive power—that is, whether all and only the possible terminal strings of a language are generated; and (ii) their STRONG generative power—that is, whether the structure assigned to these strings describes correctly how the idealized native speaker would understand these strings. On the other hand, linguistic theory, constructed as an explanatory system whereby descriptions of specific phenomena are deduced from general principles, may be evaluation on internal grounds. The problem of evaluating grammars becomes one of devising procedures for deciding what are 'similar processes' and 'natural classes'—that is, what are significant generalizations. As Lees (1957) has clearly indicated, attention is diverted from unrealistic operational demands for mechanical procedures in deciding between alternative theories—typically expressed in so-called 'crucial experiments'. It is now focused on formulating rigorous criteria of relative excellence within a theory. One important corollary of this notion is that a general linguistic theory will be concerned with studies of language acquisition which aim to discover necessary features of a Language Acquisition Device (cf. McNeill, 1966). Chomsky is concerned with 'the predisposition of the child to search for certain types of regularity in natural language'. An explanatory theory will evaluate grammars

78

as to how far they correctly specify the form of the regularities used by the child in the acquisition of language. This takes us beyond the mere specification of linguistic universals, to what Fodor (1964) called a 'phase-one theory'—where the features are functionally defined.

Let us put all this another way. If the questions the observer proposes to ask are about what native speakers will accept as grammatical utterances, then he needs a competence model $L(C)$* of the native speakers' tacit competence $L(C)$. If the questions have to do with the actual production and understanding of language under various conditions, then he needs a performance model $L(P)$* of the actual linguistic behaviour, both productive and interpretive, $L(P)$. But according to Chomsky's conception of the task, it is not adequate for the construction of $L(C)$* to find a set of rules capable of generating any grammatical utterance, and none that is ungrammatical. Nor will such considerations as economy serve as criteria for preferring one set to another. The criteria must relate to the 'faculté de langage'. The aim is to explain WHY certain features are common to all human languages.

What sort of model do we need to answer these questions? Neither $L(C)$* nor $L(P)$* as defined above can do it. We need to discover what determines the form ultimately taken by 'tacit competence'. One approach to this, is to ask such questions as: under what constraints does it develop—what limits are set to its possible variations? As answers to these questions more is needed than a succession of static competence models at different stages of development. We need to know how the child, and adult, STRUCTURES the language system—that is, we need a model of how organisms structure their behaviour.

Now the structuring of language is not the only kind of structuring that goes on (cf. Piaget, 1954, for indications of this in early life; and Lashley, 1951, for more general considerations). So ideally we require a model of structuring behaviour that will take these general behavioural considerations into account. One approach is to see how far other kinds of behaviour can be appropriately described with similar formal systems to those developed within linguistics. Following Miller, Galanter & Pribram (1960), Miller & Chomsky (1963) make some tentative suggestions along these lines about the description of complex behaviour; and some accounts applying similar systematic notions are: Kirsch (1964) and Clowes (1966) on pattern perception; Marshall (1966), re-interpreting some ethological data; and Alexander (1964), on handling and relating information in planning and design. Linguistic structuring probably has some special features, but anything which tends needlessly to isolate it is obviously disadvantageous. Some expressions of insistence

79

on innate determinants of linguistic structure might have just this effect. This is not to deny that 'predispositions' to notice certain kinds of regularity exist at the point where children start to acquire language. But it may be possible to relate these predispositions to other features of early development and relate these in turn to features of a general functional theory of behaviour. Alternatives here will need to be evaluated—perhaps partially in relation to correlative physiological theories. However, at this point we call a halt as we proceed into the realm of metatheoretical futuristic dreams.

Discussion

A. L. BLUMENTHAL

I shall not attempt to discuss the vast range of data on the psychology of language that Wales & Marshall have covered.[1] They have set themselves a difficult task—if not an impossible one—in surveying such a large sample of the literature in the hope of extracting an explanation of how the human organism is able to use language. Yet they do not, in fact, attempt to present a theory of linguistic performance, but rather to present a heuristic for future research and theory. Such a presentation could be quite useful in several ways. For example, there has been considerable confusion among psycholinguists over fundamentals of theory. Most troublesome are confusions concerning competence and performance, and also confusions concerning the surface-structure and the deep-structure of syntax. The occasion of this assembly of psycholinguists provides an excellent opportunity to examine these very matters.

In spite of its title, the paper by W & M analyses competence perhaps to a greater extent than it does performance. And it does not keep the two distinct, even though the authors initially separate and define them. Much of the psycholinguistic research reviewed by W & M shows a similar confusion between the two concepts. Therefore the issue might profitably receive further discussion, and I will devote to it most of my comments. Please allow me to state once more, quite briefly, the outline of fundamental notions. I shall make a few distinctions that were not explicit in W & M.

1. Dr Blumenthal was unable to attend the Conference and, through no fault of his, his valuable comments on the paper by Wales & Marshall arrived just too late to be presented for him in his absence, as was his intention. We are very pleased to be able to publish them in the proceedings. (*The Editors*)

A GRAMMAR is a theory of a language; it is a theory for pairing sounds with meanings. At present we divide grammar into three sub-components: phonetics, syntax, and semantics. The first two of these sub-theories have been successfully advanced in the last ten years. There is little agreement concerning the present status of semantic theory. W & M did not include semantics within grammatical theory. They imply that semantics is a theory of concept formation. (One might then arrive at the conclusion it is not a part of the study of language.) But the form of the theory of language as an abstract system is that of a phonetic component which is indirectly related to a semantic component; the relating of one to the other is accomplished through syntax.

The syntactic component is, first, a description of the nature of the relations (deep-structure) that connect the parts of a sentence and there-fore that influence sentence-meaning; and, secondly, it is the phrasing (surface-structure) of the linear string of word-formatives which are the basis for the output of the phonetic system. The deep-structure is a set of relations-plus-semantic features that may be transformed into a surface-structure and then into sound. Chomsky gives strong arguments for these distinctions.

But so far my discussion has been an outline only of the theory of language structure. When followed through, it goes a long way in des-cribing WHAT a language user understands when he says that he 'under-stands a sentence'. It does not tell us how he arrives at this understand-ing. If language were a game, competence would be the rules of the game, while the actions of its players would constitute performance. The two are not the same. A person who does not know the rules of the game may briefly observe its players and attempt to imitate their actions. The imi-tator will soon be accused of making 'stupid mistakes'. In just as brief a time this erring player could have had the rules explained to him. He would then be acceptable, for he plays by rules rather than by imitation. On the other hand, he could observe and imitate for a much longer time and gradually invent rules that approximate and finally match those of the other players.

The lack of the direct availability of competence for empirical observa-tion is of concern to W & M. But this is no more of a difficulty than it is for the other sciences that must infer laws for complexly-determined events. Competence and performance are not simply the two sides of one coin; competence is only one of many systematic factors that deter-mine observable performance. Also contributing to performance are the structure of memory, the nature of attention, the mechanisms of per-ception, and the psycho-motor skills. More explicit and fundamental

81

mechanisms, for language behaviour may yet be identified. Psycholinguistic experiments deal with combinations of these systems. The Fodor & Bever (1965) experiment was a perception study; at issue was the difference between an 'active' and a 'passive' theory of speech perception. Blumenthal's (1965) memory experiments, on the other hand, were intended as a competence study in that their purpose was to show experimental verification of the competence model; use of the memory modality was incidental. W & M might have attempted such classifications for other experiments. Their statement that 'competence and performance can be usefully and adequately integrated in the explanation of linguistic behaviour', is tautological because PERFORMANCE and LINGUISTIC BEHAVIOUR are the same thing.

We have been presented with a discussion and comparison of the possibilities for finite-state, phrase-structure, and transformational performance models. Separate performance schemes are implied for phonetics, syntax, and semantics. W & M's orientation thus discloses a repetition of grammatical theory under the guise of a performance theory, which they supplement with the conclusion that any absolute separation of performance from competence means there must be a homunculus manning 'internal sentence generators'. Elsewhere they speak of some deep-structures that are more difficult to 'generate, in a psychological sense', than others, where by 'generate' they mean arrive at the surface structure. Here is the heart of the difficulty: GENERATE is a technical term that was borrowed from mathematical logic by theoretical linguists. A 'generated' sentence is one that has been described through grammatical analysis. W & M use the term in the sense of mechanics to refer to a mechanism for the production of behaviour.

We can find similar confusions in much of the psycholinguistic research. For example, there is Miller & Isard's (1963) study of the perceptual consequences of linguistic rules, which raised many of the issues that prompted W & M. The confusion results in the view that, when perceiving language, people must infer a syntactic structure before they decide on words. This implies that performance proceeds 'from the top down', through a phrase structure derivation, and ending, finally, with selection of words. Such a notion is extremely implausible. The same implausibility holds for production, which is that we decide first on the structure of a sentence and then choose its words. (Notice the same problem in Yngve, 1960, and in Johnson, 1965, and many others.)

Savin (1966) describes his experimental subjects as 'computing' the structure of self-embedded sentences. However, he gives no test to determine whether or not his subjects actually understood the doubly-embedded constructions in terms of embedded grammatical relations when they were asked to recall them. I disagree with Savin who says that people must recover underlying grammatical structure in order to remember a sentence. They must do this only to understand a sentence fully. But understanding only makes a sentence easier to remember; it is not necessary for memory. Obviously, self-embedded sentences can be reproduced without being 'computed', just as a string of unrelated words may be recalled in a given order. Some preliminary results from our laboratory at Harvard indicate that subjects seldom ever consider or attempt to process multiply-embedded sentences as such, presumably because the performance mechanism does not work that way. Subjects often, however, attempt to process these sentences as having only one embedded clause that in turn contains a compound subject followed by a compound verb. Such an interpretation of the embedded sentence of course renders it semi-grammatical because it lacks certain co-ordinating conjunctions, and sometimes lacks verb concordance. But, nevertheless, it is usually interpreted (and remembered) in a way not intended by the experimenter, who sees his language-user too much as being a generative grammar. What this means, again, is that the rules of grammar and the techniques of performance must be kept separate.

I find no obvious or natural connection between the voluminous research on word-association or on list-learning and the present line of psycholinguistic theorizing. Natural language is unique, but not because it is patterned, not because it is a communication system. Its uniqueness is as dramatic as the difference between men and other animals, including the primates, who after thousands of trials have been taught associations between binary numbers and arbitrary symbols. (We must withhold our judgement on dolphins until their communication system is analysed.) A performance theory, or 'heuristic schema' might take a comparative orientation. What is it that distinguishes language behaviour from other forms of communicative behaviour? What is it about sub-human behaviour that renders language usage impossible? Animals certainly have adequate neuromuscular apparatus for speech: certain birds can easily be taught to utter complete sentences. The bird's utterance, whether an English sentence or a mating call, is under specific stimulus control and doesn't show much variation. We say that human language is not 'stimulus bound', but instead that it is 'appropriate to the situation'. The difference is great and is important. The form of the human verbal response in the mating situation or under conditions of pain or hunger is infinitely varied. The capacity for the creative and novel use of the human communication system is unique. The corres-

83

ponding human performance capability may lie at a more cognitive level then usually considered: for instance, in the ability to make propositional judgements.

A performance schema might well suggest the techniques, mnemonics, and cues that the language user employs. W & M's schema is too lofty an abstraction to be of heuristic value in this sense. Also, it may be in error in that it suggests an order of input processing that proceeds from surface-structure to deep-structure to semantic interpretation, and these terms were used in the sense of the linguist's description of language. Such an ordering in performance is, at least to this commentator, a rather counter-intuitive notion that would require more justification from what we can learn about perception and production if it is to be considered seriously.

A. R. JONCKHEERE

I feel particularly embarrassed by this long paper by Wales & Marshall because I am hardly competent to discuss the finer points of linguistic theory; but I want to make one or two points which I hope will arouse some discussion, particularly with reference to the notion of competence and performance, which seems to be one of the central issues in the interaction between the psychologist and the linguist today. The first thing is that the notion of competence is nothing new in psychology: one might say that it is a traditional notion, in the sense that it is implicit in the idea of intelligence and intelligence testing. There is a sense in which this notion of intelligence could be considered as a disposition. We present to people a series of test items; on the basis of their responses to these test items we try to make an inference about their intellectual capacity. Piaget has been one of the few people who might perhaps be thought of, in this context, as trying to formulate the child's intellectual competence in a sense very closely allied to the notion of competence as applied to language by linguists. And it is interesting that Piaget, in doing this, has had to resort, for better or for worse (possibly worse), to various rather curious notions—his 'groupement' and various other logical calculi which he has tried to develop, in order to characterize the various stages through which a child goes, in terms of his intellectual competence. It is perhaps not surprising, from this point of view, that Piaget has had very little regard for current learning theories as being of any use to him in trying to give an account of the child's performance with respect to what he feels to be the child's competence. The same problem, in a certain sense, arises for Piaget, in the sphere of intellectual capacities, as arises for the psycholinguist when he tries to account for the performance of people with language with reference to their competence as defined by linguists.

Let us take another look at this notion. Another area of psychology, where this is perhaps exemplified, is in the attempts made by scholars such as Newell & Simon (1963) to construct a machine which is claimed to go through the successive steps in the derivation of various theorems in the propositional calculus. This is not necessarily the most efficient way of deriving these theorems from a given set of axioms and substitution and deduction rules, but it is claimed by Newell & Simon that this is the way which in some sense simulates how human beings actually go through this process; that is to say, in many cases the simplest proof or the shortest proof is not produced by the machine. It may, in fact, be rather a circuitous one, and great stress is laid by the authors on the fact that what the machine does matches quite closely the successive steps made by a human subject, although another machine could be constructed which would perform far more efficiently.

There is a sense in which the machine has a competence: given a certain input, it can go through the moves of trying to derive this expression by the application of the various deductive rules, and so on. Nevertheless, the explanation of the working of the machine is surely quite a different thing from the account of its competence; and it is not even clear in what sense the rules (the machine's competence) are built into its operation. It is one thing to say that the operation of the machine is in conformity with the rules and another thing to say that the formulation of these rules, which may be done in numerous ways, plays a very important part in the explanation of its working.

In defining this competence, linguists go through a number of stages in their thinking. One of these is what I would like to call the 'idealization' (in some sense) of actual language. They cannot be blamed for this. The natural scientist or physicist also has (in some sense) to 'idealize' the world around him; for instance, he assumes that there are continuous quantities, when he knows well that he can only measure down to a certain limit and that he should really be employing a discontinuous kind of mathematics, using finite differences; but it is very much simpler for him to work with continuous variables in the formulation of his theories. He knows, in that sense, that it is an approximation to what can possibly be observed. In the same way, the linguist 'idealizes' language and, having 'idealized' it in a certain way, then tries to characterize it and so get to this notion of competence. One major aspect of this 'idealization' is the notion that there is no limit to the length of sentence that can be produced, on the one hand, or understood, on the other. This is obviously

85

not true: there is a natural limit on the length of sentence that can be handled either by the emitter or the receiver. I am not sure that this is a trivial point. What the length is will depend on a large number of things. It will depend, for instance, on whether the sentence is spoken or written, and whether it is heard or read (in the cases of reading and writing, there is the possibility of back-tracking; and so the memory load is not so great). Similarly, one might say that there is a limit to what an adding-machine can handle. Numbers containing more than a certain number of digits cannot be put into the machine, because the register is just not big enough. Nor can one go on adding indefinitely on the machine: the store would overflow.

There is a sense in which we can describe the competence of this machine by saying that it is an adding machine and specifying the rules for addition in any number of different suitable ways; but the performance is clearly different from the competence in that there is an actual upper limit to its performance. I am inclined to believe (although one cannot decide about this *a priori*) that, because of the limitation on length, amongst other things, one would be led astray, if one tried to introduce competence notions as an explanation of performance. It does not necessarily follow that the characterization of the rules which a person is following in some form of rule-conforming behaviour has to go into the explanation of how he follows these rules or performs behaviour in conformity with them.

This question of an upper limit depends on a number of things, not only the way in which a sentence is emitted and so on, but also on the actual syntactic structure of the sentence. One sentence could be very long because the syntactic structure is relatively simple to follow, whereas other types of sentence, with different kinds of syntactic structure, will be much harder to follow. This has been clearly exemplified by Yngve's work with left- and right-hand branching systems. I point this out because it comes up in a number of contexts in the paper by W & M. For instance, Osgood's theory is criticized on the grounds that, *inter alia*, the possibility of infinitely long sentences cannot be incorporated in it. It is clear that Osgood is not trying to give a competence model here, but an account, perhaps a causal account, of human verbal behaviour. To criticize him, therefore, for not being able to produce infinitely long sentences seems to me to be a rather unreasonable thing to do, although of course his scheme may be well criticized on other grounds.

The same point comes up in connection with Yngve's work. One important implication of Yngve's 'depth' hypothesis is that there are finite memory restrictions on depth, so that left-branching contributes as much to unacceptability as does nesting and self-embedding. I am not quite clear precisely to what W & M are objecting in their reference to Yngve's hypothesis. I should have thought that all the empirical evidence at this point suggests that there is a finite memory. The upper limit, in terms of sentences, does therefore suggest that one can make a frequency count of different types of sentences. The count could be made with reference to their base structure: the probability of the occurrence in various contexts of different types of sentence ('type' now being defined in terms of the base structure) will not be zero.

Linguists often argue that language behaviour cannot be handled in terms of Markov chains, because the frequency of occurrence of any particular sentence is virtually zero. This is true, if one takes the actual sequences of words themselves; it is true, possibly, in terms of surface structure; but is it true of a base structure characterization of sentences? Is it not feasible to make probability statements about the frequency of occurrence at this level? And if one can do that, one can once again start putting stochastic elements into the generation of sentences at a deeper level. On this basis one could construct a machine that would produce intelligible sentences of one form or another on a 'quasi-random' basis. This random basis is important in the explanation of choice behaviour between one sentence and another. The fact that one can show experimentally that some types of sentences are handled in some ways with greater difficulty than others, may mean that ease of handling is a function of the frequency with which the base structured sentences occur in everyday discourse. (We have to take account of this when, for instance, we look at experiments on subliminal perception in which words of different frequencies occur; we allow for this, and control for it, in order to make inferences. Here, too, the frequency of occurrence of the basic structures may be a factor which has to be considered.) Of course, if one had the frequency count, one should still be faced with the question why some basic structures are more frequent than others. There may be a particular economy in one type. (I am now speaking psychologically, in terms of possible psychological mechanisms.) Although the absence of an upper limit to sentence-length obviously makes easier the formulation of what the linguist calls competence, the suggestion I want to make is that the transference of the notion of infinite sentences to the psychological mechanism which is to give a causal account of human performance may create difficulties for the psychologist.

Another point where the linguist's standards seem to be rather strongly influencing those of the psychologist has to do with the way in which linguists choose one grammar in preference to another in trying to give an account of competence. This depends on a number of factors, including the consideration of what are considered 'deviant' or 'non-deviant' sentences. Presumably any grammar (if it is precisely formulated) has the function of dividing all strings of words into two classes; those which, with reference to this grammar, are deviant and those which are not. How does one check this? I would think that it is not a question of taking a Gallup poll, but rather of sitting down and thinking about the more sensitive and deeper aspects of language and then deciding that certain statements are deviant and certain others are not. If a particular grammar accepts the set of deviant sentences as non-deviant, then one says that it is not so good as another grammar which rejects this set. Obviously this question of deviance and non-deviance may be correctly treated from the linguist's point of view (although, up to a point, it is a little arbitrary), but from the behavioural point of view one must have different reasons for deciding that a sentence is deviant. The psychologist has different reasons for considering a sentence to be deviant. Well, I can imagine a context in which it might be used: after all, *History admires John* or *Fate admires John* are acceptable. Sincerity, apparently, cannot be personified in this way. But it is difficult to take a sentence in complete isolation and decide whether it is deviant or not —from the psychologist's point of view at any rate. Sentences are usually admitted in various contexts; contexts of other sentences, contexts of reference, where the sentence is actually omitted, and so on.

Another criterion, which has already been mentioned, for assessing the validity or value of various types of grammar, is the resolution of different kinds of ambiguity; syntactic ambiguity, semantic ambiguity, and so on. Once again (and this was pointed out in the discussion of Thorne's paper), ambiguity rarely arises in the actual day-to-day use of speech, because the context makes clear (to put it crudely) what is meant. While it is perhaps an important thing for linguists to be able to resolve syntactic ambiguity, one wonders whether the ability to resolve this ambiguity should be a deciding criterion for the psychologist. It may be that the criterion for ambiguity which the psychologist needs when he is studying the language production of human beings is different from that of the linguist, whose task after all is essentially different. Hence the wrong grammar, from the point of view of the psychologist, may be chosen by linguists searching for their competence description because these various criteria (such as the infinite length of sentence, etc.) are not perhaps the ones that are important for psychologists. All this matters only to the extent that there is a fairly wholesale incorpora-

88

tion into the psychologist's explanatory scheme of the competence model made by the linguist.

The point that interests me about W & M's schema of linguistic performance is this: there is no input for producing sentences, but only for analysing them. Presumably the input for production should be a little arrow at the top into the conceptual matrix—just a cloud above it with 'thinks' inside it! This is not perhaps a serious criticism, but it does raise the thought that, while we can at least pose very clearly the problem of what is involved, or what has to be accounted for, in a language-comprehension system, it is extremely difficult to know what the input is for a machine that will produce a sentence as its output. It is perhaps unfair to raise this question now, but it must be faced some day. This may be the point, by the way, where my earlier mention of a probabilistic basis for the relations or interrelations between strings of what we might call the basic structure components is important. Interestingly enough, in this question of input and output the reverse is the case when we are actually doing experiments. It is far easier to study the output of subjects because they produce the sentences, whereas the input is usually something we cannot handle very well. It is an instruction like 'press the button', or something of that sort, where we cannot specify in very much greater detail what is going on.

General Discussion

B. Bett, Ruth Clark, L. J. Cohen, D. J. Dakin, Julie Greene,
P. N. Johnson-Laird, Kate Loewenthal, J. Macnamara, D. McNeill,
J. C. Marshall, J. Morton, R. C. Oldfield, R. J. Wales, and Y. Wilks.

The main points raised had to do with: (i) the sense in which sentences can be said to be of potentially infinite length; (ii) the relevance of frequency of occurrence to the construction of models of linguistic competence and performance; (iii) the notion of context; (iv) the psychological relevance of the linguist's distinction of competence and performance; (v) evaluation procedures.

In reply to Jonckheere, Marshall pointed out that Wales and he had carefully stressed the fact that such psychologists as Lashley, Tolman and Hull had made distinctions comparable with that drawn by Chomsky between competence and performance; Piaget was particularly important in this connection, being one of the few psychologists who had seriously tackled the question 'What kind of competence does the child acquire?' Jonckheere did well to draw attention to the ambiguity in W & M's references to Osgood's model: what they had intended to say was that self-embedding contributes more to difficulty (in terms of psychological processes) than does left-branching, and that this result contradicted the predictions of Yngve's depth measure. As for the possibility of carrying out frequency-counts on deep structures: these would necessarily be based upon a corpus of actual utterances, so that all the constraints known to inhibit the occurrence of unacceptable utterances of various kinds (e.g., *Black crows are black*) would operate to bias the statistics. What did such frequency counts tell one anyway? The interesting question was why some forms occur more frequently than others. With regard to context: until we had a theory of context, it was inappropriate to suggest that a knowledge of 'context' would enable us to dispense with certain parts of syntactic or semantic theory. (Wilks referred to the work of Olney, of the Systems Development Corporation, and to that of the Cambridge Language Research Unit as being of relevance to the construction of a theory of context.)

There followed a long discussion of the notion of 'infinity', as applied to the length of sentences (Morton, Cohen, McNeill, Oldfield, Wales, Bett; Cohen's contribution is printed below). It was stressed by McNeill that the condition imposed upon grammars that they should allow for the generation of sentences of unbounded length made it unnecessary to include *ad hoc* rules. The fact that 'infinitely long' sentences obviously cannot occur did not affect the nature of the rules introduced into the grammar under this condition. Cohen had asked how one would know at any point, as one was progressing along an 'infinitely long' sentence, that it was ungrammatical at that point (its structural description being incomplete); the answer was implicit in the question: the grammar must have recursion as one of its properties, and this was the reason why linguists imposed upon grammars the condition allowing for the generation of sentences of unbounded length. Oldfield suggested that the term 'infinite' was being used rather loosely in this connection and distinguished between various kinds of 'unboundedness', in particular between infinite and transfinite series. Various other aspects of this question were taken up by the other speakers. Wales granted the importance of clarifying the various senses of the term 'infinite', but stressed that it was in fact 'unboundedness', as explained by McNeill, that was important for psychology.

In the discussion of competence and performance, several speakers wondered whether there was any useful purpose served by bringing together the views of Hull, Lashley, Piaget, and Chomsky: their differences of approach were far more striking, and far more important, than their similarities. There was some discussion whether the distinction between competence and performance (as drawn by linguists) was appropriate in relation to psychological processes (Julie Greene, Kate Loewenthal, Wilks, Ruth Clark: the contributions of Kate Loewenthal and of Wilks are selected as representative of the views expressed and are printed below.)

Taking up the reference by Wilks to Chomsky's 'levels of adequacy' (see below), Marshall agreed that this would ultimately be of vital importance for psychology: Chomsky had originally introduced the notion of 'observational' adequacy in order to clarify the question of a lexically-unbounded corpus; he had then defined the notion of 'descriptive' adequacy to take account of the speakers' 'intuitions' about syntactical similarities, relations of paraphrase, and so on, in the corpus; finally, he had raised the question of deciding between two (or more) 'descriptively-adequate' grammars—this was the question of 'explanatory' adequacy. Linguists were still far from being able to tackle 'explanatory' adequacy, but when they were able to, one would expect that the psychologist might contribute materially to the solution of this question, since the answer depended, presumably, upon what was represented 'ontologically' in the brain.

Johnson-Laird returned to the question of frequency-counts: one could conceive of a simple experiment in which the subjects were asked to assess the relative frequency of such virtually-synonymous pairs as actives and passives. Suppose that the subjects agreed that the passive versions were in fact more probable: wouldn't this result enable one 'to break the circle between relative frequency and intelligibility', since there was a lot of evidence to suggest that passives are harder to comprehend than actives? And would this result have implications for the theory of competence or merely for the theory of performance? Wales thought that the results of an experiment of this kind would be relevant only for the theory of performance: passives, negatives, interrogatives, and so on, could be combined in so many ways that frequency-counts were impossible to interpret for even the simplest practical purposes. Marshall added that in many experiments of the kind proposed we really had little idea of what we were asking the subjects to do; since we did not know how they had interpreted their instructions, we could not interpret the results of the experiments.

At many points in the discussion the problem of 'accessibility of consciousness' was raised: some speakers, including Wales and Marshall, felt that little insight into a number of psycholinguistic problems would

91

be obtained until 'accessibility to consciousness' and related notions were reinstated in experimental psychology.

With regard to frequency of occurrence and context: Morton suggested that the circularity involved in the use of measures of frequency could be eliminated, or reduced, by taking account of what the subject would accept as an appropriate context; by relating, tentatively and hypothetically in the first instance, the frequency of the behaviour in question and its underlying neural determinants, and by investigating the way in which the neural determinants translated contextual information and stored information about frequency into elicited behaviour (see below). Wales said that, even if context were found to be sometimes relevant to disambiguation, the psychological reality of ambiguity still remained as a problem to be reckoned with.

MORTON: I would first of all like to compliment Wales & Marshall on producing a masterful interpretive survey of recent literature; in effect the only one available. I am very grateful to them.

Until recently I have had no firm views on the order of applying syntactic and semantic processing to the input string. W & M may have derived this impression (see above, p. 57) from the fact that I have used the term 'dictionary' to describe the assemblage of logogens (units which operate terminally to make a word available as a response). But the term 'dictionary' was, however, not meant to be taken literally. My present views are very like those of the authors (and indeed are influenced by them), except that I believe there may be a direct connection to the 'Semantic Interpretation' (see their schema of linguistic performance) which by-passes the deep structure analysis, and give to this connection a greater importance than they seem to do in their writing. I would like to put this connection after the 'Preliminary Surface Structure Analyser' rather than, as they do, before it, since the PSSA is rapid in its action and operates sequentially (cf. Thorne et al., 1965), and will therefore contribute some useful information for the 'look-up' procedure.

With regard to the role of probability and the reciprocal relationship between guessing and intelligibility measures, I would like to refer to a similar notion I have put forward elsewhere (1964c: 217), which appeared to lead to a useful way of referring to recognition without having to talk about perception. Where I think probability may have a neural counterpart is at a higher level than of words—what I have previously called 'thought units' (1964a: 61-3) and now call 'ideogens'. This is the kind of system to which I think Jonckheere was referring.

COHEN: If we are to consider the feasibility of constructing machines to simulate speech-competence, one item that needs clearing up is the

92

question whether a person should be ascribed the ability to construct infinitely long sentences, as part of his grammatical competence. There seem to me to be strong reasons against this, although several speakers have suggested it, if by an infinitely long sentence is meant a sentence of which the morphemes stand in one-to-one correspondence with the series of natural numbers. First, there would then be strings of which no finite creature could determine the grammaticalness. Secondly, in any language in which the main verb normally appears at the end of certain types of sentence, there could be no infinitely long grammatical sentences of that type. Thirdly, if a theory of grammar were to allow infinitely long sentences, its definition of the concept of a sentence's structural description could no longer be constructive—in the meta-mathematical sense. On the other hand, even if no grammatical sentence is infinitely long, the following series may well be infinitely long, namely the series which has as members the sets s_1, s_2, s_3 ..., where each s_i has as members all and only those grammatical sentences that contain exactly i morphemes. In other words, the length of grammatical sentences, so far as a theory of competence is concerned, is probably unbounded, though finite. Intuitions to the contrary tend to rely on the natural splitting up of very long conjunctive sentences into separate, shorter sentences. But suppose such a very long conjunction to occur in the antecedent of a conditional sentence, and one can no longer rely on such an escape-route.

KATE LOEWENTHAL: I would like to refer to the place where Wales & Marshall deal with the problem of distinguishing between competence and performance. They quote from Minsky and suggest that there could be no distinction between 'coding' and 'knowledge' structures on empirical grounds, and that anyway, 'some KNOWLEDGE is likely to be used in the encoding and interpretive processes'. It seems to be a slight evasion of an issue—to say that 'anyway it is in some sense true that performance incorporates competence' (i.e. knowledge).

One way of resolving this issue is to ask what is meant by 'knowledge'. When someone applies rules, does he know the rules in the sense that he is aware of them and can explicitly state them? Or does he only 'know' rules in the sense that they are reflected in performance? This is reminiscent of the situation in concept attainment tasks, in which some people can recognize and use concepts without being able to say what they are; a similar situation arises in learning experiments, where people can often recognize things without being able to produce them. I think then that it is possible to make a distinction in psychological terms between competence and performance (perhaps rather a naive one). If a person is

93

able ONLY to apply rules in his performance without conscious knowledge of what they are, then he lacks competence. If however he 'knows' rules in the sense that he is able to state them in a 'meta-language', then he could be said to have competence. This would distinguish between a SPEAKER'S competence and performance. It does happen, of course, that a LINGUIST is able to extract a competence model from a speaker's performance. But this does not tell us whether the speaker has the SAME competence, or indeed ANY competence. I think we have to assume that it is unimportant whether an individual has competence. The problem for psycholinguistics is how an individual can perform according to a set of rules which the linguist can abstract, but which the individual may be unaware of. I feel that language performance probably depends on a mechanism which is non-linguistic, or sub-linguistic—a purely cognitive ability to conceptualize, which, as has been concluded from researches on deaf children, is highly developed in individuals who have no language. Investigation into these conceptual mechanisms would, I feel, give more of an explanation of language behaviour, for I would agree with Jonckheere and Julie Greene that competence models have far more predictive than explanatory value.

WILKS: I feel I must say that nothing in the admirable paper by Wales & Marshall has helped me to see the difference between a competence-model and a performance-model. The distinction they suggest at one point between a battery of abstract rules and an algorithm is, unfortunately for them, a distinction that most metamathematicians do not accept! [At this point Wales intervened to say that in their paper he and Marshall explicitly rejected this interpretation of the distinction.] I cannot see what a competence-model would be like; or rather, where I can see what it would be like, I cannot see why anyone would want to construct one. It would be a codification of the grammar that we are taught at school, or rather of our memories of it. I do not see that one need not set out to make a model for ALL performances, for mistakes, squeaks and grunts. If competence just means freedom to make a selection, this is all right, but trivial. What Chomsky (1964) means by it comes out fairly clearly when he talks about 'levels of adequacy': if we have a number of (observationally-adequate) grammars describing the data, we might reasonably choose (a descriptively-adequate) one that also accords with our intuitions about structure. The trouble with this, of course, is that Chomsky assumes that one of the observationally-adequate grammars will be descriptively-adequate. He does not consider the fact that his is not a necessary truth! However, Chomsky's own account does have the merit that it does not assume that one must

94

START by constructing a model for intuitions, even though one may call in their help later. [At this point McNamara intervened to point out that Chomsky had never suggested starting with data.]

What I cannot follow is the suggestion made throughout the paper by W & M that there is a choice as to which kind of model one constructs. There can be no choice of a competence model, if these words are inter-related in the same way as the words in the phrase *electron model* ('a model for the electron'). On the other hand I do not see that this real difficulty is avoided by the kind of coyness that the authors show when they say that their schema of linguistic performance is 'IN NO SENSE to be understood as a model'. If that is true, then there is no point in drawing it, describing it, or discussing it. Of course it is a model, and a very sensible one too!

Third Session

David McNeill
The creation of language by children

with prepared comments by

Colin Fraser and
Margaret Donaldson

Chairman Boris Semeonoff

David McNeill

Superficial acquaintance with young children reveals one of the problems with which a theory of language acquisition must be concerned. At the age of eighteen months or so, children begin to form simple two- and three-word sentences. At four, they are able to produce sentences of almost every conceivable syntactic type. In approximately thirty months, therefore, language is acquired, at least that part of it having to do with syntax. The process of acquisition, as the title of this paper somewhat fancifully puts it, is one of invention. On the basis of a fundamental capacity for language, each generation creates language anew, and does so with astonishing speed.

A second problem for theories of language acquisition concerns the nature of what is acquired. A transformational grammar entails a distinction between the superficial and underlying structure of sentences. The underlying structure must be so arranged that transformations can apply—a requirement which, in general, means that superficial and underlying structures differ. The linguistic information included in the underlying structure is essential for comprehending sentences; yet it is abstract information, never directly manifested in the surface form of speech. Somehow, children acquire such abstractions.

These problems are separate—the acquisition of abstract structures and the speed of acquisition, although an argument can be made that the solution to one is a solution to the other. More will be said on this below. But first, it is necessary to describe the general point of view to be explored here. As suggested in the first paragraph, this is that children are endowed with a biologically-founded, inborn capacity for language acquisition. This hypothesis is not new. The existence of an inborn capacity for language was taken for granted during the nineteenth century. Horatio Hale, for example, in his Vice-Presidential address to the Anthropology Section of the American Association for the Advancement of Science in 1886 made large use of a presumed capacity for language in accounting for the origin of different linguistic stocks among Oregon and California Indians. Although seen as conservative, his theory was well received. However, stated so simply, the view that children are endowed with a capacity for language is not a particularly interesting hypothesis. It merely repeats the observation, apparently true, that man is alone among all animals in possessing language. To make the hypothesis interesting, it is necessary to show what some of the specific features of this capacity might be. On this, some definite suggestions can be made.

Chomsky (1965), Katz (1966), and others as well, have argued that the specific content of a child's capacity for language is manifested in the form of linguistic universals. These are features that define the general form of human language and so appear in natural languages everywhere, regardless of physical or cultural setting. A brief review of their argument will set the context for what follows.

One may think of the problem of language acquisition as being essentially the same as the problem faced by linguists in evaluating grammars written for particular languages. In constructing a grammar, a linguist hopes to reconstruct the tacit competence possessed by fluent speakers of the language. A child hopes to become such a speaker, so he, too, must reconstruct the competence of fluent speakers. In other words, he must formulate the grammar of the language to which he is exposed. One way a linguist has to evaluate the accuracy with which a grammar represents linguistic knowledge is to become a fluent speaker himself, and test the formulations of the grammar against his own intuitions. A child, however, cannot do this. He cannot evaluate the grammar that he supposes to underlie the language he overhears by becoming first a fluent speaker and then judging the grammar against his intuitions. It is acquisition of the grammar in the first place that poses the problem. A child must evaluate proposed grammars in a different manner; and this, too, corresponds to a method of evaluation available to linguists.

In addition to testing a grammar against the intuitions of a native speaker, a linguist may use linguistic theory to select one grammar from a set of candidates, the selected grammar then representing the competence of native speakers. The selection is based on the existence of various linguistic universals. It is in this sense that linguistic theory is a hypothesis about the general form of human language. Evaluation conducted in this manner leads to what Chomsky (1965) calls 'explanatory adequacy'. Explanatory adequacy is obtained when linguistic theory gives a PRINCIPLED basis for accepting one way of representing the competence of the speakers of a language over other possible ways. A grammar descriptive of linguistic competence is explained when it can be derived from linguistic theory.

Language acquisition by children can be regarded in the same way. The terms of linguistic theory, if they were available to a child, would allow him to make a principled choice of the grammar by which to represent the competence of fluent speakers of the language to which he is exposed, and thus to become such a speaker himself. According to the argument advanced by Chomsky and Katz, this is precisely what a child does because linguistic theory describes his inborn capacity for language.

100

An innate capacity for language, therefore, can be represented by the set of linguistically universal statements that are organised into linguistic theory. The acquisition of language can be regarded as the guided (principled) choice of a grammar, made on the basis of a child's innate capacity, a choice consistent with the evidence contained in the corpus of speech provided by the mature speakers to which a child is exposed.

Linguistic theory is under development and is far from complete. Linguists cannot yet make principled choices of grammars. Nonetheless, it is fairly clear what some of the universal statements in linguistic theory will be. They will include such matters as the formal distinction between rules of formation and transformation; the distinction between base and surface structure; the definitions of various grammatical relations, such as subject-predicate, main verb-object, and, possibly, modifier-head; plus many more. Some comment will be made below on each of these, particularly the last set—the basic grammatical relations. First, however, it is necessary to clarify two implications of these proposals of Chomsky and Katz. How does this theory account for the acquisition of abstract features, and how does it account for the speed of acquisition?

As to the first question, the answer is that it is badly put. The question should be instead: why do languages have abstract features at all? The answer to this revised question is quite simple: children place them there. It is possible for languages to contain abstract features because in each language these features correspond to aspects of children's capacity for language acquisition. Along with much else, the general notion of abstract phrase structures being transformed into surface structures is included in linguistic theory. This decision is independently motivated by many linguistic considerations, and does not depend on the effort to formulate a theory of language acquisition. The implication for language acquisition is that much of what children acquire consists of particular transformations, since most universal features of language are related to the base structure (Chomsky, 1965).

In answer to the second question—how to account for the speed of language acquisition—it is necessary to suppose that the features of language that correspond to the linguistic universals are among the first acquired. This hypothesis leads us to expect that children's first grammatical efforts will include the abstract features contained in linguistic theory. If it should be otherwise, an inborn capacity for language acquisition could NOT account for the speed of acquisition. However, if it should be the case that children display abstract features of language in their earliest grammatical productions, then one hypothesis—that these features reflect a child's biological endowment—can account for both

101

DAVID MCNEILL

the speed of acquisition and abstractness of what is acquired. Some
evidence in support of this hypothesis is presented in the next section.

THE BASIC GRAMMATICAL RELATIONS

The basic grammatical relations are the concepts of subject and predicate of a sentence; main verb and object of a verb phrase; and modifier
and head of a noun phrase. They are defined in linguistic theory as configurations of the base structure of sentences (Katz & Postal, 1964;
Chomsky, 1965). The subject of a sentence, for example, is the NP
directly dominated by S in the base structure. The predicate of a sentence is the VP directly dominated by S (or, alternatively, dominated by
Pred P—the difference will be ignored here, but see Chomsky, 1965, for
discussion). The object of a verb phrase is the NP directly dominated by
VP, whereas the main verb of a verb phrase is the V directly dominated
by VP. Although not mentioned in the reference cited, the modifier of a
noun phrase will be taken to be some kind of determiner directly dominated by NP, whereas the head of a noun phrase will be defined as the N
directly dominated by NP. These definitions appear to be universal,
which is to say that all languages appear to possess the configurations
necessary to apply them, and so the definitions themselves are entered
in linguistic theory. They may be written as follows, in a formulation
that will become convenient later on:

Subject of NP, S
Predicate of VP, S
Main verb of V, VP
Object of NP, VP
Modifier of D, NP
Head of N, NP

The configurations to which these definitions apply are located in the
base structure of sentences, not the surface structure, because of sentences like *John is easy to please* and *John is eager to please*, where the surface structures are the same, yet the word *John* stands in two different
grammatical relations—object in the first, subject in the second. Thus,
the definitions are 'abstract' in the sense used here.

The hypothesis given above—that abstract features mentioned in
linguistic theory will appear in children's earliest grammatical productions—requires that the basic grammatical relations will be honoured in
very early speech collected from children. One source of support for this
hypothesis comes from a child exposed to English, a little boy called
Adam by Brown & Bellugi (1964).

102

At the time his speech was first recorded, Adam appeared to have three grammatical classes—verbs, nouns, and pivots. The evidence for distinguishing these classes was distributional. This is to say that English verbs had privileges of occurrence in Adam's speech different from those of English nouns. Adam's pivot class had a third privilege of occurrence, but it was grammatically heterogeneous from the point of view of English.

A little arithmetic shows that with three grammatical classes, N, V, and P, there are $(3)^2 = 9$ different possible sentence-types two words long, and $(3)^3 = 27$ different possible sentence-types three words long. If a child were combining words at random, all (or nearly all) these nine and twenty-seven different combinations should occur. However, not every combination is a manifestation of one or another basic grammatical relation. Only four of the nine two-word possibilities correspond to one or more of these relations, the remaining five being inadmissible from this point of view. An admissible combination would be N + V (e.g., *Adam run*), corresponding to the subject-predicate relation. An inadmissible combination would be P + P (e.g., *my that*). Among the three-word combinations, only eight manifest one or another basic grammatical relation, the remaining nineteen being inadmissible. An example of an admissible combination is V + N + N (e.g., *change Adam diaper*), corresponding to the verb-object relation, whereas an inadmissible combination would be V + V + N (e.g., *come eat pablum*).

Examples of every admissible combination were contained in the first three samples of Adam's speech that Brown & Bellugi collected. In itself, this result is not surprising. Altogether, some eight hours' recording were involved, and some 400 utterances from Adam. If the child were placing words together on some principle that allowed most of the possible combinations, those corresponding to the basic grammatical relations would be expected on grounds of the large sample size. However, all 400 of Adam's sentences were of the admissible type. There were no others. Thus, although *change Adam diaper* might have occurred, *come eat pablum* did not; for details, see McNeill (1966).

That this should be the outcome is certainly not obvious, *a priori*. In fact, one might have supposed that the result would have been different. Superficially, adult speech contains many examples of inadmissible sequences of Adam's grammatical classes. For example, the sentence-type represented by *come and eat your pablum* is common enough. To judge from some of Braine's (1963a) experiments with artificial languages, people find it difficult to avoid acquiring patterns to which they are exposed, even when told that the patterns do not exemplify what they are to acquire. If we assume that the same sensitivity holds true of young children, then some explanation must be offered for the fact that Adam did not produce sentences like *come eat pablum* after hearing examples like *come and eat your pablum* in parental speech. The explanation that suggests itself is that Adam was attempting to use only those sentence patterns that express the basic grammatical relations. An adult sentence like *come and eat your pablum* did not serve as a model utterance because it does not directly manifest these relations, being instead a rather complex construction involving several transformations not yet part of the child's grammatical competence. In short, Adam may have been actively searching for ways to express the basic grammatical relations in his speech. As a result, his own earliest grammatical constructions were limited to direct expressions of these relations.

Thus, there is indication that children's earliest speech contains abstract linguistic features, in this case, the basic grammatical relations. The same conclusion is reached from an examination of the early speech of children acquiring Japanese.

I have recently begun collecting samples of speech from two children who live in Tokyo. Each child is visited twice monthly, in her home, where everything said to and by the child is tape recorded. Both girls are (at the present time: February 1966) approximately two years of age. Neither is especially gifted at Japanese; and from one exactly seventeen word-combinations have been recorded during the past three months. The second child, however, produces large quantities of patterned speech, and the evidence described below comes from her. In the interest of maintaining the tradition begun by Brown, she will be called Izanami, after the goddess of Japanese mythology who helped create the world.

In certain respects, Japanese is particularly revealing for the study of language acquisition. It contrasts with English in several ways, of which one is especially relevant to the question now under consideration. Japanese is a postpositional rather than a prepositional language. Very roughly, postpositions are comparable to prepositions in English (although not all English prepositions can be translated into Japanese postpositions, and conversely). Among the postpositions that have no English equivalent are two that obligatorily mark, in the surface structure of Japanese sentences, the grammatical subject of the sentence.

The two subject markers are *wa* and *ga*. Although both follow the subject NP of a sentence, they are not identical, and receive different analyses in a transformational grammar of Japanese (Kuroda, 1965). The differences between *wa* and *ga* will first be introduced by a few examples, then, following Kuroda, they will be characterized somewhat more systematically:

A man-ga is standing on the corner
The man-wa is standing on the corner
Man-wa is mortal

In answer to the question, 'which man is sick?', one would reply

That man-ga is sick

whereas in answer to the question, 'who is sick?', one could reply

That man-wa is sick

A person, naming some object, would say

This-wa is a digital computer,

whereas hearing someone refer to the vending machine in the corner as a computer, one could correct him by saying

This-ga is a digital computer.

The distributional similarity of *wa* and *ga* is as close in Japanese as in these English examples, so that what is presented to a child in parental speech will not distinguish them. However, as the examples indicate, *wa* and *ga* play very different grammatical roles. Subjects of sentences that state general truths, subjects that have attributes given to them by the predicate, subjects that function like the logical premises of judgments, and words like *this* and *that* when they are used in definitions, all take *wa*. Quite often, *wa* can be translated into English with the expression 'as for...'. Thus, the examples given above can all be rendered:

As for that man, he is standing on the corner
As for man, he is mortal
As for that man, he is sick
As for this, it is a digital computer

In each case, an attribute—standing on the corner, mortality, computerhood—is judged applicable to the subject of the sentence. Kuroda calls this usage 'predicational judgment'. So much for *wa*.

The postposition *ga* differs from *wa* in two ways. That is to say, *ga* has two distinct senses, both different from *wa*. In one sense, *ga* is used in simple description. Instead of the predicate of the sentence being a property judged applicable to the subject, the subject and predicate stand in some roughly equal relation to one another. They are merely

105

linked (see Weinreich, 1963, for a discussion of this relation). The connection is always felt to be momentary, as in *a man is standing on the street corner*. Typically, the subject of the sentence is a specific, yet indefinite noun, as in the example just cited. One does not attribute a property to an arbitrary member of the category, *man*. One merely observes what he is doing at the moment. The descriptive sense of *ga* reflects such momentary linkage.

The second use of *ga* excludes possibilities from a known set of alternatives. In this sense of *ga*, information is conveyed not only about the subject of the sentence, but also about the members of the set of alternatives not mentioned in the sentence. Thus, to use one of Kuroda's examples, if three people, John, Bill, and Tom are lying side by side in three beds, and a doctor arrives asking, 'Who is sick?', the answer *John-ga is sick* means not only that John is ill but, in addition, that Bill and Tom are well. Heavy stress often conveys this meaning in English —*Jóhn is sick*. The corresponding sentence with *wa* conveys information about John alone. If the reply is *John-wa is sick*, meaning 'as for John, he is sick', nothing is learned about the state of health of Bill or Tom. The vaporous quality of much Japanese philosophy may exist because of this postposition, *wa*.

To turn now to the acquisition of Japanese: the proposal made before, and supported by the evidence of Adam's speech, strongly suggests that the postpositions *wa* and *ga* will appear early in Izanami's speech. This is because the subjects of adult sentences are consistently marked by *wa* and *ga*, which, in turn, relate to the base structure through fairly simple transformations. If Izanami is attempting to express the grammatical relation of subject in her sentences, she would have a basis for discovering and then using these transformations. If, on the other hand, she is not attempting to express the relation of subject, there would be no basis for her to formulate the transformation, so *wa* and *ga* should not appear.

What of the distinction between *wa* and *ga*? Izanami's mother uses *wa* twice as often as she uses *ga*. Presumably, this would favour acquisition of *wa*. Moreover, *wa* is involved whenever the mother introduces new vocabulary, describes permanent states and general truths, or attributes properties to objects. Some examples addressed to Izanami are *this-wa is a tape recorder* (pointing to it), *grandmother-wa lives in Kyoto*, and *papa-wa is big*. We can be certain that such sentences from Izanami's mother are understood, inasmuch as they are the principal means of introducing new vocabulary and information to the child, and there is no doubt that Izanami acquires both. Moreover, all these sentences involve a concrete object as the designated subject of the sentence (*this* accompanied by ostensive definition, *grandmother, papa*), as opposed to the *ga*-marked subject of a sentence, which is always an arbitrary member of a general category. For all these reasons, therefore, we might expect *wa* to appear.

The mother uses *ga* both in simple descriptions of transitory states and in the exclusion of alternatives from a known set. Some examples of the former are *you-ga sit well* (as Izanami manages not to topple over while sitting Japanese-style on the floor), and *yes, a bird-ga is on the fence*; whereas some examples of the latter are *which-ga do you want?* and *your other friends-ga want to play with you.* It is not clear what to expect Izanami to do with the descriptive *ga*. On the assumption, often made, that children develop grammatical relations by the labelling of enduring physical relations in the real world (e.g., the names of objects, or the relation of agent to action, as in the fact that people walk, children cry, houses stand, etc.), one would not expect *ga* to be acquired early. *Ga* is never used when these conditions prevail; *wa* is the required postposition. On the other hand, assuming that this kind of relation with the physical world is irrelevant to the acquisition of syntax, one would expect *ga* to appear as well as *wa*. The exclusive use of *ga*, because it requires a child to hold alternatives in mind and to exclude all but one, ought not to be acquired early.

The facts are as follows. Izanami uses only one of these postpositions, and it is *ga*. In eight hours of recorded speech, there were approximately 100 occurrences of *ga* and six occurrences of *wa*. All occurrences of *wa*, save one, were with the same word. Moreover, about one-quarter of the occurrences of *ga* were of the exclusive type, as in *this one-ga I like* and *the airplane-ga I prefer.*

In short, Izanami sharply distinguishes *wa* from *ga*, despite their distributional similarities in parental speech, selecting the descriptive use of *ga* as the principal concept to be encoded. It is clear from this fact alone that she is not working solely from the surface clues available to her, since on this basis *wa* and *ga* are virtually indistinguishable. *Ga* is included almost whenever called for in her speech, whereas *wa* is almost never supplied when required. *Ga* is never used in contexts calling for *wa*. Evidently, Izanami knows the transformation that introduces *ga*.

Izanami's sentences at the present stage of development are mostly two, three, and four morphemes long—which means that she is still in the earliest phase of producing patterned speech. Hence, there is strong support here for the proposal that children attempt to express the abstract relation 'subject of' in their most primitive grammatical efforts, which confirms what we have already seen in the speech of Adam. The child's use of *ga* and her exclusion of *wa* clarifies the cognitive implications of the effort to express the grammatical relation of subject. The conceptual correlate of this relation is the linkage of subject and predicate as in momentary description. It is not the discovery of enduring relations between specific agents and actions in the physical world, nor the kind of relation involved in the application of names to objects. Izanami belies this hypothesis. Indeed, on Izanami's evidence, naming appears to be completely separate from grammatical development, since appellation in Japanese requires *wa*, which Izanami invariably omits, although naming of objects is common in her speech. If the development of appellation led to developments in grammar, Izanami's postposition would have to be *wa*.

The conceptual content of *wa* thus appears to lie outside a child's attempt to express the subject relation. It is important to note in this connection that Kuroda came to the same conclusion on completely independent grounds. The postposition *wa*, although it marks the subject of a sentence and never co-exists with *ga*, nonetheless represents an essentially different concept that is added to the notion of grammatical subject. Accordingly, the situations that call for *wa* do not represent to a child the basic grammatical relation of subject (if by this, we now mean momentary description), even though it is a grammatical subject that should be marked. Hence, Izanami omits *ga* and ignores *wa*. This would seem to be very strong evidence of a child's impositions of conceptual constraints on to the speech he produces.

There remains the problem of Izanami's use of the exclusive *ga*. It appears to indicate that she can hold in mind several alternatives at once, select one of the set, and simultaneously exclude the rest. Presumably, children are not able to perform mental gymnastics of this order until they reach the age of seven or eight (Bruner & Olver, 1966), so its appearance in Izanami at the age of two occasions some surprise. It is possible, of course, that the linguistic evidence should be interpreted at face value. However, there is an alternative explanation. According to at least one Japanese informant (Nobuko B. McNeill), *ga* in its non-descriptive use not only encodes exclusion but also subjective certainty. Apparently one can easily tell the self-confident from the timorous in Japanese debates by noting who uses *ga* and who uses *wa*. The *ga*-sayers are the self-confident ones. The Japanese Milktoast prefers *wa*. All Izanami's uses of *ga* in its non-descriptive sense were statements of preference—*this one-ga I like, airplanes-ga I prefer*, and so on. If we can assume that a two-year-old knows what she likes, perhaps the apparently exclusive use of *ga* would be explained. Unfortunately, this account is *ad hoc* because there is no general reason to expect children to express subjective certainty through grammatical means.

In addition to the findings already cited from children acquiring Japanese and English, Slobin (1966) has presented evidence that children acquiring Russian also attempt to express abstract grammatical features in their earliest speech. Unlike adult Russian, where inflections carry information about the grammatical relations in sentences and word order is highly flexible, the earliest sentences of Russian children lack inflections and are composed in rigid order. This phenomenon can be explained if one assumes that Russian children attempt to express abstract structures but lack transformation rules of introducing inflections. Indeed, rigid word order is precisely what would be expected on the hypothesis that children include abstract features in their early speech, but must add to this inborn structure the particular transformations employed in their native language. As Slobin (1965) writes: 'The most economical representation of an inflected language like Russian would order the language in the underlying representation. Inflections could then be added to the characteristic positions of parts of speech, and an additional rule or rules would then re-order this string.'

The basis on which a child chooses to build sentence order may depend on what he believes to be the local manifestation of the basic grammatical relations. For the Russian child described by Slobin, sentences were produced in the order subject-object-verb, whereas the statistically predominant order in parental speech was subject-verb-object. There are several ways in which such a difference could arise. In general, the attempt to express the basic grammatical relations means producing sentences with an underlying structure of the type conventionally represented by labelled brackets or tree diagrams. The attempt to express the basic grammatical relations does not, however, determine the order in which constituents will appear (and, indeed, this is one of the idiosyncratic aspects of language). Linguistic theory can offer no guidance to a child at this point, so order must be discovered from parental speech. In the case of the Russian child described by Slobin, it is possible that occasional appearances of SOV sentences in parental speech led him to conclude that SOV is the preferred order in Russian. But deviant orders can arise in other ways as well. Consider, for example, the English sentence fragment, *hit the ball*. In fact, it is a verb phrase, manifesting the verb-object relation. However, to a child who expects the basic grammatical relations to hold in parental speech but does not yet know the order of constituents in English, the fragment *hit the ball* is ambiguous.

109

Depending on a child's interpretation of the meaning of the fragment, it can be taken to manifest either the verb-object relation or the subject-predicate relation. If he thinks the fragment means 'the ball hit something', then he must analyze it as corresponding to the relation of subject-predicate. Such a child would be expected to produce sentences backwards for a time. As a matter of fact, reversal of constituents occurs in the early speech of children. One of Braine's (1963b) subjects, for example, produced sentences like *allgone shoe, allgone lettuce*, which are inversions of the corresponding sentences in adult English (*the shoe is allgone, the lettuce is allgone*). It is possible that the Russian child's s o v order also arose from such initial 'ambiguities' in parental speech.

We have seen three indications that children include abstract linguistic features in their early speech. In every case, the abstract feature appears to have been one or another basic grammatical relation. Since the evidence comes from children acquiring three very different languages, it appears that children do identical things in the face of radically different conditions of learning. The proposal that linguistic theory represents children's inborn capacity for language accordingly gains empirical support.

Other abstract features that appear early in children's speech can be briefly mentioned, also. In particular, the forms underlying negation (Bellugi, 1964; summarized in McNeill, 1966) and interrogation (Bellugi, 1965) appear early and can be taken as evidence in favour of the proposal. In general, one would expect that the capacity for language acquisition is very rich, governing many (if not all) abstract aspects of language. Future observations of children developing linguistic competence will provide opportunities to evaluate this expectation.

One characteristic of children's early speech is the appearance of the so-called 'Pivot-Open' construction. The terminology, Pivot (P) and Open (o), was introduced by Braine (1963b) to describe the primitive grammatical classes that he had observed in children's speech. Others have observed a similar division of children's vocabulary (Brown & Fraser, 1964; Miller & Ervin, 1964). The P-class typically has a fixed position with respect to the o-class, sometimes before and sometimes after, although more often before; it always contains few members compared to the o-class; and each member is generally used with relatively higher frequency than individual words in the o-class. Most new vocabulary enters the o-class, whereas the P-class is relatively closed. All these are stable characteristics of the P-o distinction.

Many workers in the area of language acquisition have assumed that this distinction marks the beginning of a child's grammatical system, subsequent developments arising from the opposition of P and O. However, the proposal considered in this paper—that children attempt to express the basic grammatical relations—suggests a different interpretation. The P-O distinction may merely be a by-product of deeper grammatical developments. To justify such a reinterpretation, however, it is necessary to consider an additional characteristic of P and O classes.

P and O classes are usually heterogeneous from the point of view of adult grammar, often containing words from several adult grammatical classes. The P class of Brown's subject, Adam, contained articles demonstratives (*this*, *that*), possessives (*my*, *your*), various adjectives, and the words *other* and *two*. The O class of one of Ervin's subjects contained nouns, verbs, and adjectives. Such heterogeneity appears to be the rule, and it raises a puzzling problem. Although heterogeneous, these classes appear to be GENERICALLY APPROPRIATE. Adam illustrates this nicely. His P-class included both the articles, all the demonstratives and possessives at his command, and all the adjectives in his vocabulary at the time, even though he was not yet distinguishing these various adult classes. Somehow, Adam placed words from these classes in his P-class before he recognized the grammatical distinctions on which the adult classes are based. Adam must have been sensitive to something held in common by these several adult classes.

One explanation is that Adam classified words according to a set of gross grammatical categories, this set in turn belonging to a hierarchy of categories. The upper levels of the presumed hierarchy would be the result of obliterating distinctions drawn at lower levels (Chomsky, 1964*b*). The lowest level of all in the hierarchy would be the classes of adult grammar. The upper levels, on the other hand, might be linguistically universal. Accordingly, the grammatical categories of all natural languages would be sub-classes of the same set of gross categories, and Adam's generic P-class could then be one of the generic classes taken from the upper regions of this universal hierarchy (McNeill, 1966).

It is conceivable that this view is correct. However, an analysis of Izanami's speech throws it into serious doubt. It is the effort to accommodate her grammar and Adam's within one consistent scheme that leads to a reinterpretation of the P-O distinction. If Izanami possesses P and O-classes (and it is not certain that she does), they would be as follows:

Pivot	Open
this	*lady*
this-one	*baby*

111

Pivot	Open
that-one	*cat*
good	*mommy*
not (adj)	*milk*
hurtful (adj)	*school*
dirty	*hold*
pretty	*look*
little	*good*
	happy
	beautiful
	.
	.
	.

Izanami's and Adam's P-classes overlap wherever possible. Japanese has no articles, and possessives are themselves constructions, so neither is expected to appear in Izanami's P-class. But her P-class does contain demonstratives and adjectives, as does Adam's, which appears to support the notion of a universal hierarchy of categories. However, note Izanami's O-class: it, too, contains adjectives, which means that neither her P nor her O-class is generically appropriate. It will be impossible for Izanami to develop the adult class of adjectives in the way that Adam did, by sub-dividing the P-class. Izanami will have to recombine P and O-classes in order to obtain a single class of adjectives.

What is needed is a theory broad enough to explain both Adam and Izanami, both generic and non-generic classification. The proposal already discussed—that the basic grammatical relations are part of a child's capacity for language—provides such a theory. In order to apply the definitions of the basic grammatical relations, it is necessary to assume that the information symbolized as N P, V P, D, N, and V is also available to a child. The definitions provided above indicated this. Accordingly, the evidence from Izanami and Adam in support of the proposal that these relations are part of the capacity for language is likewise in support of the proposal that the information contained in the definition of these relations is part of the capacity for language.

The suggestion here is that children sort words, not according to a hierarchy of categories, but according to where they occur in sentences that manifest one or another basic grammatical relation. Words are classified in terms of which symbol (N P, V P, D, etc.) forms the context of the word sorted. If children do this, they would, in effect, be using the basic grammatical relations as a source of basic grammatical features.

There are six possible features, the six symbols included in the definitions of the basic grammatical relations. Presumably all six are available to a child. Two are used here to illustrate how classification might proceed. Whenever a child observes a word in parental speech fulfilling the definition of a MODIFIER, the word is tagged (—N); on the other hand, whenever he observes a word fulfilling the definition of a PREDICATE, it is tagged (NP—). A given child may use only one of these features, or he may use both. If both are used, they may be applied disjunctively or conjunctively—disjunctively when every word is given only one feature or the other, conjunctively when some words are given both features. The following would be the result:

Either feature applied alone would lead to a generically appropriate class. Adam's P-class, for example, would result from using (—N) alone, since *this, that, a, the, two, my, your*, and various adjectives all fulfil the definition of modifier in parental speech. Applying both features disjunctively would lead to the cross-classification that Izanami displayed —some adjectives would be tagged (—N) whereas others would be tagged (NP—). Hence, some would be used in one position in sentences, some in the other position. Moreover, some adjectives, those that happened to be classified (NP—), would fall together with nouns and verbs, both of which would also be classified (NP—). Verbs, nouns, and adjectives are exactly the contents of Izanami's O-class. Finally, applying the two features conjunctively would yield a separate class of adjectives for both Adam and Izanami.

If this is what children do, the implications for the status of the P-O distinction are not encouraging. P-O ceases to be a basic step in the acquisition of grammar. Instead, it is a superficial characteristic of children's sentences, derived from the effort to assign features to words. The statistical imbalance between P and O that Braine observed, which is used to define the two classes, simply reflects the fact that parental speech presents relatively few words fulfilling the definition of a modifier. Words classified (—N), therefore, occur with high frequency in a child's speech and the set of words so classified expands only slowly. Words classified by features other than (—N) would appear in speech as O-words of various types, the latter classification being based on their greater numerosity and smaller frequency.

A CODA

If we accept the proposal that linguistic theory describes children's inborn capacity for language, a further question may be (and often is) asked. The question concerns the specificity of this capacity. There is

113

occasionally a feeling that if children should possess specific capacities, the capacities must be specific to something other than language. A common suggestion is that children have a specific capacity to process data in wonderful ways, one outcome of which is linguistic competence (cf. some of the discussion contained in Smith & Miller, 1966). The assumption implicit in these suggestions is that a capacity not specific to language will be simpler than one specific to language. The assumption is probably false and certainly it is unjustified. There remains, nonetheless, a question as to the extent that language rests on specific abilities, and something should be said on the implications of assuming that these abilities are not unique.

The argument will be that if the abilities underlying language are not specific to language, then cognition generally must have properties matched by the universal aspects of language. At the very least, cognition must possess the universal features of the base structure, plus the notion of a transformation rule.

In grammar, transformations relate the surface structure of sentences to the underlying base structure. An infinite variety of surface types is reduced to a finite variety of base types. The implication of assuming that the capacity for language is a general ability, not one specific to language, is that there is a set of general principles of cognition whereby superficial complexity and diversity are traded off against abstract simplicity and uniformity. In this sense, transformational grammar may provide a model of cognition in general, differing from a theory of cognition primarily in the terminology used.

It follows from this proposal that the variety of abstract types available to cognition is strictly limited—it is to this limited set that all superficial diversity is reduced. Among the abstract types included, however, presumably there would be fundamental methods of combining concepts, corresponding to the basic grammatical relations. The basic grammatical relation, in fact, would be special cases of such fundamental methods of combination.

The present proposal is, of course, highly programmatic. Its only merit is to make reasonable the suggestion that language acquisition rests on more general cognitive abilities. Although programmatic, the proposal is open to empirical tests of various kinds. Suggested cognitive abilities can be rejected by showing that they do not appear in non-linguistic cognitive development at the time that they appear linguistic development. It would be important to know, for example, if Piaget's (1952) examples of sensori-motor and pre-operational development could be interpreted as the unfolding of a transformational system. It

114

should be noted in passing that there is no justification for supposing that linguistic development is more rapid than cognitive development, previous claims notwithstanding (as in McNeill, 1966). Without an analysis of the system acquired in cognitive development that is comparable to the linguistic analysis of syntax, a comparison of the speed of cognitive and linguistic development is simply not possible. That cognitive development apparently continues until the age of twelve, whereas linguistic development is apparently complete by the age of four, may only mean that the acquisition of a system of general knowledge is three times as complex as the acquisition of English.

Discussion

COLIN FRASER

Like many interesting things, McNeill's paper comes in three parts. I shall concentrate my comments on the first part, on McNeill's statement of the background from which he proceeds. My co-discussant will improve the balance between comments and paper. In large part, I shall be supplying background to the background and I shall be discussing, not so much 'The creation of language by children', but rather 'The creation of theories of children's language'. My remarks will be directed at psychologists rather than linguists.

Until recently, in so far as there was any theory of language development, it was some sort of learning theory. Language, it was felt, was THE instance of a complex learned skill, with a minimum of specific biological mechanisms being necessary for learning to take place. It would have been conceded that man needed control over the motor mechanisms of speech and that he required some sort of general intellectual capacity to acquire language; but apart from those, language was well and truly a learned achievement. As Carroll (1964) has put it: 'Human language...is always learned. Each child must learn his language from scratch....' And, starting from scratch, a child learned language by means of a mixture of imitation, selective reinforcement and generalization.

It might be safer to regard the foregoing as not so much a theory, more a way of life, and, needless to say, it was not a way of life to which all students of language acquisition subscribed. But it was the standard view of how language development took place and, as such, it posed a problem for the psychologist who, like myself, found (and finds) the phenomena of language acquisition much more fascinating than theories

115

which supposedly explain them. If such a psychologist took seriously the standard account, then, on the one hand, he felt that somehow language acquisition had been explained, but, on the other, he could not see how the complexities, the intricate details of children's speech had in any way been illuminated. He may well have felt that learning theory obscured rather than revealed the phenomena of language development, and inhibited rather than encouraged research.

Thus, an alternative view of the development of language is to be welcomed. Such an alternative has recently become increasingly familiar and is, in fact, the position espoused by McNeill. To paraphrase McNeill: it is now proposed that, first, children are born with a biologically-based, innate capacity for language acquisition; secondly, the best guess as to the nature of the innate capacity is that it takes the form of linguistic universals; thirdly, the best guess as to the nature of linguistic universals is that they consist of what are currently the basic notions in a Chomskian transformational grammar. Metaphorically speaking, a child is now born with a copy of *Aspects of the Theory of Syntax* tucked away somewhere inside. Given the present state of knowledge regarding innate capacity and language universals, the above seem defensible guesses.

The child, presumably, still requires experience of hearing language in order to trigger off the inbuilt mechanisms and to acquire the details of English, French, Navaho, or whatever language the child happens to be in the process of acquiring. The exact balance between innate and experimental factors would seem to depend on the extent to which presumed universals prove to be real universals and the extent to which additional universals are discerned.

As I said, a plausible alternative to learning theory is to be welcomed but, from the viewpoint of the person studying language development, it would be unfortunate if the alternative went the way of its predecessor, that is if it served to obscure the language acquisition process rather than to open it up for study. It may be the pessimist in me, but I feel I already detect signs of such a thing happening. On the other hand, perhaps the recentness of the position means that, as yet, certain working assumptions have not yet been looked at more closely. In which case, I would like to indicate briefly a few aspects which deserve expansion and perhaps rethinking. A quotation from Chomsky and Miller (1963: 275-6) will serve as introduction:

How an untutored child can so quickly attain full mastery of a language poses a challenging problem for learning theorists. With diligence, of course, an intelligent adult can use a traditional gram-

116

mar and a dictionary to develop some degree of mastery of a new language; but a young child gains perfect mastery with incomparably greater ease and without any explicit instruction. Careful instruction and precise programming of reinforcement contingencies do not seem necessary. Mere exposure for a remarkably short period is apparently all that is required for a normal child to develop the competence of a native speaker.

That last sentence deserves particular attention, because it makes two assertions that normally go unchallenged in the writing of Chomsky and his associates, first, that language is acquired very quickly (McNeill refers to the 'astonishing speed' of acquisition) and, secondly, that it is done so by 'mere exposure'.

But what is the speed of acquisition? How long is it before we can say that a child has mastered his native language? We do not know with any precision. McNeill suggests that, thinking particularly of syntax, we could say it takes approximately thirty months, from the age of one and a half to the age of four. But this seems like a considerable underestimate, even for syntax. On a number of indices it is possible to demonstrate later development. Menyuk's (1963) work, for example, provides some evidence of gaps up to the age of about six and a half and one suspects that a finer analysis than hers would reveal much more room for development.

Perhaps more interesting is the question of where syntax begins. McNeill, like a number of other writers and researchers, suggests eighteen months, when the child starts to produce two- and three-word utterances. But it may be important to remember that the child has been responding, apparently appropriately, to speech for some six months prior to this. It seems quite conceivable that there are definite regularities in what the child is responding to, that these regularities might make up a passive grammar or a grammar of comprehension and this might be predictive of the elementary grammar of production which the child reveals when he starts to speak for himself. Thus, by taking one year as our starting point and insisting on development past the age of six, we have, with very little effort, more than doubled the time a child is supposed to take to acquire language. Clearly further extensions could be argued for at either end.

Even if the speed of acquisition was known, on what grounds would one be justified in describing it as 'astonishing'? Is it so astonishing, if one is convinced that, for five or more years, the child is working very hard and for long hours on mastering language? After all, what else is there for a young child to do with his time! I think recent research has demonstrated that some children, at least, do tackle the job most assidu-ously. Again, is it so astonishing, if one feels that the absence of inter-ference from prior learning or development is relevant?

But perhaps the real basis of astonishment lies in the assumption that, in mastering what is unquestionably an extremely intricate and complex task, exposure, 'mere exposure', is enough. But what is exposure? At times it simply seems to be something other than learning by means of carefully controlled reinforcements; in so far as all parents do not sys-tematically give peanuts (or even verbal peanuts like *Good!*) whenever their child says something vaguely recognizable, then it must mean that exposure is sufficient. Alternatively, exposure is something other than 'careful instruction'. On this point, it is interesting to read the recent views of a Japanese linguist, Shiro Hattori. He claimed (1965: 104) that children begin to speak, not as a result of hearing normal rapid adult conversations, but by imitating words and short utterances that adults have spoken repeatedly and clearly. Hattori claimed that his own daughter failed to acquire Tatar, although she heard normal, rapid con-versations in it, whereas she quickly acquired Japanese, in which she was 'instructed'. Admittedly, one brief anecdotal account is hardly decisive evidence, but it is perhaps one inadequate piece of evidence more than has been forwarded for the counter-view. Furthermore, a similar type of situation, with adults using a clear, simple English when talking to children, has been reported in recent American studies (e.g., Brown & Bellugi, 1964). The fact that a number of well-educated, professional parents do indulge in what might be called tuitional exposure does not in itself demonstrate that such exposure is a necessary condition for lan-guage acquisition. But it seems reasonable to ask for some clues as to what is necessarily involved in exposure. If a child were kept in a dark-ened room, fed by machine and hit over the head at five-minute intervals would he acquire English even if normal adult conversation were pro-vided twenty-four hours a day? Perhaps not. Perhaps one needs 'normal' exposure. But if this involves a normal mother-child relationship, then the door is wide open for primary and secondary reinforcement as an invariable part of acquisition by exposure.

In addition to 'astonishing speed' and 'mere exposure' there are other aspects of the innate-capacity view that merit scrutiny. One is the claim that the task of the first-language acquirer is essentially the same as the job of the linguist who wishes to write and evaluate grammars of a lan-guage. Another might be the apparent assumption that all language universals are biologically-determined, rather than culturally-deter-mined, universals. But I hope I have already succeeded in making the

118

general point that, if the view of language development which McNeill has adopted is to end up as something other than an opaque screen between the observer and the phenomena, then that view will have to be spelled out in much more detail. I very much hope that this clarification will take place.

I shall not try to do justice to the second part of the paper, the attempt to demonstrate the early appearance of basic grammatical relations. Being a worrier over details, I shall content myself with asking for additional information at various points.

In the analysis of the material from Adam, I would like to know more about what the admissible types of two- and three-word combinations were, and how McNeill decided if a particular utterance was an example of an admissible or inadmissible type. For example, an admissible combination was v + n + n (e.g. *change Adam diaper*). Does this mean that any v + n + n would be taken to reveal basic grammatical relations? What if *change diaper Adam* or, even, *eat chair Mommy* had appeared? Furthermore, why does *change Adam diaper* represent a verb-object relation rather than a disordered subject-verb-object relation? Presumably, because McNeill assumes that *Adam diaper* is a cut down version of the adult *Adam's diaper*. I wonder to what extent guesses and personal interpretation were essential for the identification of examples of basic grammatical relations.

With regard to the *wa/ga* distinction in Izanami's speech, *ga* appeared early, *wa* did not. Why does this pattern support the idea of the initial appearance of abstract features? Should not both *wa* and *ga* have appeared?

I would also welcome further information regarding the proposed re-analysis of the pivot/open distinction, which has been thought to occur early in the speech of English-speaking children. In an attempt to accommodate both Adam and Izanami within a consistent scheme (at this point theologians boggle), McNeill suggested the occurrence of tagging in terms of context, where context was defined by basic grammatical relations. This analysis seemed to depend on some words being tagged in only one way, and other words being tagged in more than one way. What determines whether tagging proceeds 'disjunctively' or 'conjunctively', and, indeed, what determines which words will be tagged and which ignored?

Finally, a comment on the coda. In discussing the specificity of an inborn capacity for language, McNeill appears to come down on the side of an extremely non-specific capacity, with presumably some very general mechanism capable of analysing all sorts of cognitive problems in a similar fashion. Obviously one might agree with the notion of an inborn capacity for language but disagree about the scope of the capacity and mechanisms. Lenneberg, perhaps the most interesting and plausible advocate of an inborn-capacity view of language, has challenged (1963) the notion of a non-specific capacity and has argued for specific anatomical and physiological correlates of language. Perhaps the argument will be resolved with the appearance of Lenneberg's promised book on the biological basis of language. More probably, due to lack of satisfactory evidence, arguments about the scope of inborn capacities and the nature of innate mechanisms for language will continue for quite some time. Meanwhile, perhaps we should get on with the job of discovering what the language behaviour is that these innate capacities and mechanisms are supposed to be explaining.

MARGARET DONALDSON

I find McNeill's paper question-provoking in the way that one hopes such a paper will be; and it seems to me that many of the questions to which it gives rise are very important ones, particularly from the point of view of developmental psychology. So I have had some problems of selection. I decided in the end to concentrate on two main topics, but I did not of course overlook the coda, as McNeill knew I would not.

The first question that I want to raise for discussion is how far one can reasonably go in drawing parallels between the problems faced by linguists when they construct a grammar and the problem faced by a child when he begins to acquire his native language. Much of the earlier part of McNeill's paper is based on the claim that we may think of the two as being 'essentially the same'. He argues that in both cases the aim is to 'reconstruct the tacit competence possessed by fluent speakers' and that, if the child is to achieve this, he must, like the linguist, 'formulate the grammar'. Further, he goes on to argue that some of the procedures involved may also be said to correspond. It is important to try to be clear about what such claims imply.

In some sense it is no doubt true that, in the process of acquiring his first language, the child acquires—or constructs—its grammar. But in what sense? Herein lies much of the problem of what we mean by an assertion that the native speaker 'applies rules' when he talks (or understands)—a problem that is currently urgent for psycholinguistics, as several of the papers in this symposium show; indeed, it seems to be the central theme.

Chomsky (1964a) speaks of 'the child's discovery of what from a formal point of view is a deep and abstract theory—a generative grammar of his language'; and it may well be essential for the understanding of acquisition to make this emphasis. But the phrase 'from a formal point of view' should perhaps be kept well to the fore. I am not entirely sure that I know what this phrase means in the context, but by keeping it to the fore we can at least remind ourselves that other points of view may also be possible. I am concerned that our understanding of some of the crucial features of the acquisition processes may be hindered if we fall too readily into a way of talking that assimilates them to the activities of the linguist.

It might be as well to begin by mentioning one or two rather obvious differences between what the child does and what the linguist does, if only to clear them out of the way before we go on to consider correspondences.

In the first place the objectives are clearly not identical. The linguist is aiming to construct a formal description or model of competence; the child is constructing competence itself (which may also involve model-building in some sense—but that is irrelevant at the moment). He is constructing the thing which the linguist is giving an account of.

Now the relation that exists between a model and that which it models does not imply an isomorphism between the activities involved in the formation of the one and of the other; and in this case it seems evident that the activities, considered as psychological processes, cannot be closely akin. The linguist has a developed linguistic competence which he uses in the statement of his formulations and in the processes of arriving at them. The child, in whatever manner he may 'formulate', presumably cannot use the very tool he is shaping, especially not in the early stages, which are of course the most puzzling. A closely related point is that the linguist has many kinds of cognitive competence, which he certainly uses for his theorizing and which the child, on all available evidence, appears to lack. The real puzzle is: how can the child do the job he has to do without these tools and what must we suppose he has instead?

What, then, is the nature of the positive correspondence between the linguist's task and the child's?

The linguist has an array of possible grammars to choose from for any given language. If he accepts Chomsky's view of the nature of his undertaking, he will not make the selection by using criteria of economy or the like. He will want his decisions to derive from considerations about the nature of the 'faculté de langage'—and consequently he will aim to make his choice by PREFERRING WHAT THE CHILD PREFERS, the argument being that if you want to give an account of competence you must know

121

under what constraints it has to operate (see, for example, Chomsky 1964a: 43). Notice that this means that the child's criteria for evaluation cannot be the same as those of the linguist. The child cannot take as criterion 'what the child prefers'. Of course it follows that the linguist will use the same criteria as the child at one remove, so to speak, once he discovers what these are.

So Chomsky's reasoning PRESCRIBES for the linguist a certain degree of accordance with the activities of the child. He must have regard to what the child does and build into his theorizing constraints corresponding to the constraints that actually limit the form human languages can take. He must favour the kinds of generalization to which the child is predisposed—or limited.

This shows the relevance of studies of language acquisition for linguistic theorizing. But what about the relevance of linguistic theorizing for studies of language acquisition? Evidence about language acquisition is a source of explanatory power for linguistic theory; linguistic theory, on the other hand, can help developmental psychologists to appreciate what it is that they have, for purposes of their own discipline, to explain. For instance it is because of developments in linguistic theory that the problem of accounting for the acquisition of 'abstract features' is currently recognized to exist. But the solution of this problem is another matter—and this brings me to a consideration of the two questions that McNeill formulates on p. 101 of his paper. He asks first of all: 'How does this theory [i.e., the proposals of Chomsky and Katz] account for the acquisition of abstract features?' And then he suggests that this question is badly put and proposes that we ask instead: 'Why do languages have abstract features at all?' Now I am not entirely sure why McNeill thinks the first question is 'badly put'. However, it is certainly ambiguous. It might be a question about the evolution of language—how did languages acquire abstract features, historically speaking? But all the earlier part of McNeill's paper seems to run counter to this interpretation. On the other hand, if he is thinking of the first question as a question about ontogenesis, then it is hard to see how he can propose to replace it by: 'Why do languages have abstract features at all?' And clearly if the first question IS about ontogenesis it cannot be disposed of by the answer McNeill suggests for the second, namely, 'Children place them there'. This still leaves us very much in the position of having acquisition to account for. How do children do it?

To say that they do this (or anything else) by using their innate capacity is not much help, as McNeill of course recognizes, unless we are able to go on to give an account of the nature of this capacity and how it oper-

122

ates. Chomsky (1964*a*) argues convincingly that language could not be learned in the ways in which it is learned by an organism 'initially uninformed as to its general character', and that the child must therefore come to the task already prepared for at least some of the basic features of the system which he has to master. But which features? And prepared by what means? Chomsky believes that the means are biologically given, and it is undeniable that they have some constitutional basis specific to the human species. But when the child begins to produce patterned speech he is normally about eighteen months old. It is, therefore, reasonable to ask whether during these eighteen months any other kinds of development, which may serve in some degree as preparation, normally occur. In so far as this search fails, then the claim that the basic features are in some fairly rigorous sense given as 'innate ideas' will of course be strengthened. But the search should evidently be thoroughly undertaken before firm conclusions about innate ideas are drawn. (Even if the search does show that preliminary preparation is relevant this of course does not mean that we dismiss the notion of some kind of predetermined structuring.)

With this in mind let us consider McNeill's claim to offer empirical evidence to support the view that the child comes to his language learning prepared to recognize and indeed to search for the basic grammatical relations of subject-predicate, and so on. In the time available, I shall concentrate on the evidence from the little Japanese girl, Izanami, about the acquisition of the subject markers *ga* and *wa*. You will remember that these mark different kinds of subject-predicate relation, and that Izanami at the age of two uses *ga* almost whenever it is called for and never uses it wrongly in place of *wa*. In other words, where *ga* is appropriate she marks the noun as subject, where *wa* is appropriate no subject-marker appears—or it appears very rarely. McNeill concludes, very reasonably, that the situation which call for *wa* lie outside the child's attempt to express the subject relation; but he also concludes that the evidence from Izanami supports the general contention about the innate nature of the child's linguistic preparedness, and this is less clear.

It is at least open to question whether this evidence can be taken to support any sweeping 'innate universals' claim. If one claims that the subject-predicate relation in general is a universal abstract feature (and clearly one cannot make a claim for universality that invokes any distinction peculiar to Japanese—that is, one cannot claim universality only for the *ga*-type), then how do we explain why Izanami is able to recognize one of the sub-divisions imposed by Japanese but not the other? If she unfailingly marked the grammatical subject but did not always know

123

whether to use *ga* or *wa*, this would seem to be, at least on a superficial view of the matter, better evidence for the operation of some universal. However, the truth may be more complicated. I want to suggest two possible—and quite sharply contrasted—explanations for the differential acquisition of *ga* and *wa*.

The first of the suggestions attempts to relate Izanami's partial success to what is known about the general cognitive development of the normal two-year-old. McNeill points out that *ga* is appropriate whenever subject and predicate are transitorily linked but inappropriate for the statement of general truths or the attribution of properties. Now a normal two-year-old child has completed what Piaget calls the sensori-motor period, extending from birth to eighteen months, and has consequently developed (*a*) a conception of a world of objects having some kind of enduring identity and (*b*) a quite extensive repertoire of 'schemas of action' that can be applied to these objects. He is, for instance, aware when the door opens, when a matchbox opens, when his mouth opens; and Piaget (1952) offers pre-linguistic evidence that different 'openings' are recognized as similar—that they belong in one schema or rudimentary cognitive structure. But the child at this stage has not organized the objects in his world according to their attributes and has little awareness of general truths. The coming together of a given object and a given schema of action is indeed for him a linkage of a quite transitory kind.

On this basis, then, one might reason that Izanami is predisposed by the age of eighteen months or so to recognize the *ga* type of relation, but not because of an innate idea—rather because she has already built up a fairly elaborate set of cognitive structures which enable her rapidly to assimilate this particular feature of the language. However, we are then left with the question of how the child can make *wa*-type noun-verb utterances at all if she is unable to recognize the subject for what it is. And at this point a rather different explanation suggests itself.

I make the second suggestion very hesitantly because it involves further consideration of the entire basis of the *ga/wa* distinction in Japanese —and my knowledge of that language is, to say the least, limited (to be exact, it is limited to *ga* and *wa*!) Even if what I am about to say is incorrect with respect to Japanese, however, it may be worth suggesting that this kind of interpretation be considered. The possibility occurred to me as a result of thinking about the nature of the difference between two of McNeill's examples:

A man-ga is standing on the corner

and

The man-wa is standing on the corner.

I could not see that the distinction between attribution and transitory linkage applied very satisfactorily in this case, and I felt I had perhaps not understood the point McNeill was making. So I consulted a Japanese grammar and found in it a comparison of the following two sentences:

THIS-*ga is red* (tells which one is red)

and

This-wa is RED (tells what colour this is).

This is, of course, the same sort of distinction that McNeill illustrates on p. 105 by reference to the digital computer and the vending machine. It then occurred to me that in the case of '*This-wa is* RED' one might reasonably maintain that 'red' is the logical subject of the sentence, though it has the role of surface predicate. We might render the sentence as: *Red is what this is.* And the same could be argued in the case of *The man is standing on the corner* (*Standing on the corner is what the man is doing*); but clearly not in the case of *A man is standing on the corner*, where the surface subject and the logical subject certainly coincide.

Now if it is the case that this coincidence tends to occur where *ga* is appropriate but not where *wa* is appropriate, we might have to consider whether Izanami's use of *ga* but not *wa* provides evidence for the operation of a very deep and very abstract theory—one which makes Izanami reject the surface subject and refuse to mark it where it is not also the logical subject. It seems clear, however, that we are at present far from being able to decide whether this conclusion is justified—and of course there is another obvious possibility: it might be that the stress given to words in the actual utterances Izanami is hearing is not irrelevant. Possibly she uses *ga* because *ga*-type subjects tend to receive emphasis in speech whereas *wa*-type ones do not.[1]

Clearly we need much more evidence. First it is important to find out whether we are dealing with a regular feature of Japanese or whether children differ a good deal in the ways in which they first handle this distinction. If *ga* regularly comes first, then we need to know, for instance, (*a*) what kind of *wa*-type utterances occur in children's speech before *wa* itself appears; (*b*) when and in what contexts *wa* does eventually appear; and (*c*) what happens, say, in the case of the early handling of passives where surface and logical subjects fail to coincide.[2]

1. At this point, McNeill intervened to say that this is not in fact the case in Japanese. (The Editors)
2. McNeill remarked that this is not true of the Japanese passive. (The Editors)

Finally, of course, it would be good to have more evidence from other languages which make similar distinction (as presumably some do). There is no doubt that comparative evidence is going to be of the first importance for the better understanding of acquisition. This is one of the reasons—though by no means the only one—why McNeill's contribution in this paper is so valuable.

My last remark concerns McNeill's coda and involves a reversion to what I said earlier about the desirability of at least making a serious attempt to relate language acquisition to other aspects of cognitive development instead of considering it in isolation. McNeill recognizes that there are arguments for trying to do this but he says that these arguments rest on the assumption that a capacity that is not specific to language will be simpler than one that is. I do not intend, in anything I have said, to make this assumption. I am assuming only that the wider the range of phenomena to which an explanation can be shown to apply, the more satisfactory as an explanation we may take it to be.

General Discussion

R. M. Burstall, Ruth Clark, L. J. Cohen, Margaret Donaldson,
A. R. Jonckheere, J. Lyons, J. Macnamara, D. McNeill,
J. C. Marshall, J. Morton, Jess Reid and R. J. Wales.

The main points raised had to do with: (i) the biological basis for language-acquisition; (ii) the distinction between the 'logical' and the 'grammatical' subject in sentences, and the relevance of this distinction to the *ga/wa* opposition in Japanese; (iii) the necessity for postulating a highly-structured, innate 'faculté de langage'; and (iv) the possibility of using a language-acquisition theory as a model for a more general theory of cognitive development.

McNeill, in his general comments on the formal discussions and on the task of developing a theory of language acquisition, distinguished between (*a*) the features of a biological capacity for language and (*b*) the process through which this capacity is put to use in the acquisition of any particular language. Ideally, one would study the latter, having first acquired a full understanding of the former, but this separation was obviously not possible in practice. As it was, we had to consider how, given SOME biological capacity for language, the child could acquire, for instance, the auxiliary verb transformation in English which, since it was linguistically unique, could not be directly specified by the biological

126

capacity. The problem then was that the child must somehow have available to him simultaneously both base and surface structure, since his task was to discover the form of the relation between them. Very little was known about the way in which this was done, but parental expansion of the child's utterances might well be relevant. Jess Reid suggested that one should study the appearance of transformations in the speech of children in institutions, since their utterances are not so often expanded by adults.

Cohen raised the question of the distinction between the 'logical' subject and the 'grammatical' subject, in general terms and with particular reference to the *ga/wa* distinction in Japanese (Cohen's contribution is printed in full below). McNeill agreed that Izanami's use of *ga* might indicate that she was attempting to express the 'logical' subject. He went on to remark that where one language makes a syntactical distinction for the expression of which another makes no provision, the speakers of the latter language may have the distinction in mind though they do not give it expression in speech. English speakers were presumably in possession of the information which provided the basis for the differential use of *ga* and *wa* in Japanese. And Adam might be making the same efforts as Izanami, although English did not make the same distinctions as Japanese. On the basis of Izanami's evidence, one would indeed expect that, where Adam's utterances seem to involve subjects, these utterances would be expressive of momentary linkages. The problem was to find some means of being sure whether this is so. Kate Loewenthal suggested that one should draw a distinction between a basic ability to name objects and a more advanced ability to generate sentences concerned with relations between things. McNeill, however, questioned the primacy of naming and argued that Izanami's failure to use *wa* implied that her earliest utterances were not of this kind.

Lyons made some comments about the question of language 'universals', and referred to an alternative version of the notion of deep-structure which might have some bearing on the specificity of the capacity for language-acquisition (see below). McNeill remarked that it was obviously desirable to have rival theoretical formulations; this could lead to the clarification of many disputed points. He went on to comment on what Margaret Donaldson had to say about the analogy he had drawn between the activities of the linguist and those of the child—this analogy must be understood as existing at an extremely abstract level. The linguist's aim was to select from among a set of rival descriptions the one most highly valued by his theory. Clearly the child was not doing that: he was devising a single grammatical system; the analogy broke down,

127

therefore, at this point. But one might consider that the child was making particular decisions in the light of linguistic theory, rather than decisions about total grammars. This was THE unexplored region of language-acquisition.

McNeill turned to the suggestion that language-acquisition depends upon a more general cognitive capacity. If this were so, then this general cognitive capacity must have all the components that until now we have insisted were specific to a language learning capacity. One might attempt to relate language acquisition to general cognitive development in either direction. Language acquisition could be selected as a primary model of cognitive development. Morton pointed out, however, that this order of priorities might miss a number of important psychological interactions —in particular that between language and memory (see below). Marshall took up the question of the relevance of grammatical theory to the study of animal behaviour: his own work on the reproductive behaviour patterns of drosophila and pigeons suggested that the former might be describable in terms of a finite-state grammar and the latter in terms of a phrase-structure grammar. The use of fairly uniform descriptive procedures for the behaviour of animals and human beings might throw light on the possible direction of evolutionary development. Marshall believed one day it might be possible to generate related sentence-constituents by stimulating the connecting neurons.

COHEN: There is sometimes a tendency to use the concept of LOGICAL SUBJECT a little fuzzily in connection with these problems, though the concept of GRAMMATICAL SUBJECT is given a sharp, theoretically-defined sense. Let us suppose that the logical subject or subjects of an utterance may be discovered by paraphrasing its declarative kernel(s) in the notation of the polyadic predicate calculus. Any expression of the original utterance denotes a logical subject of it if its counterpart in the paraphrase is an individual constant or definite description, and where the paraphrase contains bound variables then the domain of these variables will also be a logical subject of the original utterance. Now it is extremely difficult to conceive of any linguistic communication between human beings that has no logical subject, and correspondingly easy to grant that any child must develop some linguistic means of denoting logical subjects. But, of course, an utterance may have more than one logical subject, even if transformation-free, like *George hit Peter*; and whereas many languages, like English, tend to use the grammatical subject typically to denote only one of the logical subjects, there seem to be other languages which, if they have grammatical subjects at all, can use these to distinguish in some way between the logical subjects. The latter

128

seems to be what happens in Japanese, where *wa* and *ga* can even occur in the same sentence; for example, *the supply situation-wa this official-ga there is preparing of a report.* Those who seek to explain such a phenomenon in every case by the occurrence of a transformation seem to be reading into Japanese the single grammatical subject pattern of familiar European languages. I think we therefore do better to explain the child's linguistic behaviour here in terms of its semantic need to acquire the means of referring to a logical subject or subjects, than in terms of some innate syntactic universal which can hardly be formulated precisely without running the risk of appearing to betray too parochial a viewpoint.

LYONS: I should like to take up the points raised by Cohen about 'logical' and 'grammatical' subjects and the dangers of 'parochialism' in syntactic description; and I want to relate my remarks to the question of whether the facts of language-acquisition by children presuppose a very specific, innate 'faculté de langage'—the question raised by McNeill in the final section of his paper.

First of all, let me draw your attention to the fact that, although Cohen introduced the terms 'logical' and 'grammatical' subject in a particular sense (a sense in which, for instance, both *George* and *Peter* are 'logical' subjects, but only *George* is a 'grammatical' subject, in the sentence *George hit Peter*), in the subsequent discussion he was assumed to have employed these terms in a quite different sense popularized by Chomsky (1965: 163)—a sense which rests upon the distinction of deep- and surface-structure in syntax. That misunderstandings should arise in discussion is of course only to be expected. But this particular misunderstanding is revealing; and there is an important moral to be drawn from it. Distinctions between various types of 'subjects' (in utterances, sentences, propositions, or judgements) have been drawn by philosophers and grammarians for centuries; and the terms 'logical' and 'grammatical' (as well as 'psychological') have frequently been employed to label these distinctions. But there has been little consistency or continuity in the application of the terms 'logical' and 'grammatical' in this connection. (For earlier discussions of the question, cf. Sandmann, 1954, with bibliography.) It must not be assumed that a particular formalization of the notion of different kinds of 'subjects' is correct or incorrect until we have examined the reasons for drawing distinctions in the first place. It is not the predicate calculus itself which forces us to say that both *George* and *Peter* are 'subjects' in the proposition underlying the sentence *George hit Peter*, but certain epistemological principles which govern our interpretation of the calculus. *George* and *Peter* are terms of an

129

asymmetrical, two-term relation; and we could readily define the notion of 'subject' in such a way that, in any expression of the form $F(x, y)$—where x and y are individual constants—it is x that is the 'logical' subject. It is important to realize, however, that Cohen's 'logical' subject is no less readily definable in terms of transformational grammar than is Chomsky's 'logical' subject in terms of the predicate calculus (if we assume that in 'paraphrasing the declarative kernels' we distinguish the uniquely-referring particular terms). The point I am stressing is, not only that Chomsky and Cohen are drawing two different distinctions which must not be confused, but that each of the two notions of 'logical' subject is important; and it is far too early to say which of them, if either, will ultimately prevail in a general theory of syntactic structure applicable to all languages. However that may be, I do believe that Cohen is right in suggesting that there is considerable danger of 'parochialism' in current work on generative grammar.

Let me exemplify this danger further by referring to the passive construction, in English and in other languages. (A number of the psycholinguistic experiments reported in the papers presented to this conference have assumed a particular relationship between the active and the passive in English.) Now there are at least three features of the English passive which, taken together, make it unusual, if not unique, among constructions of this kind in languages known to me: (i) it is very commonly used (more commonly, for instance, than in French, Russian, German, Spanish, etc.); (ii) it is restricted to transitive verbs; and (iii) it is freely used with the explicit mention of the 'agent'. By contrast (to give just one example), the Turkish passive, although it is as common as the English passive, is not restricted to transitive verbs and is very rarely used with an 'agent'-phrase (there is in fact no agentive construction in Turkish which is strictly equivalent to the English by + NP). As long as we confine our attention to English, it might seem reasonable to derive sentences such as *John was killed* by deletion of an agentive 'node' and to say (although this is surely counter-intuitive) that *John was killed* is syntactically more complex than *John was killed by Bill*. It is, however, a commonplace of traditional syntactic theory that the principal function of the passive in all languages (and in some languages its only function) is to make possible the construction of 'agentless' or 'impersonal' sentences. It is possible, therefore, and indeed it seems to me very probable, that, when fuller transformational grammars have been written for a wider range of languages, even the English passive might be treated in such a way that *John was killed by Bill* is shown to be syntactically more complex than *John was killed*. In any case, the relationship between the

130

active and the passive in English is far less straightforward than current transformational work suggests. The point I am making is simply this: if the conclusions drawn from psycholinguistic experiments depend upon assumptions of universality in the linguistic categories manifest in the data, in the present state of linguistic theory such conclusions should be regarded as highly tentative.

To take up now the more general question whether the facts of language-acquisition presuppose a highly specific, innate 'faculté de langage'. I have no views on the plausibility of this as a psychological hypothesis; but I am a little disturbed by the readiness with which some psychologists have interpreted Chomsky's arguments (1965) about the formal and substantive 'universals' of syntactic theory as evidence in support of this. Very few languages have been studied so far in any detail from a generative point of view; and I, for one, feel that quite radical changes will be made in the description of even such well-studied languages as English when we begin to take seriously the implications of universal features in deep syntactic structure.

Indeed, it seems to me that there are fairly strong reasons for recognizing elements of two different types in the base component of a transformational grammar: 'categories' (lexical items, considered solely from the point of view of their combinatorial possibilities in the underlying strings) and 'features' (for the most part, distinctions of tense, mood, aspect, definiteness, number, etc.). I will not develop the implications of this view here (cf. Lyons, 1966), except to say that, if we assume that some part of deep syntactic structure is common to all languages, this distinction between 'lexical categories' and 'grammatical features' seems to impose itself upon anyone who considers more than a typologically narrow range of languages. By the time that the child arrives at the age of eighteen months or so, he is already in possession of the ability to distinguish 'things' and 'properties' in the 'situations' in which he is learning and uses language. And this ability seems to me quite adequate as a basis for the learning of the principal deep structure relationship between lexical items (the subject-predicate relationship), provided that the child is presented with a sufficient amount of 'primary linguistic data' in real 'situations' of language-use (cf. Chomsky, 1965: 33). As for the 'grammatical features', which vary considerably from language to language, the acquisition of these would seem to depend, not only upon such general notions as 'number', 'sex', 'animacy', and so on, but more particularly upon what might be called the 'deictic co-ordinates' of the spatio-temporal situations of utterances. Briefly then, what linguistic evidence there is does not seem to me to lend any support whatsoever to

131

the view that a knowledge of the 'substantive universals' of syntactic theory is genetically transmitted as part of an innate 'faculté de langage'. MORTON: The preceding speakers have been referring to the possibility of explaining language-development by reference to mechanisms concerned with the predicate calculus, causality, generalization. The implication of this line of thought is that language is not unique by virtue of its structure, this structure in fact being rather just one manifestation of more general logical systems.

But other species manifest behaviour which indicate the presence of such mechanisms. We seem then to be discussing language in terms which are not qualitatively different from the terms we might use to describe other behaviour, human and animal. One might note here that Bartlett and those he influenced have for more than thirty years written about memory and skills in terms which are in one important respect identical to our present way of thinking about language. Thus they have been concerned with describing behaviour transfer of training not in associational terms, but rather in terms of the generality of the underlying principles.

Granted the possible universality of transformational descriptions, we are faced with the problem of having to reconsider what it is that enables human beings to develop language so readily. I would like to throw out the possibility that it has something to do with memory. I find it possible to conceive of a species which has a well formed language, but has an organizational memory which is no more complex than that of a chimpanzee. The members of such a species would not be able to remember who said what to them, or what they said to whom. They would only be able to refer to the past in the most general terms, and while they could talk about the future, they would not be able to remember what they said. Thus, although the language could be very rich syntactically, it would have a negligible influence upon their other behaviour. The reason why such a species has never appeared could be that the system would be a handicap as far as survival is concerned. Talking would be a form of play, and unlike other forms of play (mock fighting, exploring) would not be of general benefit to the species.

Fourth Session

J. Fodor and M. Garrett

Some reflections on competence and performance

with prepared comments by
N. S. Sutherland and
L. Jonathan Cohen

Chairman W. H. Walsh

J. Fodor and M. Garrett

The pre-positivist view of science—widely if not universally accepted until the beginning of this century—held that science is primarily concerned to understand the laws that determine the behaviour of ideal objects (like point masses and bodies falling freely through perfect vacua), and the character of ideal events (like interactions between literally pure chemical samples, or the acceleration of masses on frictionless planes).

Ideal objects are, of course, inherently unobservable. In order to determine their behaviour, the scientist is required to experiment upon physical objects whose properties differ from those of their ideal counterparts in ways and amounts the experimenter can, in principle, control. Considerations of simplicity are then invoked to determine which of the experimental observations are attributable to the character of the ideal objects under investigation and which must be attributed to the inherent noisiness of the experimental situation.

The positivist movement in philosophy succeeded, to a very impressive extent, in changing the VIEW of scientific inquiry held by working scientists even when it had negligible effects upon scientific practice. By and large, the change in ideology was not salubrious. Among the more influential mistakes of which positivism was guilty was that of confusing the question 'What is the proposition p about?' with the question 'What is the evidence for p?' This error was pervasive. In the philosophy of language, it emerged as the notorious 'verifiability criterion', the doctrine that the 'cognitive meaning' of a proposition is exhausted by enumerating the conditions under which it would be true. In the philosophy of science it appears as the contention that a science is about its data, namely, that the goal of scientific inquiry is primarily to catalogue the interactions between experimental manipulanda rather than to arrive at an account of the behaviour of theoretical entities. In the philosophy of psychology it emerged as the view that psychology is the science of behaviour.

There is, in fact, every reason to distinguish between the meaning of a proposition and the grounds for assenting to it. Evidently, the grounds for propositions about super novae, or the Roman Empire, or what life will be like in the twenty-first century are, in general, things I can exhibit and investigate here and now (e.g., inscriptions in books, statistics about production trends, traces on photographic plates, etc.). Equally evidently, the propositions to whose truth these data are relevant are about things that happened, or will happen, at very distant times or

135

places, and unless one understands that, one has not understood the propositions.

As in the general case, so in the particular. There is no reason at all to suppose that, because the evidence for psychological claims is (often) the occurrence of one or another bit of behaviour produced by some organism, psychology is therefore primarily in the business of arriving at generalizations about behaviour. On the contrary, psychology is primarily concerned with understanding the nature and capacities of the mechanisms which underlie behaviour and which presumably cause it. The observation and experimental manipulation of behaviour is of interest in so far as (and almost solely in so far as) it sheds light upon these mechanisms and capacities.

Psychologists betrayed some awareness of these points even in the darkest days of behaviourism. The ethologists, for example, never doubted that the ultimate object of their study was the behavioural repertoire of organisms. They realized, too, that even the most careful observation and experimentation were likely to elicit only a fragmentary and somewhat fortuitous sample of that repertoire. The rest was to be pieced together by diverse techniques among which simple inductive extrapolation was less important than physiological model-building, genetic and zoological analysis, and so on. It was indeed a constant complaint of the ethologists that if it is the behavioural repertoire of the organism, rather than techniques for modifying its behavioural performance, that you are studying, then a T-maze or a Skinner box is hardly the place to elicit a representative sample of that behavioural repertoire.

Even within the tradition of learning theory there have been occasional realizations that it is the competence of the organism one wants to understand and that its performance is of interest primarily as a clue to that competence. To cite the most famous case, positivistic strictures never quite managed to convince psychologists that there is no problem about 'what is learned'. On the contrary, it has repeatedly occurred to psychologists to wonder whether the discrimination they were attempting to teach their subject was, in fact, the discrimination the subject was mastering. It is not always possible to dismiss the feeling that a subject's discriminative performance may be misleading as a clue to the perceptual competence he has acquired. Where the subject is a non-verbal organism, the development of experimental procedures capable of eliciting behaviour that DOES bear directly upon competence may prove to be a very difficult undertaking.

But while analogies to a performance/competence distinction are discoverable throughout psychology, it is perhaps only in recent theorizing in psycholinguistics that the full implications of that distinction have begun to be clear. In this paper we wish to consider some of the ways in which that distinction is illuminating and some of the ways in which it is problematic.

It is clear that Chomsky's insistence upon the competence/performance distinction in linguistics amounted to a major methodological clarification. So long as the linguist held that the object of his study was literally the behaviour of speakers, his data was impoverished in two important ways. In the first place, it is obvious that the utterances speakers in fact produce are a small, finite, and from the linguistic point of view, fortuitous, subset of the infinite set of sentences that comprise their language. It is not the fault of English that we do not often say, for example, *My friend owns three-eighths of an elephant*; clearly we must not represent the failure of the corpus to contain instances of such utterances as a consequence of the structure of English. Indeed, what we say is probably so fortuitous from the point of view of language structure that there is no reason to suppose a theory of the CORPUS would be other than arbitrarily related to a theory of the language. Further, many of the relevant structural relations in the language would likely fail to be exemplified in the corpus, and many generalizations that are true of the corpus would fail to be true of the language.

Secondly, there are all sorts of things that speakers know about their utterances that do not emerge as features of a corpus; whether, for example, their utterances are grammatical, or ambiguous, and so on. So long as the linguist supposed himself to be studying the corpus, there was no way for him to avail himself of this data. If, on the other hand, he thinks of the corpus as merely a clue to the informant's competence, which latter is the primary object of scientific scrutiny, there would seem to be no good reason why he should not also avail himself of whatever other clues he can find; among these, the informant's perception of grammaticality, ambiguity, and other linguistic relations have proved to be particularly revealing.

Linguists thus have very good reasons for saying that they are interested in the study of competence in the sense in which studying competence contrasts with studying behaviour. But linguists often also claim to be studying competence in a rather more restricted sense. They sometimes wish to suggest that what they are studying is linguistic capacity independently of the other psychological mechanisms and competences with which linguistic capacity must be supposed to interact in the production of verbalizations. Here linguistic competence is opposed

137

not only to linguistic performance but also to whatever non-linguistic abilities enter into the production of linguistic performance. The contrast is thus between the speaker's information about his language and whatever psychological mechanisms may be supposed to enter into the exploitation of that information.

For example, it seems evident that no speaker can fully exploit the linguistic information at his disposal if only because every speaker has certain bounds on his memory. Such bounds make it impossible to produce or process sentences of more than some fixed length or complexity. Since the memory limitation of speakers clearly ought not to be represented as part of the structure of their language, linguists are inclined to say that their account of linguistic competence must abstract from them. Linguists thus represent themselves as providing a formulation of the linguistic information at a speaker's disposal. Linguistic performance is the exploitation of this information in a way that is somehow supposed to be determined by psychological mechanisms which, like memory and motivation, are not language-specific. The question of HOW linguistic information is put to use in the production or processing of sentences is left to the psychologist. His problem is to construct a 'performance model' where this means not a model of behaviour but a model of how the speaker's linguistic information interacts with other psychological mechanisms in the production of behaviour. It should be noted that this sense of the performance/competence distinction cuts across the earlier one, for the mechanisms the psychologist studies are as theoretical as the grammar the linguist formulates. Hence in the sense in which distinguishing between performance and competence is distinguishing between behaviour and the mechanisms underlying it, both linguistic and psychological models are models of competence.

There are in short two performance/competence distinctions more or less confused in the methodological literature of psycholinguistics. The first, which insists upon the distinction between studying behaviour and studying the mechanisms underlying it, seems to us pre-eminently worth honouring. We shall not discuss it further here. The second is, however, less obviously sound; for the contrast between linguistic information and 'psychological mechanisms' is often interpreted not as a point of methodology but rather as a theory (or proto-theory) of the way speech is produced. It suggests that a performance model ought to consist of a model of linguistic competence (a grammar) plus some further component or components at present unknown; jointly these components are somehow to issue in the utterance or understanding of sentences.

That clearly is the picture that has dominated theorizing and experimenting in psycholinguistics in the last decade. We would like to suggest that it is at best one of a number of possible pictures; that unlike the distinction between capacity and behaviour, it is not to be defended on *a priori* grounds. We would also like to suggest that that picture is perhaps a little *simpliste*.

It is one thing to say that a grammar formalizes the speaker's linguistic information. It is quite another thing to argue that a grammar is THEREFORE a component of whatever system of mechanisms is involved in the production of speech. Some models for speech recognition and production do, in fact, use grammars in this way. 'Analysis-by-synthesis' models, in particular, work by using the grammar in conjunction with some system of heuristics such that the former affords a source of structural descriptions, while the latter requires these descriptions to converge upon the analysis of an input.

A grammar G of L may be thought of as an axiomatic representation of a set containing precisely the sentences of L with their structural descriptions relative to G. A perceptual model relative to G may be thought of as a device which converts an arbitrary string s_i into its structural description in G, just in case s_i is a sentence of L. If we know of a given string that it in fact lies in the set represented by a grammar (i.e., that it is well-formed in L), a perceptual model can provide an analysis of the string by employing the grammar to effect a disciplined search of that set. For example, given that restrictions are placed upon the deletions that may be effected by the rules of a grammar, the sentences that are generated by the grammar can be ordered so that they increase monotonically in length. One may then determine the structural description for any s_i of length M by generating all the derivations for sentences of length less than or equal to M.

Clearly this way of using a grammar as a component of a perceptual model is vastly inefficient. The number of sentences n words in length increases roughly exponentially with n, and no serious model of language processing could require exponential searches as a routine part of sentence recognition. Indeed it is a psychological point of which too little has been made that, within rather wide limits, increasing the length of a sentence in words does not grossly increase its perceptual complexity. It is difficult to see how a model of language processing in which analysis-by-synthesis procedures play a central role could, in principle, be reconciled with that fact.

The methodological virtue of analysis-by-synthesis procedures is that they envisage an extremely unabstract relation between the competence model (the grammar) and the performance model (the perceptual analyser). The former is literally held to be a proper part of the latter. The defect of these virtues is that such models decline to operate in anything like real time. It has become increasingly evident that such models derive what interest they have from the ingenuity of the feed-back and pre-analysis routines they employ to reduce the size of the space that must be searched synthetically in any given recognition.

Part of what is wrong with the analysis-by-synthesis model is precisely that it uses grammatical information in the same form in which that information is represented by the grammar. This may be seen clearly from the following rather trivial example.

Suppose we have a simple generative grammar in which lexical items are introduced into trees by rewrite rules; hence, the last syntactic rule employed in a derivation might be:

(1) N → *boy*

etc. Consider what would be involved in using such a grammar in a straight analysis-by-synthesis routine. Given as input, *The boy went to the store*, and given that the second word has been identified as N in a candidate analysis, the analyser would be required to search the entire store of nouns in the lexicon of its grammar simply to find out WHICH substitution instance of N the sentence contains. Clearly, this difficulty is artificial. What we want is to allow the analyser to employ a 'reversal rule': a rule that expresses the same grammatical information as (1) (roughly, the information that *boy* is a member of the set of nouns) BUT THAT HAS LEXICAL ITEMS IN ITS DOMAIN, for instance:

(1′) *boy* → N

That is, even in trivial cases, if the grammar is to be employed efficiently as a source of information we must allow ourselves a more abstract view of the relation between the grammar and the performance model than strict analysis-by-synthesis routines suggest. Suppose (counterfactually) that a recognition routine could be constructed by providing, for each rule in the grammar, a counterpart rule related to it as (1′) is related to (1). Such a routine would, presumably, be enormously more efficient than an analysis-by-synthesis routine, but the price of that efficiency would be that THE GRAMMAR WOULD NOT APPEAR AS PART OF THE ROUTINE. Rather, the routine would include a system of rules that are arrived at by a systematic distortion of the rules in the grammar. The relation between the performance and the competence model would be, to that extent, abstractly conceived.

A less trivial example of the abstract employment of grammatical rules by sentence recognition routines can be adduced from recent work on computer recognition of sentences in natural languages (cf. Petrick, 1965; Zwicky, Friedman, Hall & Walker, 1965). In some such routines, reversals of the BASE structure rules of a transformational grammar are employed to assign tentative SURFACE structures to inputs to the recognizer. Sometimes, however, no base structure rule can be employed to analyse subtrees occurring in the surface structure; for example, because the subtree is transformationally derived. Thus, there is no phrase structure rule: $N \rightarrow A + N$; hence no reversal rule: $A + N \rightarrow N$; hence no way of using the base structure rules of the grammar to assign the node N to phrases like *tall boy*, *big house*, etc.

The way out of this problem chosen in some recent routines is to associate with transformational rules, like those that produce AN phrases, phrase structure analogues. Thus, in the case sketched above, while the grammar derives *the tall boy* from *the boy is tall*, the recognition routine assigns N to the surface structure of *tall boy* by using a phrase structure rule.

The interest of this point is that such routines exemplify a particularly abstract relation between the grammar and the recognizer. They do not suppose that the recognizer contains precisely one rule for each rule of the grammar, or even that a structure must be assigned by employing the same number of rules employed by the grammar in generating it.

We have (finally) reached a point where empirical evidence may be seriously adduced. We have already had reason to object to certain primitive performance models on the grounds that they fail to represent realistically the time required for sentence processing and because they erroneously suggest that sentence length must be a major determinant of sentence complexity. The entire question of the degree of abstractness of the relation between the performance model and the competence model is susceptible to similar, but subtler, empirical constraints. If, for example, the grammar is involved in sentence processing in anything like the way that analysis-by-synthesis models suggest, then we have a right to expect a very general correspondence between such formal features of derivational histories as, for instance, length in rules, and such performance parameters as perceptual complexity, ease of recall, and so on. If, on the other hand, the relation between the performance and competence models is relatively abstract; if, for example, grammatical information is employed in the form of heuristics which do not involve direct appeals to the grammar as a source of derivations, then we would

141

expect an inexact correspondence between formal features of the deri-vations of a sentence and the performance of subjects who are required to manipulate the sentence in experimental tasks.

Let us try to be clear about precisely what is at issue. The perceptual analysis of a sentence presumably involves (although it is not exhausted by) the recovery of the structural description of that sentence. A struc-tural description, in turn, is a theoretical representation of the sentence which marks such semantically and phonologically relevant syntactic relations as the subject and object of the sentence, its segmentation into phrases, and the constituent types to which those phrases belong.

That it is the full structural description of a sentence which is the psychologically pertinent output of a recognition device is not now open to serious doubt. It is only in terms of the relations the structural des-cription marks that such intuitively available notations as grammaticality and syntactic ambiguity can be reconstructed, and only by reference to these relations that a general characterization of syntactic similarity be-tween sentences can be formulated. To put it slightly differently: the structural descriptions assigned by generative grammars automatically provide formal counterparts for grammatical relations, the recognition of which lies within the perceptual capacity of speakers. This fact can be explained only if we assume that the perceptual recognition of sentences involves the recovery of their structural descriptions.

Moreover, an increasing number of experimental results have sug-gested that the subject's recognition of relations marked by full struc-tural descriptions (but not presumably, by less abstract representations of sentences) can determine his performance on experimental tasks. To consider only two examples: Fodor & Bever (1965) and Garrett, Bever & Fodor (1966) have demonstrated that the subjective location of noise heard while attending to sentences is in part a function of the surface structure of the sentence. Mehler (1964) has shown that recall of a sen-tence is a two-phase process in which recall of the base structure is rela-tively independent of the recall of its T-marker.

There is, therefore, both psychological and linguistic support for assurance that the structural description of sentences is 'psychologically real', and hence for understanding the task of developing a performance model as involving the construction of a device capable of converting a sentence into its structural description.

But while it is a primary constraint upon grammars that the structural descriptions they enumerate should mark precisely the psychologically real syntactic relations—the relations in terms of which sentences are understood—it is far from evident that grammars equally satisfy the

142

constraint that psychological reality can also be claimed for the operations whereby these descriptions are generated. While there can be no serious doubt that a speaker who understands a sentence does so by recovering its structural description, it is by no means obvious that the processes by which he converts a wave form into a structural description are identical to (or isomorphic with) the operations by which a grammar converts an axiom string into a structural description.

We have seen that the hypothesis that grammatical operations (as opposed to structural descriptions) are psychologically real, turns in large part upon whether there exists a correspondence between such formal features of the derivation of a sentence as length and such performance characteristics of the sentence as the perceptual complexity. A very large part of the serious experimental work in psycholinguistics in the last five years has assumed or attempted to demonstrate a direct correspondence between formal features of derivations, like length in rules, and perceptual complexity. The early results were a series of most impressive successes. There appeared to be very good reason for claiming that a quite simple relation holds between increasing the length of a derivational history by one or more rules, and variations in performance parameters, like increased latency for recognition, increased difficulty in recall, and so on. These experiments serve as a sort of model for the empirical investigation of the relation between performance and competence. We will briefly review some of the most important ones before turning to more recent and more equivocal findings.

The first experiment aimed at revealing the psychological relevance of grammatical (specifically transformational) operations was performed by Miller, McKean & Slobin (cf. Miller, 1962). They attempted to demonstrate that the relative difficulty of producing certain systematic changes in sentences could be predicted as a function of the relative transformational complexity of the sentences.

The subjects taking part in the experiment (henceforth abbreviated as 'Ss') were given two columns of sentences and required to match the members of one with their counterparts (systematically altered) in the other. The sentences in the two columns were assumed to differ by one or two transformational operations and were, of course, randomly distributed between the columns. For example, a sentence in one column might have been *Jane liked the old woman* (Simple, Affirmative, Active, Declarative, hereafter, SAAD), while its passive counterpart in the other column was *The old woman was liked by Jane*. Before beginning the task, Ss were instructed which operations were to be performed in a particular pair of columns (as Active → Passive, or Affirmative → Negative, etc.).

Each pair of columns tested an operation or a pair of operations (as in the case of SAAD → Passive Negative). Base search time was determined by having *S*s locate untransformed versions of sentences in a scrambled list (as SAAD → SAAD, or Passive → Passive).

It was assumed that differences in the time taken to perform these matches would reflect differences in the time taken to perform the various transformational operations. That is, given a SAAD, to find its match in the other list *S*s must perform the required transformation and then look for a sentence which matched the result of the transformation.

Of the relationships among the types of sentences studied by Miller *et al.*, two were considered to require two operations, and four, only one operation. For instance, where a P (Passive) sentence was required (or given), and an N (Negative) sentence given (or required), it was assumed that one 'undid' the work of the negative transformation and then applied the passive. But for the same initial condition (given an N sentence) where a PN sentence was required, *S*s were assumed to apply the passive while not being required to 'undo' the result of the negative transformation. On this view, it would be predicted that the result of the experiment should find SAAD → (N or P) and PN → (N or P) comparable while SAAD → PN and N → P should both be more difficult (although comparable to each other). In fact, the order in the results was just that:

SAAD ↔ N	1.1 seconds more than base search time
SAAD ↔ P	1.4
P ↔ PN	1.7
N ↔ PN	1.9
SAAD ↔ PN	2.7
N ↔ P	3.5

The view that the complexity of processing these sentences can be indexed by looking at the steps in their derivational history seemed to be supported. Further, there was the suggestion that these operations produced a linearly additive perceptual complication (sentences involving both negative and passive transformation required a time approximately equal to the sum of the average time required for negative and passives applied separately).

Because of some dissatisfaction with the pencil and paper method used above, Miller & McKean (1964) carried out a refined version of this same experiment. In the later version a sentence was presented tachistoscopically. When *S* had performed the required transformation of the sentence, he pressed a button which presented a search list (and stopped a timer which had started on presentation of the sentence). In this technique the search time is separated from the presumed process-ing time and is employed only to provide a check on the accuracy of the task performance. An independent measure (S's subjective estimation) of the transformation time is thereby obtained, and variance introduced by the search is eliminated. The results here were comparable to those with the pencil and paper method, but there was some rearrangement within the two 'equivalence' sets (i.e., among those sentences requiring two operations vs. those requiring one operation). In the Miller & McKean results, applying the negative transformation to a passive sen-tence is easier than applying the passive to SAAD (i.e., P → PN is easier than SAAD → P). This makes the Miller & McKean results more uni-form than those of Miller *et al.*; for application of a single transform the negative is easier than the passive, and of each of the two applications of the two transformations, the one involving transform from SAAD is the easier of the pair (i.e., SAAD → N is easier than P → PN, and SAAD → P is easier than N → PN, and SAAD → PN is easier than N → P). Negative transforms are easier than passive transforms, and SAAD forms are easier to handle than any other.

Another experiment (McMahon, 1963) with negative and passive sentence types provides information of a different kind. McMahon's test of these sentence types required S to judge whether a presented sentence was true or false (by depressing a labelled key which stopped a timer activated when the sentence was presented). His sentences were of the form *5 precedes 13* or *3 is preceded by 7*, and so on.

McMahon found that negative sentences required longer to judge than did passives or active affirmatives. The order of difficulty was (from easiest to most difficult):

Act Aff
    —small difference
Pass Aff
    —large difference
Act Neg
    —small difference
Pass Neg

These results are interesting when compared to those of Miller & McKean. The transformation easiest to perform is apparently the one whose effect upon truth value is most difficult to determine. It is not clear how to interpret the difference between the Miller & McKean re-sults and those of McMahon unless it is assumed that semantic considera-tions play a central role where questions of truth value are raised in the experimental situation. On that assumption one can account for the observed proximity of synonymous forms (actives and passives), and for the recording of types.

An extensive study of the effects on recall of the differences between SAAD, Q (Question), P and N sentences was carried out by Mehler (1963). The addition of Q sentences yielded eight sentence types (SAAD, Q, P, N, PQ, PN, NQ, and PQN). Mehler used eight lists of eight sentences each; each list contained one of the eight syntactic types; each sentence on a given list was derived from semantically disparate (i.e., non-synonymous) SAADS. S was presented with the eight sentences one after another. After he had heard all eight, S attempted to recall the sentences in the set. Then the sentences were presented again and S was again tested for his recall—and so on, for five presentations. Ten Ss were run for each of the eight lists.

Scored for ease of acquisition (which is NOT predicted by length in words), SAAD is much easier to learn than any of the other types. This conforms to the results of both the Miller & McKean studies and the McMahon study.

Mehler assumed that S recalled the sentences by using a strategy in which the underlying form of the sentence is stored independently of the transformations which determine the sentence's syntactic form; that is, the sentence is assumed to be represented in memory, not in its surface form, but in some form minimally necessary to specify semantic content and with a set of transformational instructions for deriving the final syntactic form. The minimal grammatical information required for semantic interpretation is represented by the deep structure of a sentence. Since SAAD forms have the minimal number of syntactic 'footnotes' (i.e., since they resemble deep structures more closely than any other type of sentence), they should be the most easily and accurately remembered.

In these results, the sentences were ordered roughly as they were in the Miller & McKean study; the order for correct recall was similar to that for ease of transformation. SAAD was much the best for accurate recall; those cases with only one transformation were next, followed by those with multiple transformations. This indicates that for these types of sentences, length of derivation is related to ease of recall.

Another experiment which represents a particularly relevant approach to the study of performance variables is by Savin & Perchonock (1965). It represents an attempt to relate the storage requirements of various sentence types to aspects of their derivational histories. The assumption is that the greater the complexity of a sentence, as indexed by the num-

146

ber of rules required for its generation, the greater will be the demands it makes on storage. Savin & Perchonock sought to confirm this prediction by requiring *S*s to recall both a sentence and a set of unrelated words. In particular, *S*s were presented with a sentence followed by a string of eight such words. *S*s had to repeat the sentence and as many of the words as he could recall. The number of words successfully recalled was the measure of storage requirements for a particular sentence type (always assuming that the sentence was correctly recalled, of course). Savin used the same sentences as did Mehler plus emphatic (E, with heightened stress on *Aux*) and *wh*-forms. Hence, Savin & Perchonock investigated SAAD, Q, P, N, E, Wh and the combinations of any two transformations.

The ordering of sentence types from the results of this experiment was as follows (ordering is presumably from least to most complex):

sentence type	mean number of words recalled	
SAAD	5.27	
Wh	4.78	
Q	4.67	
P	4.55	
N	4.44	(presumably one rule)
Q^{neg}	4.39	
E	4.30	
PQ	4.02	
PQ	3.85	
EP^{neg}	3.74	(presumably two rules)
NP	3.48	

Note that in every case those sentences with one transformational operation required less storage (interfered less with recall of word strings) than those with two operations and that SAAD was least interfering of all.

More strikingly, Savin & Perchonock found a constant effect of given transformations. That is, a particular transformational operation apparently took the same storage space, whatever other transformations it was associated with (as—Q transform added the same difficulty whether the sentence queried was P, E, SAAD, etc.). In this experiment (as for Mehler, etc.) length of the sentences in words will not account for the results adequately.

Taken together, the experiments just reviewed would appear to supply rather striking evidence for the claim that the length (in transformations) of the derivational history of a sentence is reliably correlated with the facility with which the sentence is understood or remembered. Hence,

147

they appear to support the view that a very close relation exists between the psychological process of analysing a sentence and the linguistic process of generating it; formal operations specified in the second process correspond directly to variations in performance parameters relevant to the first.

A few points should, however, be noticed about these findings. In the first place, they concern a rather limited set of grammatical manipulations. Without exception the experiments we have reviewed were concerned with relations between sentence types like question, passive, declarative, negative, and so on. There is a clear historical reason for this: in early versions of transformational theory, the transformations which produce these types were distinguished as 'optional singularies'; that is, they were thought of as a determining class of formally-specifiable and linguistically-related forms. It is not surprising (although it may have been unfortunate) that sentences so interrelated became objects of sustained experimental attention.

Secondly, it may be noticed that some, though certainly not all, of the predictions based on transformational complexity are confounded with what might be predicted on the basis of length and/or meaning. If *Does John run?* is transformationally more complicated than *John runs*, it is also longer. To which of these factors should its relative complexity be attributed? Similarly, if in one's experiment one compares *John isn't here* with *John is here*, one is comparing not only sentences that differ in length and transformational structure, but also sentences that differ in meaning. Perhaps negatives are more complicated than affirmatives simply because they are negatives. It is worth remarking that synonymous sentence types like active and passive or question and negative question generally tend to come out more similar on performance tasks than non-synonymous sentences comparably related in structure.

Such remarks hardly amount to a devastating criticism of the experiments under review. They do, however, suggest that it might be well to attempt experimental examinations of the relations between formal complexity and performance parameters in cases of sentence types other than simple declarative, question, passive, negative, and so on. Ideally it would be well to determine the nature of such relations in cases where length and meaning are controlled and ONLY the performance effects of variation of structural complexity is at issue. Experimental data satisfying either of these conditions are hard to find in the literature; results for experiments in which length and meaning were systematically controlled are extremely fragmentary. However, such data as has become available is worth considering, because it suggests a rather different

148

story about the relation of derivational length to performance than the one that emerges from the experimentation reviewed above.

A result of Miller & McKean (1964) is relevant here. Using the look-up technique described above, they carried out tests of sentences that differed in the expansion of the verb auxilliary. Sentences differed as follows: *Joe warned the boy*; *Joe had warned the boy*; *Joe was warning the boy*; *Joe had been warning the boy*. These differ by (i) adding *had*, (ii) adding some form of *be*, or (iii) adding both *had* and *be*. The predictions here were analogous to those for the transformations reviewed above—difficulty was expected to increase with complexity of the verb phrase. The results showed that there was no significant difference as a function of the changes introduced, except that the addition of *had* was very much easier than any other operation (.19 secs. added, compared with from .54 to .63 secs. added for the other operations).

Mehler also used his experimental procedures to test the effect of the expansion of *Aux*. More complicated expansions (involving modals) were used than those of Miller & McKean (*The boy hit the ball*; *the boy has hit the ball*;...*could hit*...;...*was hitting*...;...*could have hit*...;*could be hitting*...;...*has been hitting*...;...*could have been hitting*...). As in the Mehler experiment described above, recall was the dependent variable. The same conditions eight lists, eight syntactic types, eight semantic types) were present here as for the first experiment.

Subjects did not show any significant tendency to learn sentences with simpler *Aux* expansions more readily than those with complex expansions. Further, there was no tendency for response errors to be simplifications, and 157 errors involved complications of the *Aux*. This result thus corresponds to that obtained by Miller & McKean in their study of *Aux* expansion.

While these experiments do not systematically control for length or meaning, they provide examples where techniques that purport to measure performance complexity are employed with a new variety of syntactic material. The results are somewhat startling. Neither the prediction based on structure nor the prediction based on length is confirmed. The shorter sentences, which in this case are also the sentences with shorter derivations, are not in general easier to process than the longer ones. The prediction required by primitive models of the performance/competence distinction, that to complicate the derivation of a sentence is to increase its psychological complexity, is not supported. To put it somewhat differently, there are indefinitely many formal features of the derivations of sentences, any of which might, in principle, provide the basis for predicting performance complexity. The present

149

result suggests that a theory which associates complexity with the number of rules applied in the derivational history is not confirmed. If, then, a metric of complexity is to be defined over features of derivational histories, that metric will need to be sensitive to more subtle features than mere length in rules.

A similar story seems to emerge in the case of experiments on sentences in which meaning or word length or both are systematically balanced. Slobin (1963) failed to find the structurally predicted relation between long and short passives: that is to say, he did not find that short passives (like *John was found*) are more complicated on performance tasks than the long passives from which the grammar derives them. On the contrary, in an experiment using the McMahon true/false procedures described above, Slobin found that both declarative and short passives are simpler (yield shorter latencies) than long passives.

An unpublished experiment by Fodor, Jenkins & Saporta studied performance counterparts to the structural relations between such variants of the comparative as (1) *John runs faster than Bill runs*, (2) *John runs faster then Bill*, (3) *John runs faster than Bill does*. Presumably the order of structural complexity is the order given here: (1) is closest to the underlying form, (2) arises from the underlying form for (1) by the deletion of the second VP, (3) arises from the underlying form for (1) by the deletion of the second V, leaving *Aux* dominating tense, which automatically receives *do* support.

When recognition latencies are measured for tachistoscopic presentations of such sentences, analogues of (1) turn out to be significantly most difficult, and analogues of (2) and (3) turn out to be indistinguishable. (It is probable that the difference between (1) and ((2) and (3)) is a dialectal artifact arising from the fact that, for many subjects, the deletion of the second verb in the comparative is mandatory when v_1 equals v_2.) Similarly, when recognition latencies for sentences containing displaced particles and adverbs are compared with the latencies for sentences containing these parts of speech in their untransformed position, one does NOT discover the predicted asymmetry. That is, while *John phoned the girl up* is derived from *John phoned up the girl*, the latter sentence is not, by the present test, perceptually less complicated than the former.

In a more recent experiment, Bever & Mehler failed to demonstrate an interaction between ease of short-term recall and length of derivational history in materials balanced for both length and meaning.

In a recall task, *S* is presented with a sentence on a flash card. An interval is allowed to elapse; *S* then counts backward for a determined period. The syntactic variable is displaced vs. untransformed position of particles and adverbs. The striking result is that NO preference for the latter is found when the interval between presentation and recall is relatively short. When, however, that interval exceeds about thirty seconds, bias in favour of the untransformed version is discovered. The results appear to invite the interpretation that although length of the derivation does not interact with the short-term memory mechanisms exploited in understanding a sentence, it does determine the version of the sentence stored in long-term memory. This is precisely, on the one hand, compatible with the view that the recognition of a sentence does not involve the same operations employed in its grammatical generation, and, on the other, with the view that it is the base structure of a sentence that is stored for long-term recall. This, in turn, suggests a claim of psychological reality for the structural description of a sentence (including the specification of its base structure) but not for the operations employed in generating it.

Recently, Bever, Fodor, Garrett & Mehler have studied particle and adverb movement in an effort to demonstrate an interaction with extraneous tasks comparable to that for questions, negatives, and so on, shown by Savin & Perchonock (1965).

The data in this experiment are still fragmentary, but it now seems fairly clear that the predicted asymmetrics are not forthcoming. That is, while the Savin & Perchonock technique yields results substantiating the view that length of the derivational history is an index of performance complexity IN THE SPECIAL CASE OF PASSIVE, NEGATIVE, QUESTION, EMPHATIC, and so on; corresponding results are not forthcoming for sentences which exemplify other syntactic relations. The difference between *John phoned up the girl* and *John phoned the girl up* is the application of one transformational rule. Hence this pair of sentences is comparable to a pair like *John hit the ball* and *The ball was hit by John*. Yet the Savin & Perchonock technique indicates a difference of complexity only in the case of the latter pair.

What is one to make of such negative findings? The simplest move (and very possibly the right one) would be to deny the validity of the experimental procedures. Quite aside from the distinctly fragmentary character of the complexity data at present available for most types of syntactic relations, it is certainly true that we know very little about the way to measure the relevant verbal performance variables. It is also true, however, that some procedures have given the anticipated results in the case of some sentence types. If one is to deny the validity of such procedures in cases where they appear to fail, it seems one will equally have to deny their validity in the cases where they appear to succeed.

It is at any event now conceivable that enough negative data will eventually accumulate to make one wonder whether it is the theory that is at fault rather than the experiments. The problem may be not that our experimental procedures fail to measure perceptual complexity, but rather that it is a mistake to claim psychological reality for the operations whereby grammars generate structural descriptions.

Clearly, any perceptual routine will require a determinable number of distinct operations to assign a correct structural description to a waveform. We have seen that, in the case of certain conceivable perceptual routines, there is a simple correspondence between that number and the number of operations a grammar requires to generate the structural description. Whether the routine that speakers in fact employ exhibits such a correspondence is an empirical matter, to be settled, at least in part, by determining how well the relative length of derivational histories predicts relative structural complexity. It must surely be possible to imagine data that would be relevant to such determinations, and it is worth speculating on what happens if the data turns out badly.

It should be emphasized that, in showing that a predicted complexity order fails to obtain, one has not shown that the grammar is disconfirmed. A grammar is simply an axiomatic representation of an infinite set of structural descriptions, and the internal evidence in favour of the structural descriptions modern grammars generate is so strong that it is difficult to imagine their succumbing to any purely experimental disconfirmation. Rather, one would best interpret negative data as showing that an acceptable theory of the relation between competence and performance models will have to represent that relation as abstract, the degree of abstractness being proportional to the failure of formal features of derivations to correspond to performance variables.

It should also be emphasized that it is not unreasonable that this relation SHOULD turn out to be abstract. In the first place, it has long been known that SOME determinants of perceptual complexity are related to features of the structural description of a sentence, not to features of its derivational history. Sentences whose derived bracketing is of the form $(A_1 (A_2 (A_3 B_3) B_2) B_1)$ (e.g., *The man the dog the girl owned bit died*) are characteristically more difficult to understand than sentences whose derived bracketing is of the form $(A_1 B_1) (A_2 B_2) (A_3 B_3)$ (e.g., *The man who died was bitten by the dog that was owned by the girl*). But this feature of the structure of a sentence need bear no direct relation to the number of rules required to generate the sentence; quite short centre-branching sentences can be much harder to understand than quite long right-branching sentences. The second point is still more serious. A grammar, we have said, is an axiomatic representation of a certain set (the sentences of a language). A perceptual analyser may be thought of as a decision procedure for membership in that set; given any string in a certain vocabulary, it applies a derivation just in case the string is in the set enumerated by the grammar. It is well known that axiomatic representations and associated decision procedures exist for sets other than the sentences of a natural language. To take a very simple case, consider the set s of theorems of the propositional calculus. s can be precisely represented by a pair (α, β), where α is a finite, non-null set of well-formed formulae in the vocabulary of s, and β is a finite, non-null set of inference rules. The pair (α, β), represents a recursive enumeration of s in the sense that the application of every permitted order of the rules in β to the axioms in α will generate all and only the strings in s. In this rather limited sense the relationship between s and the pair (α, β) is analogous to the relationship between an adequate English grammar and English.

One might imagine a tribe of very rational people who speak propositional calculus as a native language. One might also imagine that some linguist belonging to that tribe (call him N) has performed the enormously impressive feat of axiomatizing the language; that is to say, he has arrived at a formal statement of the pair (α, β).

Although rational, the tribe contains psycholinguists; the foremost of these (call him G) is interested in developing a performance model to explain how the information expressed by the axiomatization is employed in the production and analysis of utterances. He reasons as follows:

Since (α, β) effects a recursive enumeration of s, appropriate constraints on β would permit the construction of a decision procedure in which (α, β) is used in rather the way that English grammars are used in analysis-by-synthesis procedures. Given an input I in the vocabulary of the propositional calculus, (α, β) is required to list theorems in some constrained manner until either I is matched or some subset of the theorems is exhausted to which it can be proved that I must belong if it is a theorem.

This performance model leads to empirical predictions. In particular, G argues if the performance model is correct, then the perceptual complexity of a theorem of his language ought to be closely correlated with the length of the shortest proof of that theorem from the axioms α that employs the inference rules β.

The relevant experiments are run, and not surprisingly, nothing works—not surprisingly, because, while the axiomatization correctly

153

represents the set of strings comprising the subject's language, the subject may use proof procedures which exploit the information the axioms represent in some quite different form. For example, he might be using a method of truth tables.[1] Such a method is equivalent to (α, β) in the precise sense that it picks out exactly the set of theorems that (α, β) enumerates. On the other hand, it is simple to choose (α, β) such that some of the formulae it generates only via long proofs are trivially proved by truth tables. The converse also holds.

What is poor G to do? He can rail at his experimental methods, but even in a rational tribe it is hard to stop psycholinguists from doing experiments. He can blame N for having misled him, but this is to misunderstand what question N's theory is supposed to answer. N was attempting to formalize the information people use in deciding which strings are theorems in their language; (α, β) is precisely such a formalization. If it does not present that information in the form in which people use it to analyse formulae, that is no fault of N's; he never said it did. Finally, G can attempt to arrive at a new, and more abstract, view of the relation between (α, β) and the performance model, which theory some later generation of experiments will doubtless also confute. Do not, however, mock G. His sorrows are ours.

1. T or F is assigned to formulae in accordance with the conventions:
    P *or* Q is T unless P is F and Q is F
    P *and* Q is F unless Q is T and P is T
    P Q is F unless Q is T and P is T
    P Q is T unless P is T and Q is F
    Not P is T unless P is T
    A formula is a theorem if and only if it is T on all assignments of T and F to the variables.

Discussion

N. S. SUTHERLAND

Fodor and Garrett's paper is long and complicated, so I shall attempt to summarise it as I go along. For convenience, I have divided their paper into six sections and I shall give a summary of each section and then one or two comments of my own.

I.

F & G start off by claiming that positivism in some way impeded the progress of science and in particular the progress of psychology. They do not state very clearly what the positivist view of science was nor do

154

they attempt to show in any detail how the positivist view influenced experimental psychologists. They claim that 'in the philosophy of psychology positivism emerged as the view that psychology is the science of behaviour' and evidently they disapprove of this view; but I am not at all clear why they should disapprove, nor do I know of what else psychology can be the science. The behaviourists insisted that psychology was about physical events and if the work of people like Thorndike or Hull is compared with that of Stout and McDougall it seems to me that behaviourism represented a great step forwards. It is of course true that the categories of physical events with which psychologists deal are extremely complicated and the early behaviourists may have underestimated this complexity. Despite this, it was the recognition that psychology is about certain classes of physical events that opened the way to the scientific study of behaviour, and in particular to the search for mechanisms.

F & G say: 'There is no reason to suppose that psychology . . . is primarily in the business of arriving at generalizations about behaviour. Psychology is primarily concerned with understanding the nature and capacities of the mechanisms which underlie behaviour. Psychologists betrayed some awareness of these points even in the darkest days of behaviourism.' I have two qualms about these statements.

First, F & G appear to take a very narrow view of science. I would have thought that establishing generalizations about behaviour was an extremely useful thing to do; it might even be regarded as a necessary preliminary to arriving at the mechanisms mediating behaviour. Some of the most noteworthy advances in science, for example Boyle's laws of gases, have consisted simply of high level generalizations. Such generalizations are often an important step towards discovering the mechanism lying behind them. Thus the behaviour of gases was subsequently interpreted in terms of laws governing the behaviour of individual molecules. In the light of the history of science it does seem a trifle odd to cavil at psychologists for wishing to establish some generalizations on which to found a science of behaviour.

Secondly, it is simply not true that psychologists have not been interested in the mechanisms of behaviour. Unfortunately, F & G do not mention by name any of the workers they are attacking, but I would assume they are referring to people working in the thirties and forties. Some of the main experimental psychologists at this time were Lashley, Hull, Tolman, Guthrie, Koffka, Kohler, and Hebb; they all proposed theories which were attempts to specify the mechanisms behind behaviour. It is true that some of these workers, particularly Hull, in their *obiter dicta* gave incorrect descriptions of what they were doing at a metascientific level; but they should be judged by their scientific achievements not by what they wrote about their own work. The only important psychologist who steadfastly refused to postulate mechanisms was Skinner, and we owe to him some of the most important and surprising discoveries made by experimental psychologists.

I am sorry to spend so much time on F & G's rather fragmentary introductory remarks, but they do seem to me to represent an unduly narrow and mistaken view of scientific activity. Moreover, I think the points I am making are relevant to understanding some of the difficulties that F & G encounter when they come to interpreting some of the recent experimental results in psycholinguistics. Part of the difficulty in relating these results to the mechanism of speech production and recognition may be that we simply have not done enough experimental work on language performance to establish sufficient generalizations about it to enable us to make reasonably well-informed guesses about what these mechanisms are.

2.

The second part of F & G's paper is largely devoted to the problem of competence. Chomsky points out that linguistics should be concerned to give generative rules not merely for the sentences speakers actually produce but for the sentences they might have produced such as *My friend owns three-eighths of an elephant*. Nobody is likely to quarrel with this since it is a standard attribute of any good scientific theory not only that it accounts in some sense for what does happen but that it will account for what might have happened in other circumstances. It is clear that there are an indefinite number of unspoken sentences that people could recognize as being grammatical and which they could generate if asked to generate unusual grammatical sentences, and people's ability to do this must be taken into account by any satisfactory theory of grammar. Moreover, the way in which people behave in unusual circumstances is likely to throw light on the way in which they behave in normal circumstances, so that a consideration of unusual grammatical sentences is likely to throw light on ordinary grammatical sentences. There is nothing very novel about this within the context of science: the behaviour of matter under very low temperatures only obtainable under artificial conditions throws considerable light on its behaviour under more usual circumstances. Any physical theory of matter that could not account for the behaviour of matter under very unusual circumstances would not be a very satisfactory theory.

156

F & G point out that linguists usually use the phrase 'linguistic competence' in a restricted sense. They use it to refer to the linguistic information a speaker has at his disposal—the actual use the speaker makes of such information will be limited by psychological mechanisms such as memory capacity, motivation, and so on. They point out that psycholinguists must study, not merely the linguistic information that is at a speaker's disposal, but also how he puts it to use: study of the latter question will also involve a study of the mechanism behind behaviour, not merely the behaviour itself. They argue that the usual view taken by psycholinguists is to arrive at a model of behaviour which consists of a linguistic-competence model plus some further mechanisms which 'will jointly issue in the utterance or understanding of sentences'. They then go on to argue that this view may be misleading, since a formalized grammar may not necessarily be a component part of the mechanism that actually results in the production or recognition of speech. Before going on to their reasons for saying this, I would like to comment on their use of the word 'competence'.

They nowhere make a clear distinction between 'competence' and 'mechanism', and indeed they appear to treat the terms interchangeably. For example, they say: 'In the sense in which distinguishing between performance and competence is distinguishing between behaviour and the mechanisms underlying it, both linguistic and psychological models are models of competence'. It seems to me that the words 'competence' and 'mechanism' have completely different meanings and that much of F & G's later puzzles come from a failure to distinguish these terms. To take an analogy from computers, both analogue and digital machines have the capacity or competence to perform the operation of addition. The two types of machines, however, involve very different mechanisms. If we studied the input-output relations of a digital and an analogue machine we might conclude that part of their competence was to perform arithmetical operations. Supposing we did not know the rules of arithmetic, we might even work out from studying the behaviour of the computers what the rules of arithmetic were. In order to do this we would have to ignore any errors the computers made, just as the linguist ignores mistakes in speech. All this would be an important step forward in understanding the behaviour of the computer, but it would not be a final answer. We would still not know what the mechanism in the computers was, nor would we know that two different mechanisms were at work in the analogue and the digital machine. To arrive at an answer to the latter question we would have to consider much else besides the ideal rules which the computer obeys in carrying out arithmetical opera-

157

tions. Two things in particular would give us a clue about the different mechanisms in the two computers. First, we would find that the actual operations they conducted departed sometimes from the ideal operations: in other words the machines would make mistakes—more importantly they would make different kinds of mistakes, and the kinds of mistakes each machine made would provide us with clues about the mechanism operating in each. Secondly, we could of course start looking inside the machines and try to make inferences about the way they worked from the way the bits and pieces inside were put together.

It should be clear from this example that studying competence and studying a mechanism are by no means the same thing. We may know what a machine is competent to do without knowing how it does it. Similarly, there is a sense in which we might know what the mechanism in a computer is without knowing all the things that the machine was competent to do if properly programmed, and indeed this is very much the position we are in at the moment with existing computers.

It may be worthwhile not only distinguishing between competence and mechanism but also distinguishing two senses of the word mechanism. So far I have used mechanism to mean the basic arrangement of the bits and pieces inside the unprogrammed computer or organism. From a knowledge of this mechanism plus a knowledge of the inputs to which it can be subjected over time, it is in theory possible to work out what tasks the machine is competent to perform. We could, however, take the mechanism of a computer at a given time to mean the state of the machine once a programme has been read in: the computer is now a different machine involving a different mechanism for every different programme. The programme would no longer be regarded as an input—the only inputs we are now concerned with are the data fed in. Similarly when we talk of the mechanism behind language, it seems important to be clear in which sense we are using the word mechanism. It is perfectly proper to study the mechanism responsible for language performance in an adult, without worrying how it got to be the way it is as a result of learning. We might also want to study the basic, genetically-determined mechanism in the nervous system and show how such a mechanism could give rise to linguistic competence as a result of the way it is affected by learning. Although the second objective is clearly the more fundamental, it may be that the first objective is easier to achieve. Thus we have some knowledge of the mechanisms of depth perception in man but we are unable to say how far such mechanisms are determined genetically or how far they are programmed in by the environment.

In summary, then, it is necessary to distinguish between competence and mechanism, though both aspects of behaviour are worthy of study. Knowing the ideal tasks that an organism can perform does not of itself tell us what is the mechanism mediating any given task. Moreover, even if we knew all the details of the mechanism inside an existing organism this would not of itself tell us what tasks the organism was competent to carry out. We could not be said to have fully explained behaviour until we had both worked out what the mechanism is and what tasks such a mechanism was capable of mediating.

Having made the distinction between competence and mechanism, it is difficult to see why the puzzles that F & G discuss in the remainder of their talk should ever have arisen. I suppose the answer is that F & G were trained or at least very heavily influenced by linguists, whose concern is with competence not mechanisms. I shall argue that the proper concern of psychologists is with mechanisms and that they must not be deflected from this aim by the long shadow cast by Chomsky.

3.

In the third section of their paper, F & G argue that knowing the rules for generating grammatical sentences does not solve the problem of how sentences are recognized; and they appear to be rather puzzled by this. In this section they call attention to some well-known problems in recognition, such as that of matching an input to a stored or generated representation of the input as analysed.

They go on to point out that if the actual recognition and generating processes in the nervous system correspond closely to the linguistic rules for generating a grammar then we might expect various performance measures of sentence complexity to correspond rather closely with the complexity involved in generating a sentence by a generative grammar.

4.

In their next section F & G mention some results of experiments attempting to measure sentence complexity in terms of behaviour. Most of these experiments are well known, but it may be worth briefly recalling the main results. Miller has obtained evidence suggesting that it takes longer to match a sentence with its transformation when two transformations are involved than when only one is involved. Both Mehler and Savin & Perchonock have obtained evidence suggesting that the memory load in retaining a sentence increases with the number of transformations required to generate the sentence from the corresponding kernel sentence. F & G rightly point out that in some of these experiments the number of transformations are confounded with sentence length; in other cases they are confounded with semantic meaning. They might have added that a further variable not taken account of in these experiments is the frequency of usage of different types of sentence and this could clearly affect ease of matching and recall. Although, therefore, these results are in agreement with expectations from Chomsky-type generative grammars, they do not provide very strong support for the notion that the mechanisms of speech recognition and production mimic closely the abstract generative grammar proposed by Chomsky.

5.

In the next part of their paper F & G cite a series of negative results; they cite several experiments in which it was found that performance measures of sentence complexity do not correlate with the complexity of the generative process in a formal grammar. In particular both Miller and Mehler found that the behavioural complexity of sentences involving the expansion of auxiliary verbs did not correspond to their grammatical complexity. Slobin found that the short version of the passive was easier to recognize as true or false than the longer version, although according to the grammar the short version is more complex, since it is generated via the long version. Fodor, Saporta & Jenkins obtained similar negative results when they attempted to measure by a performance variable the complexity of different versions of comparative sentences.

6.

In their final section F & G consider what should be done by workers in psycholinguistics about such negative results. They present an ingenious and illuminating analogy. They consider the case of an imaginary tribe whose native language is the propositional calculus. They imagine that a linguist has succeeded in axiomatizing the language and pose the problem of what is to be done if a psycholinguist comes along and finds that performance measures of sentence complexity do not correspond to measures of complexity based on the number of steps required to derive a theorem in the language from the basic axioms. They rightly point out that this would not come as any great surprise, since there are numerous procedures for testing whether a given proposition is a theorem. If speakers used truth tables to determine whether a string was a theorem the length of time taken to test different strings would be very different from if they used a particular form of axiomatization.

It is clear that this example could be elaborated indefinitely, and I believe it is worth elaborating somewhat further. For instance, it is known that it is possible to axiomatize the propositional calculus in more than one way and the number of steps involved in the proof of a given theorem will vary enormously depending on what axioms we choose. This suggests a possibility not considered by F & G: namely, that although the type of grammar developed by Chomsky may be one way of axiomatizing language it is not necessarily the only way nor need it correspond to the axiomatization system (if any) represented in the brain.

Moreover, it is abundantly clear that the ease with which a logician is able to prove a particular theorem does not correspond in any simple way with the number of steps involved in deriving the proof from the basic axioms. Logicians do not attempt to derive proofs by randomly applying axioms in succession. They develop strategies; and the proof that is difficult is not simply the one that is longest when broken down into elementary steps, but the one which involves some very unusual steps. Moreover, when a logician wishes to derive the proof of a new theorem he does not start with the elementary axioms: he often starts from theorems that he can remember and which he may well have forgotten how to prove.

Just as the logician makes use of heuristic devices in proving theorems, so it seems to me certain that the human brain must do so in recognizing and producing sentences. It does not seem to me to have been proven that all sentences must be completely decomposed into their deep structure in order to be uttered or understood. It seems possible that performance may be controlled more by a system of analogies than by a more rigorous generative procedure in which the axioms of linguistics are directly represented in the brain. For example, if the brain can categorize words into types, new sentences could be formed not by directly looking up a very general rule but by looking up an instance of the use of a word of a similar type. The formal rules governing the output of such a system might be identical with those of a linguistic grammar, but the mechanism would be very different from a mechanism directly incorporating a generative grammar.

The dilemma in which F & G claim to find themselves as a result of the negative findings on sentence complexity seems to me to be of their own making. It arises through a failure to distinguish between competence and mechanism. The task of psycholinguistics is not to confirm Chomsky's account of linguistic competence by undertaking experiments. To the extent that Chomsky has succeeded in axiomatizing grammar, his account does not stand in need of such confirmation. The task of psycholinguistics is to my mind very much more difficult and

161

interesting. It is, by doing experiments, to find out what are the mechanisms which underly linguistic competence. Arriving at these mechanisms may even involve discovering first some low-level generalizations about language of the sort that F & G began their talk by condemning.

SUMMARY

I will finish by trying to summarize what I have been saying. I have been trying to insist that there is a big difference between competence and mechanism. One might take the task of the linguist to be the study of competence and the ultimate task of the psycholinguist to be the discovery of the mechanism that gives rise to that competence. Whereas the linguist can afford to ignore errors in speech, the psycholinguist cannot since it is precisely the nature of the errors made that may give one of the best clues as to the underlying mechanism. There can be no question that a knowledge of linguistic competence is likely to be of enormous help to the psycholinguist in arriving at the mechanism underlying language performance. There can also be no question that thanks to the work of Chomsky (I feel I should cross myself every time I mention that name!), Halle, and others, our knowledge of competence is at a much more advanced stage at present than our knowledge of the mechanism. This is likely to remain true for some time. In fact it seems to me unlikely that we shall make much progress with the mechanism of language until we have solved other fundamental problems in perception and learning. In the case of perception we often have a reasonable knowledge of competence. For instance, in making size judgements it is clear that people conform to the rule 'Multiply retinal size by the distance an object is away'. Although we know what they are competent to do, we still have no very clear idea of the mechanism by which they do it. Although people do follow rules in carrying out other tasks, the rules followed in language behaviour are much more complex than in any other kind of behaviour; and it is Chomsky's great achievement to have given us a systematic account of these rules. Admiration for Chomsky should not, however, lead us to suppose that there is nothing left to do.

Finally, it may be worth repeating a point made by Wales & Marshall (cf. pp. 54ff.). It is possible to specify a mechanism at different levels of abstraction. For example we might be able to specify the successive steps taken in processing information in speech recognition and production, without necessarily being able to specify the details of the physiological mechanisms involved at each stage. The final proof of the correctness of any mechanism postulated must come from showing at a physiological level that the suggested mechanism is the one instantiated in the nervous system. There is of course another side to this coin. If we had a complete wiring diagram of the brain, we would not necessarily understand the mechanism behind language. We would still have to understand how the detailed physiological mechanism gives rise to performance, and this would almost certainly involve us in treating the physiological mechanism in terms of abstractions at a considerably remove from the basic elements that make up the nervous system. This is why neurophysiology and experimental psychology are likely to remain distinct sciences.

L. JONATHAN COHEN

In their very interesting paper Fodor & Garrett seek to achieve two main objectives. They wish to draw attention to the risk of conceptual confusion—confusion that might obstruct the advancement of knowledge—in prevalent ways of using the competence-performance distinctions in psycholinguistics; and they also wish to show that experimental results do not fit the view that hearers always assign a correct structural description to a wave-form by a process that varies directly in its order of complexity with the procedure by which a fully adequate grammar generates that description.

I am not altogether sure that F & G have achieved their objectives and my doubt about this exists at three different levels. I suspect that they may have introduced more conceptual confusion than they have dispelled. I suspect that the experimental evidence they cite may not support the conclusions they draw. And, at a more fundamental level, I suspect that the question they ask could profitably be replaced by a rather different one. But on all three of these matters I speak with the diffidence appropriate to a critic who is neither a linguist nor a psychologist by profession, and has had very little time indeed to prepare his remarks.

According to F & G there is a 'pre-positivist', pre-twentieth-century view that science is primarily concerned to understand the laws determining the behaviour of ideal objects and events, as such unobservable, from an experimental study of physical objects that differ from their ideal counterparts in controllable respects. This view was succeeded, we are told, over a very wide field by a 'positivist' theory that science is about its experimentally-discoverable data and not concerned with theoretical entities in any way at all. Now, it would be very easy to spend a lot of time arguing that this is a grotesque travesty of historical fact. One could point out, for instance, that the view of science that F & G describe as positivist was quite clearly and influentially expounded by Bishop

Berkeley, who was very far from being a positivist (in the ordinary sense of being anti-metaphysical) in the early eighteenth century; and that, whatever the situation has been in the philosophy of psychology, a concern for theoretical entities of one kind or another—electro-magnetic waves, sub-atomic particles, fields of force, genes, molecules, and so on —has dominated a very great deal of twentieth-century thought about science, whether this be the thought of professional scientists like Bohr and Heisenberg or of professional philosophers like Duhem and Popper. But for present purposes it is obviously far more important to concentrate on how we should conceive scientific theory now, in the field in which we are interested, than to hold a historical inquest of any kind.

On this point it seems to me to create, rather than dispel, confusion if we suppose, as F & G seem to suppose (pp. 135-9), that a theory which seeks to determine the behaviour of a certain kind of ideal object under ideal conditions, and to explain at least some aspects of observed behaviour in terms of this idealized counterpart, is *pro tanto* a theory that seeks to explain observed behaviour in terms of mechanisms that underlie it. These seem to me to be quite different types of theory that may or may not be combined in particular cases. As a very simple paradigm we can consider the IDEALIZED DESCRIPTION of an ordinary clock's behaviour as rotating one hand at twice the speed of the earth's rotation on its axis and the other hand at twenty-four times that speed, although of course actual clocks are rarely, if ever, as accurate as this in their performance. But the UNDERLYING MECHANISM here is the clockwork or electric motor responsible for actual clocks' actual performances, not any ideal clock's behaviour. Again, ideal counterparts are unobserved or unobservable because, like perfect clocks, they are rarely, if ever, to be found; mechanisms, on the other hand, are unobserved or unobservable because they are too small or too well-hidden by nature. Finally, theories about ideal counterparts represent a simplified description of observable data. Theories about mechanisms purport to explain observable data rather than to describe it in any way. I fully endorse F & G's view of the importance of Chomsky's insistence upon the competence-performance distinction in linguistics. I think it very useful to be able to think of an ideal speaker's speech-potential as a competence, to which actually observed linguistic behaviour may be related as performance. But such a conception of competence has nothing whatever to do with any mechanism of any kind, as F & G seem to suggest (p. 138). If, on the other hand, we do wish to talk about the psychological mechanisms that causally underlie linguistic performance it is bound to create confusion if we call such a theory of a mechanism either a theory of competence or a model of performance. It is surely better to call it a theory of the speaker-hearer's mechanism.

There is one other point, rather late in their paper, on which F & G seem to me to be likely to create confusion. They talk of a generative grammar sometimes as an axiomatic representation of the set of sentences of a language (p. 153), and sometimes as an axiomatic representation of the set of structural descriptions of those sentences (p. 152). Now the former description of a generative grammar seems to me to be both legitimate and useful. As axiomatizations of sets of sentences generative grammars no doubt have their peculiarities; but one can clearly distinguish between the elements axiomatized (the sentences), the axioms (generative rules), and the proofs or derivations. But what else can be meant in this context by the structural description of a sentence than an account of its derivation or generation, namely, a phrase-marker plus a transformation-marker? Hence it seems to be just a kind of nonsense to speak of generative grammar as an axiomatic representation of the set of structural descriptions of the sentences of a language—it is like speaking of Russell's axioms for the propositional calculus as an axiomatic representation of the proof of its theorems. The point is that given a set of supposed theorems we may conceivably find it very hard work to discover an adequate set of axioms for them. But given a set of supposed derivations we can normally just read off the postulates, rules, and so on, which produce and control them. Perhaps it will be thought that, in criticizing the description of a generative grammar as an axiomatic representation of a set of structural descriptions, I am just being pedantic in a typically, and annoyingly, philosophical way. But I shall shortly suggest that this misdescription may be closely connected with a mistake that F & G seem to have made in the interpretation of the experimental evidence they cite.

F & G are concerned in general with the nature of the hearer's psychological mechanism, and the specific question they would like to answer seems to be: by what operations does the hearer map a wave-form on to its structural description? Earlier experiments seemed to support the view that these operations varied directly, in the time they took, with the number of steps (i.e., the number of applications of rules) necessary to generate the sentence or its structural description in the appropriate generative grammar, and these earlier experiments were therefore compatible with some kind of analysis-by-synthesis theory of the mechanism under investigation. However, there are, in any case, considerable implausibilities in this kind of theory, as F & G rightly say, owing to the order of time that would appear to be involved; and a number of experimental results are now reported that seem clearly incompatible with the view that a hearer maps a wave-form on to its structural description by operations that directly match the steps taken in generating this description within a grammar.

F & G conclude from these later results that the relation between the grammar, as a theory of linguistic competence, on the one side, and a theory of the hearer's mechanism, on the other, is more abstract—more indirect, they must mean—than has previously been supposed. It was open to them to suggest that perhaps the grammar itself was at fault, and that by suitable alterations of the grammar a direct relation might be re-established between the theory of linguistic competence and the theory of the hearer's psychological mechanism. But F & G explicitly (p. 152) reject this interpretation of the experimental results: 'The internal evidence in favour of the structural descriptions modern grammars generate is so strong', they say, 'that it is difficult to imagine their succumbing to any purely experimental disconfirmation'. But if F & G are speaking of just THESE structural descriptions as being assigned by hearers to wave-forms, then the complexity of the structural description itself will vary directly with the number of steps necessary to generate it in the grammar. So unless one is to suppose an unbounded number of structural descriptions existing preformed in the hearer's mind, the hearer's mechanism that assigns a structural description to a wave-form has in any case to articulate a description that varies directly in complexity with the number of steps taken to generate it in the grammar. Hence F & G's abstract, or indirect, operations of mapping wave-forms on to structural descriptions are not at all analogous to the method of truth-tables they refer to at the end of their paper (p. 154); for the method of truth tables is an effective procedure for generating, in relation to each theorem of the calculus, a table that constitutes a demonstration of that theorem by reference to the principles of truth-table construction. Such a method would be analogous to the use of a quite different grammar—a grammar generating the same strings but with different structural descriptions. Instead, if one can find any analogy at all in regard to the propositional calculus, it would be a method of assigning proofs to theorems without the need to make successive references back to the axioms, and I find it difficult to conceive of such a method without self-contradiction. To put it another way, the trouble is that the articulation of the structural description can hardly be distinguished from its generation. I think that F & G's misdescription of a generative grammar as an axiomatic representation of a set of structural descriptions, to which I referred earlier, has led them to suppose that such a distinction can have psychological reality. On the one hand they want to stick to existing grammars and their structural descriptions: on the other hand they want to speak as if the articulation of a structural description can be realistically distinguished from its proof or generation. They cannot have it both ways. Again, if that distinction is not possible, F & G's interpretation of the data seems to require that we should posit an operation within the hearer's mechanism which preserves a direct correspondence between the relative complexities of some structural descriptions and the relative latencies of the wave-forms to which they may be assigned, but counteracts a lack of correspondence where this is found to exist: that is to say, in the former type of case it either does not operate at all, or varies directly in the time it takes with the relative complexity of the structural descriptions, or always takes the same period of time; while in the latter type of case it must operate, cannot always take the same time, and, roughly speaking, must vary inversely in time taken with the relative complexity of the structural descriptions. It seems to me that this is not a very illuminating hypothesis unless some indication is given of why a hearer should have a mechanism that behaves in this odd and irregular way.

So what are we to say here, if we are to say anything at all? A simpler alternative to F & G's hypothesis is obviously to modify the grammar. For example, if Mehler has shown that there is no significant tendency to recall sentences with simpler *Aux* expansions more readily than those with complex expansions, it may be that the grammar should be content to treat each of these expansions (*could, could be ... ing, could have been ... ing*) as single units for purposes of syntactic description. But I wish to suggest instead a rather more drastic reconsideration of our views about the psychological mechanism than F & G envisage, a reconsideration which I think has been hinted at also by some speakers at earlier meetings—not that I have any strong confidence that my own sketch of a hypothesis is in the right. But at least the case for it should not be lost by default of presentation, and clearly far too little is known as yet about actual performance for any precise theory of the hearer's mechanism to be advanced at all and even for any partial and imprecise sketch of a theory (like mine) to be advanced with confidence.

What I want to suggest is that we should reconsider not just our views about the process by which a hearer maps a wave-form on to its structural description, but the whole question whether he does it at all. This is, after all, an empirical question. Presumably the purpose of a theory about the hearer's mechanism is primarily to explain how a hearer understands utterances in his own language; and it is worthwhile pausing a moment to ask what we mean by 'understand' here before we go on to try and explain how this understanding takes place. I do not find some sort of answer to this, philosophical, question quite as difficult to give as some speakers were suggesting in the discussion of Thorne's paper. A man is normally said to understand an utterance if, when necessary, he can draw the right conclusions from it, or can tell what would count as an answer to it, or can judge whether it is true or false, or act appropriately, and so on. But he does not actually have to DO these things in order to have understood what was said. He only has to be able to do them. He only has to have filed the information he has received in a way in which he can retrieve it, if necessary, for the successful execution of one or other of these tasks. It is very important here that we should distinguish between what a hearer does when he understands an utterance and what he does when he shows that he understands it, because the latter is much more closely tied up with the SPEAKER'S role in speaker-hearer activity. We must distinguish, as F & G advise us to do in another connection, between the question 'What is the proposition p about?' and the question 'What is the evidence for p?', where in this case p is a proposition that someone understands something. Of course, if the utterance heard, or read, is in a foreign language, then no doubt the hearer has to map it on to its structural description in order to effect a translation of it into his own language (i.e., a translation of it into a form in which it can be filed for convenient retrieval). But one should no more suppose that a hearer's understanding of an utterance in his own language must involve some process of translation or paraphrase because his understanding of an utterance in a foreign language does, than one should suppose that his learning of his own language involves the learning of lexical equivalences because his learning of a foreign language involves this. If we insist on taking the foreign language learning-understanding set-up as a model for the native language learning-understanding set-up, we shall inevitably conjure up some bogus mental counterparts to the native language words learnt or the native language utterances heard, and the existence of these counterparts will explain nothing at all because they will themselves constitute just another set of linguistic units to be learned or understood. Indeed, I suspect that the Katz-Fodor theory of meaning, which identifies the whole of the speaker-hearer's semantic competence with what is in fact only a part of it, namely, with the ability to analyse, paraphrase, and detect anomalies

168

and ambiguities (Cohen, 1966), is particularly liable to lead psycho-linguists into this barren error.

So the hearer's mechanism I am proposing is one that will map wave-forms on to memory-storage instructions. Such a mechanism must be capable of recognizing occurrences of those morphemes and combina-tions of morphemes (i.e., nouns, verbs, adjectives, etc.) that constitute categories under which information is usefully stored alongside estab-lished relevant rules for identification, individuation, inference, and so on; and it must be capable of distinguishing those morphemes from morphemes that are not of this kind (i.e., articles, conjunctions, etc.). It must also be capable of reversing certain transformations that have taken place in the generation of the utterance, in order to identify the appropriate filing categories (e.g., reversing displacements, like *George put his own friends up* from *George put up his own friends*), and breaking down logically compound sentences into their constituent kernels plus the relations between these. It must be capable of filing under each appropriate category a morphophonemic description of the kernel sen-tence or sentences plus transformation-markers which CAN be pro-cessed for a full structural description if the hearer needs to show, or utilize, his understanding in a way that requires this processing. And the hearer's mechanism must also be capable of treating its description of the wave-form as a cross-reference to other filings of the same wave-form, and of filing alongside this description a description of certain contextual circumstances of the wave-form's utterance (in order to identify the denotations of personal pronouns, demonstratives, etc., and to assist in residual disambiguation; I assume that in most cases con-textual circumstances will have determined the initial filing of poly-semes). But I really cannot see why the mechanism of a hearer's under-standing need be supposed to produce a full structural description for each wave-form understood: it does not seem even to have to produce all the transformation-markers (e.g. semantically redundant displace-ment markers, as in *phone up→phone...up*, can be omitted), let alone the phrase-markers. To produce a full description would seem to be an ex-traordinarily uneconomical procedure, when we reflect on the number of utterances we hear and understand (boring lectures, uninteresting books), and yet never act on, linguistically or non-linguistically, in any way at all—that is, never paraphrase, translate, infer from, answer,—so that we never need to make use of a full structural description. Our guiding principle, I suggest, should be to look for the most economical means of storing information for the purpose of showing that we do understand it.

169

In short, what I am suggesting is that for a hearer to understand a speaker's utterance correctly is to file a partial description of it under the same memory-storage categories, and to be prepared to take to at least some extent the same linguistic and non-linguistic action on it, as the speaker would be prepared to take if the roles were reversed. To misunderstand is to file it under different categories, or to file a misdescription of it; and to fail to understand it is not to file it at all, or not to file a description of it that is adequate for the purposes of eliciting implications, answering questions, checking truth-values, and so on.

How does such a theory fit the experimental data? I have time here only for a brief and highly selective survey, but I do not know of any yet reported data which fail to fit:

1. The fact that subjects are quicker to recall grammatical sentences they have heard than ungrammatical ones, especially at higher speeds (Miller, 1962), is quite compatible with the filing-instruction theory of understanding, as I have very crudely outlined it. For if we accept such a theory we shall suppose that the shorter latency of grammatical sentences is due to the greater difficulty that the SPEAKER'S mechanism has in producing ungrammatical ones (a familiar experience even outside recall situations) rather than in the greater difficulty the HEARER'S mechanism has in recognizing these.

2. The fact that displacement of the clicks in the experiments of Fodor & Bever, and of Garrett, Bever & Fodor, was found to be related to the constituent structure of the sentences is perfectly compatible with the requirement that a hearer's mechanism should be capable of describing a wave-form in terms of its constituent morphemes plus transformations undergone.

3. The results of Miller, McKean & Slobin (1962), of Miller & McKean (1964), of Mehler (1963), and of Savin & Perchonock (1965), that are cited by Fodor & Garrett, are obviously accommodated by a theory of this kind. So are McMahon's results. His experiment is particularly interesting because it is the only one cited by Fodor & Garrett which seems to require Ss to UNDERSTAND what they hear, as distinct from merely recalling it. Not surprisingly, therefore, we find that sentences generated by a negative transformation take longer to process than those generated by the semantically redundant active-passive transformation. The storage procedure will be more complex if there is a more complex semantic content to store.

4. As for the experiments of Miller & McKean, and of Mehler, that test the effect of *Aux* expansions, these can be construed as showing which groups of morphemes are treated as combining to constitute

170

single categories for filing purposes; that is, semantically speaking, *Ss* must be taken to treat *could, could be . . . ing, could have been . . . ing,* and so on as single units. This is by no means counter-intuitive, especially when one takes into account the way in which the number of words used to express these notions varies widely from language to language.

5. Slobin's result again fits my theory reasonably well. Short passives yield shorter latencies because they yield less semantic content to file: cf. *John was found* with *John was found by George.*

6. As for Fodor, Jenkins & Saporta's result that *John phoned the girl up* has the same latency as *John phoned up the girl,* even though the former sentence is transformationally derived from the latter, it seems again here that we have a case of semantic redundancy. The phoning up can be recorded and filed away under the category of *phoning* without any need to conjoin a transformation-marker with the phonetic description of the string. (It is a little different here from the case with passives: the passive transformation may be semantically redundant, but, unless he notices that it has occurred, a hearer may not be able to recover the standard declarative form on which he operates to construct his inferences.) However, if *John put the girl up* turned out to have the same latency as *John put up the girl* it is obvious that my explanation of the *phone up* case will not do, since *up* is not semantically redundant in the *put up* sentences. It would be interesting to know what results an experiment would produce here.

7. There are also certain familiar facts of which my theory makes quite good sense. Children often seem to hear and understand grammatical sentences perfectly well long before they can speak them. Similarly, they often seem to read and understand grammatical sentences long before they can write them. It is rather more difficult to explain these facts (IF they are facts) if one has to suppose the hearer's mechanism maps wave-forms on to complete structural descriptions than if one merely has to ascribe to it the capacity to map wave-forms on to filing instructions with appropriate cross-references. Some imbalance, or asymmetry, between the speaker's mechanism and the hearer's seems suggested. Again telegraphese is probably the most successful way to communicate with children after they have passed the holophrastic stage and before they have mastered any adult syntax, and is also the way they seem to speak themselves. Perhaps this is because such telegraphese has the closest structural isomorphism with the filing instructions a child is capable of operating with at that age.

8. The normal reaction of a hearer, at least outside experimental situ-

171

ations in the laboratory, is to suppose that what he hears both makes sense and is unambiguous. He will tolerate what in fact may be a fairly high degree of ungrammaticalness in order to make some sense of an utterance. He will attach some sense even to the first few words of an utterance that is broken off thereafter. He will interpret utterances of sentences that a grammarian might cite as lexically bizarre, or a logician as self-contradictory, as if those utterances had some perfectly good sense. And unless he hesitates some time over an utterance he certainly does not search for ambiguities in its syntax: to expound syntactic deviance or ambiguity is a very special kind of activity, which most speaker-hearers are able to perform, but is not necessarily part of their ordinary process of understanding the utterances of others. Even random strings of words are liable to be understood as lists, rather than as nonsense. I do not find it at all easy to accommodate these facts to the view that a hearer's mechanism maps each wave-form it hears on to a complete structural description. On such a view one would suppose some substantial inhibition to exist that always delays and complicates the understanding of ambiguous or ungrammatical sentences. But no delay of this kind is REGULARLY apparent in ordinary speech, and the theory I am, albeit very tentatively, proposing seems to be more compatible with the fact that a normal hearer seems to look for sense first, and only on later reflection, if he fails to understand something, gets worried about ungrammaticalness and ambiguity.

10. I have, of course, said nothing about the nature of the operation by which a hearer's mechanism scans a wave-form for cues to the transformations it has undergone, or analyses it into its morphemic constituents; and also nothing about the nature of the conceptual network which structures the hearer's filing-system, or about the problem of context-description. But these problems arise on any theory. There are however certain fairly obvious ways of testing a theory of the kind I am proposing by exploring the importance of semantic variables in latency experiments. For example (after due allowance has been made for differences in degree of familiarity with different words, for different numbers of phonemes or morphemes, and for other possibly relevant variables), do *S*s react to *George has a square, red, wooden box* as rapidly as they react to *George has a long, wide, capacious box*, where the two sentences seem to differ in complexity of semantic filing instructions but not in complexity of syntactic description? Or do *S*s react less rapidly to *George is easy to please* than to *George is complacent*, where the two sentences seem much more alike in semantic complexity than in syntactic? And there is probably a large range of other experiments—in particular, experiments in-

volving speakers of different languages—that can be brought to bear on our choice of theory here.

Finally, I should like to ask your indulgence for the crude and schematic way in which, owing to the short time available, I have had to formulate my views on this subject. But if the theory I have been suggesting is of any value it can be elaborated at another time in a more sophisticated form; if it is not of any value, no one will regret that it has not been so elaborated on this occasion.

General Discussion

Ruth Clark, L. J. Cohen, M. Garrett, Sheila Jones,
Kate Loewenthal, J. C. Marshall, J. Morton, J. P. Thorne,
R. J. Wales, and W. H. Walsh.

The main points raised had to do with: (i) the relationship between transformational rules and psychological processes or mechanisms; (ii) the necessity of having a preliminary hypothesis governing the collection of data; (iii) the degree of interdependence between linguistics and psychology in the study of the development and use of language.

As chairman, Walsh opened the discussion by stressing the fact that both Sutherland and Cohen had expressed surprise that there should have ever been any temptation to confuse linguistic competence with performance (or with the mechanisms determining performance). He himself wondered whether there was any more justification for bringing linguistics and psychology together as 'psycholinguistics' than there was for uniting logic and psychology as 'psychologic' (something like this had been attempted by Hume, who regarded formal logic as a relatively uninteresting system). He suggested that speakers might first discuss the distinction between the psychological and the linguistic approach to the study of language and then devote some time to a consideration of Cohen's hypothesis that understanding an utterance is to be accounted for in terms of 'filing a partial description of it under the same memory-storage categories'. Both of these points were touched upon, subsequently; but were not discussed in any detail.

Garrett felt that there had been some misunderstanding of the claims made in the paper by Fodor and himself (Garrett's comments are collected together and printed in full below).

Sheila Jones maintained that psychologists should deal with language from the pragmatic, rather than the syntactic, point of view. It was not

173

to be assumed that the psychological processes involved in speaking and understanding sentences are illuminated by grammatical analysis. There was evidence to suggest that transformations are 'instantaneous' (cf. Miller & McKean, 1964); (for Garrett's comments see below.) Wales expressed his scepticism with respect to the term 'instantaneously' (or 'suddenly') in reports of experiments: one must keep in mind the limitations of the experimental situation, and of the instruments used. Ruth Clark, assuming that Sutherland was advocating the priority of data-collection (this was stoutly denied by Sutherland), advocated the necessity of an initial hypothesis. Kate Loewenthal suggested that there might be a case for postulating different mechanisms for speaking and listening, and that in listening meaning might be far more important than syntax (so that, in the sentence *My uncle brought me a jug from India*, the distinction between *a jug from India* and *an Indian jug* might be lost).

In the discussion of whether it was necessary to postulate the internal reconstruction of a structural description before 'filing' the information from an utterance (for Garrett's comments see below), Cohen forestalled a possible misunderstanding of his own position: he was not suggesting that there was a radical discontinuity between the theory of grammar and the speaker/listener mechanism; rather, that a full structural description may not be necessary, if one abstracts separately a theory of the hearer's mechanism. Psychologists must certainly take note of, and any theory of psychological mechanisms must seek to explain, the theory of competence put forward by linguists; for this theory of competence has drawn upon intuitions about grammaticalness—psychological data. However, the syntactic theory might be more relevant to the production than to the understanding of utterances; and the theoretical problems might be simplified somewhat if due allowance is made for this possibility.

Morton referred to the claim made by Savin (1966; cf. Wales & Marshall, pp. 71-2 above) that the difference in the recall time of branching and self-embedding sentences resulted from the amount of computing space that is required for the RECOGNITION of self-embedding sentences. He pointed out that, if a different amount of 'storage-space' were required for the 'reconstitution' of the two kinds of sentences, then some of the words would be 'wiped out' during the process of 'reconstitution'. This observation was relevant to the suggestion that grammar was involved in production, but not in recall. If anything, it pointed to the contrary conclusion.

Thorne felt that Fodor & Garrett were making essentially the same point as he had made in his paper: that linguistic units, but not linguistic rules, were psychologically 'real'.

GARRETT: Let me restate briefly the burden of our paper in order to clarify what seems to me a misunderstanding of its claims.

We take it as obvious that a grammar explicates what is a certain variety of psychological facts—intuitions which speakers of a language have about their language; for example, notions of what is or is not a sentence, notions of when a sentence has two or more interpretations and what they may be, notions of inter-sentential and intra-sentential relationships—in short, a set of complexly-interrelated observations about language structure. These are just the facts the linguist has demanded that the structural descriptions produced by his grammar should mark. In this sense it is undeniable that, to the extent the observation statements are sound, and to the extent the linguist has been successful in writing his grammar properly, the structural descriptions produced by the grammar are 'psychologically real'. It is to a structural description as the specification of such a set of relationships relevant to the understanding of sentences that we refer in the paper.

The manner of PRODUCING those descriptions—that is, the matter of how the relevant structural facts come to be marked by the speaker or hearer—is not clear at all. The set of rules used by a grammar is one way of specifying the relevant set of structural relationships, but not the only way. A search for an analysis of the connection between the way the structural description is specified by the grammar and the way it is 'specified' by speakers and hearers during the production or understanding of a sentence is one way of formulating the psycholinguistic problem; the abstract nature of this connection between grammar and recognition device is emphasized in the paper.

In this same vein we refer to the problem of WHICH aspects of the structural description are relevant to explanations of particular performance tasks. It may be, for instance, that mechanisms relevant to recognition or perception of sentences are not the same as those relevant to recall over varying periods of time. It does seem clear that different aspects of structural descriptions are differentially related to perception and recall (cf. our discussion in the paper of Bever & Mehler's recent findings relating regularization of displaced particle forms to the delay interval for recall.)

It was in aid of this view of the linguistic task and the psycholinguistic task that we distinguished in our paper the two senses of performance and competence which we find in the literature. That is, one inevitably distinguishes between what we observe organisms to DO and the

175

competence presumed to underlie the observed behaviour, but the separation of those aspects of the organism's competence which are language specific from those that are not is asserted to be properly viewed as a strategy for inquiry, as the result of a decision to investigate a particular phenomenon (human language) in a particular way. Hence, the question raised in our paper is of the status of the formal objects produced by linguists when they study selected aspects of human competence. How shall grammars be related to models which purport to explicate such performance variables as latency to paraphrase, or recognition and identification of ambiguity, or recognition of sentences under noise, and so on?

We no more than point out that perhaps—in light of the experimental evidence we cite—our approach may have been too simple-minded. Our assumptions about the relationship between grammar and recognition device, made in order to generate predictions about overt behaviour, have consisted of the straightforward adoption of the linguists' grammar as a sub-component of some 'performance model' to be accessed for information as an independent entity.

Obviously we cannot at this stage suggest what is the relationship between grammar and recognition device. We can suggest by example, however, the kind of fruitful relationship between linguistic formulations of the grammar and conclusions about constraints on a recognition device reached on experimental grounds. You will perhaps recall from earlier discussions references to so-called 'click experiments'. Briefly, these are experiments which purport to demonstrate the perceptual segmentation of sentences presented auditorily in terms of errors made by subjects in the location of short bursts of noise superimposed on the sentences. Initially, the explanation offered by Fodor, Bever, and myself for these errors was that they reflect the constituent structure of the sentence—its surface structure segmentation. Some inconsistencies in our results have recently led us to believe, however, that the explanation of the effect does not lie in just the number of constituent structure boundaries at any point in the sentence; rather, it has looked to us as though the significant boundaries were those of surface constituents which are dominated by an s node—that is, that only an embedded version of a sentence produces the boundary effect in location of clicks. I notice from my reading of Wales & Marshall's paper (in the present volume) that they have come to the same sort of conclusion from their experiences with the phenomenon. Having formulated such a notion, however, we naturally desired to make an explicit test of it, and we are now doing so; but there are difficulties. I want to detail those difficulties

176

and their eventual (partial) resolution because they are instructive of the kind of relationship which obtains between the information which linguists provide for us and our attack on problems in analysis of performance variables.

When we considered the structural description provided by the grammar, we found not only the desired set of surface elements dominated by s, but others as well. For instance, while the constituent *which he hit* in *the little dog which he hit went home* is dominated by s (just what we might have expected), so, too, is the constituent *little*. This latter unfortunate circumstance (from the point of view of accounting for our results with clicks) arises from the fact that in the grammar Adj + Noun constructions are formed from an underlying structure: Noun-*which-is*-Adj. In the example above, *little dog* comes from *the dog which is little*. In order to save our notions about the role of s nodes in the determination of click location by subjects, it was necessary to make a distinction between varieties of s—those that branch and those that do not. This at least was our first tentative move—to make a distinction among aspects of structural descriptions on grounds of our experimental results. You must understand that at that stage it was not a very satisfying move; it was a distinction hanging by an experimental thread, so to speak, and no more.

Let us now return to the linguists. They were not happy about the s nodes on adjectives, but neither were they willing to give up a well-motivated account of their derivation. In a recent paper John Ross, a linguist at MIT, proposed a rule for dealing with the problem. That is, in order to avoid having the grammar make counter-intuitive claims, he proposed such nodes should be deleted from the structural description. The deletion of embedded s nodes that do not branch (i.e., do not dominate both NP and VP) would be considered a condition on the well-formedness of structural descriptions. But to avoid having the grammar produce counter-intuitive results by the simple device of throwing away unwanted parts of the description is unsatisfactory for the linguist. He wants a MOTIVATED restriction on the grammar—that is, he wants to impose the rule of 'tree-pruning' for causes, so to speak, internal to the system. This is just what Ross does; he shows by several examples that the operation of the s node deletion rule interacts with other rules of the grammar in a general way.

I will cite one example, because I want to make especially clear the kind of grounds used to justify this rule. Ross points out the operation of two rules in the grammar which taken together, give unsatisfactory results: the extraposition rule and the rule of relative-clause reduction.

The extraposition rule moves a sentence embedded in an NP to the end of the sentence containing the NP, as (from Ross): *A student who had been drinking came in* is changed to *A student came in who had been drinking heavily*, or *A proof that this problem is unsolvable will be given* is changed to *A proof will be given that this problem is unsolvable*. In the relative clause reduction rule, phrases like *A jug from India* are derived from *A jug which is from India* by deletion of the *which is*, and similarly *someone heavy* comes from *someone who is heavy*. Notice the result of applying the extraposition rule to reduced and unreduced relatives. The unreduced relative clause in *Someone who is heavy must have slept in this bed* can take extraposition (*Someone must have slept in this bed who was heavy*) as can the unreduced *A jug which is from India* (*A jug which is from India got broken* is 'extraposed' to *A jug got broken which is from India*); but extraposition applied to the reduced forms produces the ungrammatical **A jug got broken from India* and **Someone must have slept in this bed heavy*. Ross points out that not only is it counter-intuitive to claim that *heavy* and *from India* are sentences, but one gets the WRONG results when the extraposition rule is applied. This unsatisfactory result can be avoided, however, by application of the s node deletion rule. Having applied the relative clause reduction rule, the s node no longer dominates both an NP and a VP and hence is automatically deleted; but with the s node deleted the string will not satisfy the structural index for the extraposition rule and the ungrammatical forms above will not be produced. Ross has a number of other examples which demonstrate the same point—that application of the s node deletion rule does more than avoid counter-intuitive labellings. It simplifies the operation of the grammar and avoids wrong results other than just those which initially gave rise to dissatisfaction.

Notice—on grounds entirely independent of each other—the psycholinguist trying to make sense of his experimental results and the linguist trying to make his grammar account for the intuitions of speakers come to roughly the same conclusion. Notice further that not only has our initial speculation about the nature of the click phenomenon received independent support but a whole range of new inferences about click location is made available. There is little doubt that both the initial s node deletion rule proposed by Ross and our notions about what affects the location of clicks in sentences will undergo considerable change.

What is important is not whether this current formulation is entirely correct, but rather that this is an illustration of the very productive interaction between linguists and psychologists interested in language behaviour. The point made in the paper by Fodor and myself was that we have been using the grammar in a restrictive way for no compelling reasons. On the other hand, as I hope the long example just given demonstrates, we do not intend to suggest that the linguists' insights are not highly relevant, indeed indispensable to our task.

Fifth Session

E. S. Klima and Ursula Bellugi

Syntactic regularities in the speech of children

with prepared comments by
Renira Huxley

Chairman **T. Burns**

E. S. Klima and Ursula Bellugi

What we have set as our immediate goal is the overall grammatical capacity of children—their general linguistic competence.[1] The question of course is how to arrive at this competence. The utterances produced —which seem the most direct access to competence—cannot give the total answer. There is really no way to determine which of the child's utterances are grammatically non-deviant in terms of his own grammar. And even if the grammatically non-deviant utterances could be reliably determined, they could only give hints as to the total grammatical capacity of the child, which includes not only what has been produced (or understood) but also what could be produced (or understood). The situation is the same as that involved in describing our own adult grammar if we limited ourselves to what had been uttered over some short period of time and faithfully gave equal weight to everything uttered, no matter how it actually came out. What is actually done, in analysing, is to select. Sentences are selected which are felt intuitively to be most free of deviances, and then one goes beyond the mere corpus to develop a more structured theory that excludes sentences which are wrong grammatically (i.e., present clear deviances) and that explains the status of the other cases. The range of difficulties that face the analyst in describing the language of children on the basis of their utterances should be illuminated by examining a sketch of grammatical structure in adult English.

Approaching the grammar of child language from the other direction answers certain of the problems—that is, from the point of view of the child's ability to understand sentences. Sentences the child understands describe the scope of his grammar more accurately than those he produces, just as with the adult. But if the child's 'understanding' of adult sentences is examined, there is some evidence to suggest that the child comprehends sentences according to his existing grammar. Where comprehension involves syntactic characteristics not present in the child's utterances it seems that this does not represent a relatively rich grammar coupled with a much poorer production device, but rather a limited grammar coupled with a liberal perceptual device that sifts out or by-

1. This work was supported in part by The Joint Services Electronics Project under contract BA 36-039-AMC-03200 (E), in part by The National Science Foundation Grant GP-2495, The National Institute of Health Grant MH 0473-05, The National Aeronautics and Space Administration Grant NSG-496, The U. S. Air Force ESD contract AF 19 (628-2487), and Public Health Service Research Grant MH 7088-04 from the National Institute of Health.

passes unfamiliar material. As an example, we tested children whose speech did not contain passives on this construction, using pairs of pictures. For instance, one picture showed a cat being chased by a dog, and another, a dog being chased by a cat. When the children were asked to point to the picture of the cat chased by the dog, they pointed to the picture of a cat chasing a dog, and vice versa (Fraser, Brown & Bellugi, 1963). We plan to use as much information on comprehension of syntax as possible in investigating the grammar of children.

A striking characteristic of the language acquisition situation is the fact that the particular linguistic ability that develops in the individual child as he gradually masters his native language is grossly underdetermined by the utterances he hears. Not only does he understand, produce, and recognize as perfectly normal countless sentences he has never heard, but he will reject as deviant in some way or other countless utterances that he has heard produced during his linguistically formative years. The child will reject as deviant all the various slips of the tongue, false starts, interrupted completions, and noises that are present in our everyday utterances. Given the external characteristics of language acquisition, the psycholinguist asks: How do any two children—to say nothing of those of a whole speech community—arrive at anywhere near the same language? How does a particular language—each time it is acquired by a child—keep from changing radically? Since language does not change radically in this situation, there must surely be some general principles at work, and it is the principles underlying language acquisition which we want eventually to illuminate.

But first, prior questions must be investigated. If one looks closely at the development of speech in children who have heard totally independent language environments during the early period of language acquisition, it may well be that each will follow an independent path in his grammatical growth and syntactic patterns. And if the limitations on what the child produces have little relationship to his grammatical capacity, one would not expect that a study of children's speech would reveal regularities in the order of appearance of structures across children. We propose to investigate the development of negative and interrogative structures in the speech of three children in order to examine some of these questions.

THE LANGUAGE ACQUISITION PROJECT

For several years, our research group (Professor Roger Brown and his

184

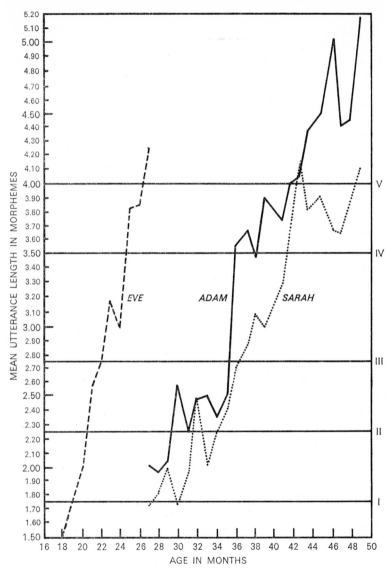

Figure I

associates[1]) has been studying language acquisition. We have as data for this research a developmental study of three children. We collected two hours of speech every two weeks in a natural setting; that is, recordings of conversations between mother and child in the home. We supplemented this data by performing small experiments to begin investigation of the children's grammatical comprehension and competence.

With these three children, each was followed by a different investigator; the families were totally unacquainted and independent of one another, and each child heard a different set of sentences as 'input'. The children were beginning to string words together in structured utterances when we began the study. One child was 18 months old, another 26 months and the third was 27 months old when we began the study. However, all three were at approximately the same stage of language development.

For each child, then, there are two to four sessions of the speech of the mother and child per month as data. These sessions were tape recorded and later transcribed together with a written record made at the time of the recording which includes some aspects of the situation which relate to the meaning of the interchange. In order to describe stages in development we picked two end points in terms of mean utterance length; the first stage is from the first month of study for each child; the last is from the month in which the mean utterance lengths approach 4.0 for each of the three children; and the second stage is between the two.

Each stage represents several thousand child utterances. From the total speech we isolated the negative statements and the questions for analysis, and have suggested outlines for a study of the development of these systems in the children's speech. We have used the children's utterances and evidence about the children's understanding of these constructions in the language of others, in attempting to consider the children's developing grammatical capacities.

NEGATION IN ENGLISH

To begin, it is necessary to specify some of the linguistic facts about the terminal state toward which the children are progressing, that is, the syntax of English negatives and interrogatives. We will consider that *negative* is a morpheme which can combine with other parts of speech to motivate negation in a sentence, and its usual expression is *no* or *not*.

1. This group has included also Colin Fraser, Dan Slobin, Jean Berko Gleason, and David McNeill.

With this notion, we can examine the facts about English negation that are relevant to the early stages of language acquisition; there are many complexities that do not occur at all in those early stages, but the basic facts about negation in simple English sentences are all relevant.

Negation and Auxiliary Verbs. The negative morpheme *no* or *not* appears most commonly in conjunction with the auxiliary verbs in English and is generally contracted with them in speech. Consider first the modal auxiliaries (*will, can, may, must, could, would, shall, should*, etc.) and notice that the negative morpheme is generally attached to the auxiliary of the sentence when there is one, and is located after the first helping verb. Compare these sets of affirmative and negative sentences:

The man will finish today.	*The man won't finish today.*
The baby can sit up.	*The baby can't sit up.*
He will have been doing it.	*He won't have been doing it.*

The negative morpheme is connected with the auxiliary verb *be*, with *be* as a copular verb, and with *have* as an auxiliary and sometimes as a main verb:

They are coming here.	*They aren't coming here.*
Her face is red.	*Her face isn't red.*
I have done it.	*I haven't done it.*

In each case, the contraction of the negative element with the auxiliary is optional. One can say either: *They can not go,* or *They can't go,* although the latter seems more frequent in informal speech.

The negative element is not attached to main verbs, nor does it stand in place of an auxiliary; thus we do not say **I wantn't it* or **I not want it,* but rather *I don't want it.* The auxiliary verb *do* occurs wherever the affirmative version of a sentence does not have an auxiliary verb, and not only carries the negative morpheme but also the tense marker. *He made one* is the affirmative sentence corresponding to *He didn't make one,* not to **He doesn't made one.* (An asterisk preceding an utterance means that this is not a possible sentence of English).

Negative Imperative. There are reasons to consider the imperative sentences of English as having a deleted subject (*you* or an indeterminate *somebody*) and modal auxiliary (*will* or *can*); and the negative imperative then begins with the negative with *do* that co-occurs with *you* followed by a verb phrase:

Don't be late, will you?
Don't trip over that.

and sometimes:

Don't you do that again!

One cannot have imperatives of the following forms: * *Can't have it,* * *Isn't coming,* * *No go,* * *Not do it,* * *Doesn't want it,* etc.

Negation and Indefiniteness. Generally, simple English sentences have only one negation in standard speech. In affirmative sentences the form of the indeterminate pronoun is *some,* as in *I see somebody* and *I want something.* The distributional facts of negative sentences suggest that if a negative element is embedded in the auxiliary of a sentence, the indeterminate form becomes an indefinite. Compare the following sets:

> *You have some milk.* *You haven't any milk.*
> *Give me some more.* *Don't give me any more.*
> *I want something.* *I don't want anything.*

When the negative element appears in conjunction with an auxiliary verb the form corresponding to the indeterminate *some* is the indefinite *any.*

Negative sentences are not only formed by embedding the negative element in the auxiliary of the sentence; the negative element may also combine with a pronoun or adverb, as in *no one, nothing, never,* or with a determiner, as in *no more, no books,* and so on. In this case, there is one negativized element per simple sentence of English, and this does not co-occur with auxiliary negation, but is an alternative.

The negative element is attached to the left-most relevant constituent; that is, the negative occurs as soon as possible in the sentence. Ordinarily it is the subject that is negated: *No one is coming* rather than * *Anyone isn't coming.* However, in a passive sentence it is the object that occurs on the left, and that would therefore be negated. Compare the negative active and passive forms:

> *No one is persuading anyone to do it.* (Subject)
> *No one is being persuaded by anyone to do it.* (Object)

The points of concern here are:

1. An indeterminate occurring in a sentence which has a negative element in it will be of the form *any.*

2. Negation tends to occur as early in the sentence as possible, perhaps as a signalling device. It is the word order in the surface structure and not the base structure which determines this tendency.

188

3. Negation can occur with auxiliary verbs, adverbs, and indefinite pronouns and determiners. Thus we find:

He never did it.
He didn't do it.
No one ever did it.

Negation not included in this study. The sections described above cover the problems which arise in relation to negatives in the children's speech as far as we have considered it in this study. Symptomatic of sentence negation in adult English is the possible occurrence of an *either*-clause (*I didn't like it and he didn't either*); the negative appositive tag (*I don't like dogs, not even little ones*); and the question tag without *not* (*He's not going, is he?*). None of those occur in the children's speech in the early stages. Negative word-marking does not occur either (*unfortunately, impossible, unmade*), nor do inherently negative words like *doubt, reluctant*.

This discussion comprises part of what we mean by the negative system, the interrogative system and the auxiliary system in adult English; that is, all the occurrences and non-occurrences involving those parts of the grammar. We will try to capture the nature of these systems by a set of rules something like those on the following pages, although undoubtedly as more is learned about grammatical systems in general and about English in particular, the form of these rules will be different. We feel that in their present state they do at least capture the spirit of this part of the grammar in a way that is compatible with other aspects of the grammar of English. One can think of the rules as giving some verifiable substance to our claim that these occurrences and non-occurrences fit together in some systematic way.

RULES FOR NEGATION IN ADULT ENGLISH

The verb phrase has at one level in its derivation the following form:

$$
\left[[T - do]_{Aux_1} (Neg) \left[\left\{ {IMP \atop M} \right\} (have\text{-pp}) \right. \right.
$$

$$
\left. \left. (be\text{-prp}) (be\text{-pp}) \right]_{Aux_2} \left\{ {V \atop {be \atop have}} \right\} \right] VP
$$

$$
or \left[[T - do (Neg)]_{Aux_1} \qquad etc. \right] VP
$$

189

This represents the underlying structure after certain transformations (the details of which are not important in this study) have already operated; for example, the positioning of the negative morpheme, the occurrence of the passive auxiliary.

Transformations

I. Replacement of *do*

$$T - do - (\text{Neg}) - \left\{\begin{matrix} M \\ have \\ be \end{matrix}\right\} \Rightarrow T - \left\{\begin{matrix} M \\ have \\ be \end{matrix}\right\} - (\text{Neg}) - \phi$$

II. Interrogative Inversion

$$Q \ [X^1 - wh + \text{indet}] - NP - Aux_1 - X^2 \Rightarrow$$
$$Q \ [X^1 - wh + \text{indet}] - Aux_1 - NP - X^2$$

III. Indefinite Colouring

1. $X^1 - \text{Indet} - X^2 - \text{Neg} - X^3 \Rightarrow X^1 - \text{Indef} - X^2 - \text{Neg} - X^3$

2. $X^1 - \text{Neg} - X^2 - \text{Indet} - X^3 \Rightarrow X^1 - \text{Neg} - X^2 - \text{Indef} - X^3$

(If Neg is treated as occurring initially in the underlying string, then a simpler formulation is possible.)

IV. Formation of Negative Pronouns

1. Obligatory

$$X^1 - \text{Indef} - X^2 - \text{Neg} - X^3 \Rightarrow$$
$$X^1 - \text{Neg} + \text{Indef} - X^2 - \phi - X^3$$

2. Optional

$$X^1 - \text{Neg} - X^2 - \text{Indef} - X^3 \Rightarrow$$
$$X^1 - \phi - X^2 - \text{Neg} + \text{Indef} - X^3$$

V. *Do* Deletion

$$T - do - V \Rightarrow T - \phi - V$$

or, expanded to include imperatives as approximately:

$$T - do - (\text{IMP}) \left\{\begin{matrix} V \\ be \\ have \end{matrix}\right\} \Rightarrow T - \phi - \left\{\begin{matrix} V \\ be \\ have \end{matrix}\right\}$$

NEGATION IN CHILDREN'S SPEECH

What it is that the child learns in becoming a mature speaker of the language is, of course, the whole system which we have tried to capture by the rules above, and certainly not those particular tentative rules. It should be understood that when we write rules for the child grammar it is just a rough attempt to give substance to our feeling about, and general observations demonstrating, the regularity in the syntax of children's speech.

We have intentionally allowed ourselves much freedom in the formulation of these rules. Even within this freedom we feel that at the very earliest stages perhaps we fitted the language unjustifiably to what we assume to be the underlying structure of adult language. These rules reflect but certainly do not describe completely the utterances produced by the child. Whenever possible we took into consideration comprehension of utterances; but comprehension, like speech, only REFLECTS the grammar. Our aim in both cases is to find basic regularities.

One of the ultimate objectives in describing such regularities is to discover—given the child's own linguistic abilities as they have developed at some particular stage and given the utterances that he hears—what system or possible systems the child will ascribe to the language.

Not very much is known about how people understand a particular sentence or what goes into producing one; but something is known about the systematicity of adult language. It has seemed to us that the language of children has its own systematicity, and that the sentences of children are not just an imperfect copy of those of an adult.

Are there hazards in considering the grammar of a child's language from the point of view of his speech? Of course there are many. One possibility is that the limitations on what is produced have nothing at all to do with the grammar but have to do with factors of memory, immediate requirements of explicitness, and the like. However, if this were the case, one would not expect the order of appearance of certain structures, and in particular certain systematic 'mistakes', to be regular across children. We want to emphasize here that we are not dealing with the expression of semantic concepts on the part of the child, or of basic grammatical notions like subject function and transitivity; rather we are concerned with the way he handles lower-level syntactic phenomena like position, permutability, and the like.

Stage I. The sentences we want to describe from stage I, are taken from the protocols of all three children:

No...wipe finger
More...no
No a boy bed
Not...fit
No singing song
No the sun shining
No money
No mitten
No sit there
No play that
Wear mitten no
Not a teddy bear
No fall!

Unless otherwise noted, the sentences included in this report represent large numbers of like utterances in the children's speech, and are not to be considered isolated examples but rather reflections of recurrent structures occurring in the children's spontaneous speech. Notice that there are no negatives within the utterances, nor are there auxiliary verbs. The element which signals negation is *no* or *not*, and this element either precedes or follows the rest of the utterance.

Let us refer to the elements *wipe finger, more, the sun shining*, in the above sentences as the Nucleus. Notice incidentally that there seems to be limited structure to the Nucleus. The sentences consist largely of nouns and verbs without indication of tense or number. Non-occurrences include inflections, prepositions, articles, pronouns, adjectives, adverbs, auxiliary verbs, and so on.

The negation system at stage I can be considered as follows:

$$\left[\left\{ {no \atop not} \right\} - \text{Nucleus} \right] \text{S} \quad \text{or} \quad \left[\text{Nucleus} - no \right] \text{S}$$

At this stage, there is no clear evidence that the child even understands the negative embedded in the auxiliary of adult speech, without at least some reinforcement. The adults at this first stage often reinforce their negative statements, as in, *No, you can't have that*, or as in the following interchange:

Mother: *I'm not sure.*
Child: *Sure.*
Mother: *No, I'm not sure.*

What is striking in the speech of the child at this stage is that he employs extremely limited means for negative sentences in his own speech, and the same system is repeated in all three subjects. In subsequent periods, the rule for negation will have a different form. In those subsequent periods there may indeed be an initial sentence adverb *no*, but this initial element is not a sufficient or even necessary part of negation.

The rule for negation that we have given serves many negative functions in the child's speech at stage 1 which will later be supplanted by other more complex rules, as the following interchanges will suggest:

Adult: *Get in your high chair with your bib, and I'll give you your cheese.*
Child: *No bibby.*
Adult: *Oh, you don't want your bibby?*

Adult: *Well, is the sun shining?*
Child: *No the sun shining.*
Adult: *Oh, the sun's not shining?*

(An adult leans over to talk to the child. Child looks up and puts up a hand in warning.)
Child: *No fall!*

Child: *No.*
Adult: *No what?*
Child: *No, Mommy.*
Adult: *No Mommy what?*
Child:...*No.* (as if she is having trouble finding words)
Adult: *No what?*
Child: *No...Oh foot...foot floor.* (pushes mother's foot onto the floor)
Adult: *Oh, you want my foot on the floor.*

Stage 2. Some of the sentences we want to describe, again from all three children, are as follows:

I can't catch you.
I can't see you.
We can't talk.
You can't dance.

I don't sit on Cromer coffee.
I don't want it.
I don't like him.
I don't know his name.

No pinch me.
No... Rusty hat.
Book say no.
Touch the snow no.
This a radiator no.
No square... is clown.

Don't bite me yet.
Don't leave me.
Don't wait for me... come in.
Don't wake me up... again.

That not 'O', that blue.
He not little, he big.
That no fish school.
That no Mommy.
There no squirrels.

He no bite you.
I no want envelope.
I no taste them.

A characteristic of child language is the residue of elements of previous systems, and the sentences produced might well be described as a coexistence of the rules at stage 1, and a new system. Let us begin with a basic structure something like:

$$S \rightarrow \text{Nominal} - (\text{Aux}^{neg}) - \left\{ \begin{array}{l} \text{Predicate} \\ \text{Main Verb} \end{array} \right\}$$

where Neg has as possible lexical representatives *can't don't, not* and occasionally *no*. The auxiliary verbs can be thought of as occurring in the speech of the children only when accompanied by a *neg*, since it is a fact that the auxiliary verbs do not occur in questions or declarative utterances at this stage. They occur only in negative sentences, and in these limited forms. This first rule can be related to the shape of sentences by the following rules:

$$\text{Aux}^{neg} \rightarrow \left\{ \begin{array}{l} \text{Neg} \\ \text{V}^{neg} \end{array} \right\}$$

$$\text{Neg} \rightarrow \left\{ \begin{array}{l} no \\ not \end{array} \right\}$$

$$\text{V}^{neg} \rightarrow \left\{ \begin{array}{l} can't \\ don't \end{array} \right\} \text{V}^{neg} \text{ restricted to non-progressive verbs}$$

where the particular selection of the negative is determined by the Main

Verb with *don't* and *can't* restricted to occurrence before instances of non-progressive main verbs.

Two auxiliary verbs appear in the negative form, *don't* and *can't*. These are considered as lexical representations of V^{neg} since there are no occurrences of *I can do it, Can I have it?, He shouldn't have it, They aren't going*, etc., but only instances of the sort described above. The negative element is also found within the sentence, but not connected to an auxiliary verb, as in *He no bite you.*

There are a number of sentences with neg (*no* or *not*) followed by a predicate. There is a limited class of subjects in this set. The negative imperative has appeared in the speech of all three children, in the form: *Don't leave me.* In the previous stage the imperative form was presumably *No fall.* There is at this stage an affirmative imperative as well, as in *Come here* and *Do it.* There are hardly any sentences with indefinite determiners or pronouns, but there are by now personal and impersonal pronouns, possessive pronouns, articles and adjectives.

It is clear that the child understands the negative embedded in the auxiliary of the sentence by this stage. Some typical interchanges suggesting discourse agreements are:

Mother: *I don't know that song, Adam.*
   Child: *Why not?*

Mother: *Well, I can't change your diaper right now.*
   Child: *Why not?*

There is also evidence that the child uses negatives to negate a preposition by this stage as in:

Mother: *Did you play in the snow?*
   Child: *No, play sunshine.*

Child: *He not little, he big.*

The system which we have suggested for stage 2, then, is the rule for stage 1, and:

$$S \to \text{Nominal} - (\text{Aux}^{neg}) - \left\{ \begin{array}{l} \text{Predicate} \\ \text{Main Verb} \end{array} \right\}$$

$$\text{Aux}^{neg} \to \left\{ \begin{array}{l} \text{Neg} \\ V^{neg} \end{array} \right\}$$

$$\text{Neg} \to \left\{ \begin{array}{l} no \\ not \end{array} \right\}$$

$$V^{neg} \to \left\{ \begin{array}{l} can't \\ don't \end{array} \right\} V^{neg} \text{ is restricted to non-progressive verbs.}$$

Stage 3. A sample of the sentences to be described, again from all three children:

> *Paul can't have one.*
> *I can't see it.*
> *This can't stick.*
> *We can't make another broom.*

> *I didn't did it.*
> *Because I don't want somebody to wake me up.*
> *I don't want cover on it.*
> *I don't ... have some ... too much.*
> *You don't want some supper.*
> *You didn't caught me.*
> *You didn't eat supper with us.*
> *I didn't see something*
> *Paul didn't laugh.*
> *I didn't caught it.*

> *I gave him some so he won't cry.*
> *'Cause he won't talk.*
> *Donna won't let go.*

> *No, I don't have a book.*
> *No, it isn't.*
> *That was not me.*
> *I am not a doctor.*
> *I isn't ... I not sad ...*

> *This not ice cream.*
> *This no good.*
> *They not hot.*
> *Paul not tired.*
> *It's not cold.*

> *I not crying.*
> *That not turning.*
> *He not taking the walls down.*

> *Don't put the two wings on.*
> *Don't kick my box.*
> *Don't touch the fish.*

> *I not hurt him.*
> *I not see you anymore.*
> *Ask me if I not made mistake.*

In the speech of the children, the modal auxiliaries now appear in declarative sentences and questions, as well as in negative sentences; so we can now begin with a basic structure like:

$$S \rightarrow \text{Nominal} - \text{Aux} - \left\{ \begin{array}{l} \text{Predicate} \\ \text{Main Verb} \end{array} \right\}$$

and suggest some rules as follows:

$$\text{Aux} \rightarrow T - V^{aux} - (\text{Neg})$$

$$V^{aux} - \left\{ \begin{array}{l} do \\ can \\ be \\ will \end{array} \right\}$$

where *be* is restricted to predicate and progressive and is optional, *can* and *do* to non-progressive main verbs.

Transformations

I. Optional *be* deletion
   $NP - be \Rightarrow NP$

II. *Do* deletion
   $do - V \Rightarrow V$

In the speech of the children at this stage the negative auxiliary verbs are now no longer limited to *don't* and *can't*, and the auxiliary verbs now appear in declarative sentences and questions, so that the auxiliary verbs can be considered as separate from the negative element of the sentence.

Indeterminates now start appearing in the children's speech, in affirmative utterances as *I want some supper* or *I see something*. The children's negative sentences have the form, *I don't want some supper* and *I didn't see something*. The negative versions are clearly not imitations of adult sentences, and indicate that the complex relationship of negative and indefinite has not yet been established. Examples of indefinite colouring or negative pronouns are rare, and do not appear with any regularity until subsequent stages.

RULES FOR NEGATION IN CHILDREN'S SPEECH

Stage i.

$$\left[\left\{ \begin{array}{l} no \\ not \end{array} \right\} - \text{Nucleus} \right] \, S \quad \text{or} \quad \left[\text{Nucleus} - no \right] \, S$$

Stage 2.

$$S \to Nominal - Aux^{neg} - \begin{Bmatrix} Predicate \\ Main\ Verb \end{Bmatrix}$$

$$Aux^{neg} \to \begin{Bmatrix} Neg \\ V^{neg} \end{Bmatrix}$$

$$Neg \to \begin{Bmatrix} no \\ not \end{Bmatrix}$$

$$V^{neg} \to \begin{Bmatrix} can't \\ don't \end{Bmatrix}$$

where the particular selection of the negative is determined by the Main Verb with *don't* and *can't* restricted to occurrence before instances of non-progressive main verbs.

Stage 3.

$$S \to Nominal - Aux - \begin{Bmatrix} Predicate \\ Main\ Verb \end{Bmatrix}$$

$$Aux \to T - V^{aux} - (Neg)$$

$$V^{aux} \to \begin{Bmatrix} do \\ M \\ be \end{Bmatrix}$$

where *be* is restricted to predicate and progressive, *can* and *do* to non-progressive main verbs.

Transformations

I. Optional *be* deletion
$$NP - be \Rightarrow NP$$

II. *Do* Deletion
$$do - V \Rightarrow V$$

INTERROGATIVES IN ENGLISH

For questions in adult English, we represent the interrogative nature of the sentence by the symbol Q, with which may be associated some interrogative word(s) (*What will that person make?*) or the element *yes/no* (*Will that person make something?*) In direct questions, the co-occurrence of Q and *yes/no* has no phonological effect, whereas in the corresponding indirect questions *whether* occurs (*I asked whether that person will make something*).

The interrogative words can be thought of as special instances of various constituents of the Nucleus of the sentence. Thus *what* in

198

What will that person make? is a special instance of a noun phrase (to wit, the noun phrase functioning as direct object of the verb *make*). To capture the similarity in syntax of the interrogative words on the one hand and the indeterminate and indefinite pronouns on the other, let us represent the interrogatives as *wh + indet*. In the presence of an initial Q, one interrogative word may be preposed (*That person will make what?* and *What will that person make?*).

The subject noun phrase of the sentence and the first auxiliary verb are inverted if Q and either an interrogative word or the element *yes/no* occurs before them (*Which person will make it?* but *What will that person make?*) Auxiliary *do* is absent as in negation, unless some element intervenes between *do* and the main verb.

RULES FOR QUESTIONS IN ADULT ENGLISH

S→(Q(*yes/no*))Nucleus
Nucleus→NP – Aux – VP
NP→(wh) + indet (provided that Q, but not Q (*yes/no*) occurs
 before Nucleus)
The verb phrase has at one level in its derivation the following form:

$$\left[[\text{T} - \text{do} - (\text{Neg})]\ \text{Aux}_1\ [(\text{M})\ (\textit{have}\text{-pp})\ (\textit{be}\text{-prp})]\ \text{Aux}_2 \right.$$
$$\left. \begin{Bmatrix} \text{V} \\ \textit{be} \\ \textit{have} \end{Bmatrix} .. \right] \text{VP}$$

Transformations

I. Replacement of *do*

$$\text{T} - \textit{do} - (\text{Neg}) - \begin{Bmatrix} \text{M} \\ \textit{have} \\ \textit{be} \end{Bmatrix} \Rightarrow \text{T} - \begin{Bmatrix} \text{M} \\ \textit{have} \\ \textit{be} \end{Bmatrix} - (\text{Neg}) - \phi$$

II. Interrogative Preposing (Optional)

$$\text{Q} - \text{X}^1 - [\text{X}^2 - \textit{wh} + \text{indet}] \begin{Bmatrix} \text{NP} \\ \text{PP} \end{Bmatrix} - \text{X}^3 \Rightarrow$$
$$\text{Q} - [\text{X}^2 - \textit{wh} + \text{indet}] \begin{Bmatrix} \text{NP} \\ \text{PP} \end{Bmatrix} - \text{X}^1 - \text{X}^3$$

P O

III. Interrogative Inversion

$$Q\left\{[X^1 - wh + \text{indet}] \left\{\begin{matrix}(yes/no)\\ \begin{Bmatrix}NP\\PP\end{Bmatrix}\end{matrix}\right\} - NP - Aux_1 - X^2 \Rightarrow\right.$$

$$Q\left\{[X^1 - wh + \text{indet}] \left\{\begin{matrix}(yes/no)\\ \begin{Bmatrix}NP\\PP\end{Bmatrix}\end{matrix}\right\} - Aux_1 - NP - X^2\right.$$

IV. *Do* Deletion

$T - do - V \Rightarrow T - \phi - V$
wh + something $\Rightarrow$*what*
wh + someone $\Rightarrow$ *who*

QUESTIONS IN CHILDREN'S SPEECH

Stage I. The questions to consider, from all three children, are:

Fraser water?
Mommy eggnog?
See hole?
I ride train?
Have some?
Sit Chair?
No ear?
Ball go?

Who that?
Why?
What(s) that?
What doing?
What cowboy doing?

Where Ann pencil?
Where Mama boot?
Where kitty?
Where milk go?
Where horse go?

Again, one can consider the elements *Fraser water, Mommy eggnog, Ann pencil, my milk go,* in the above questions as the Nucleus. As with the negative, in stage 1 there is very limited structure to the Nucleus, which consists primarily of nouns and verbs without indication of tense and number. If one considers the Nucleus of questions, negatives and interrogatives, there are few distributional distinctions which one could make at this stage. The sentences include *Want bibby, Get it, Mom sandwich, Baby table*, and so on.

The questions without an interrogative word can be thought of *yes/ no* – nucleus, where the *yes/no* marker is expressed as rising intonation. There are no other identifying characteristics of yes/no questions in adult English, since there are no auxiliaries, and there is no form of subject-verb inversion. From the context of mother-child interchange, it seems that these rising intonation sentences are frequently responded to by the adult as if they were *yes/no* questions. The formulation suggested is:

S: *yes/no* – Nucleus

The *wh* questions can be described as a list which includes only a few routines that vary little across the three children. The most common questions are some version of *What's that?* and *Where Nounphrase (go)?* and *What Nounphrase doing?* It is not at all clear that the *What* in *What cowboy doing?* has any relationship to a grammatical object of the verb *do* (that is, that it is a special case of Q Nucleus where the particular interrogative occurs as the object of *do*). What might be said, with reservation, is that, indeed, there is a relationship in the child's speech between sentences like *go NP* and *Where NP go?* but that the special interrogative form is bound to the particular word *go* and does not at all have the generality of the adult structure. Paraphrases of the above questions for the child might be: *I want to know the name of that thing*; *I want to know what you call that action*; and *I want to know the location of that object*. One might tentatively suggest a formulation as follows:

$$\rightarrow Q^{what} - NP - (doing)$$
$$\rightarrow Q^{where} - NP - (go)$$

Let us take as an example the interrogative word questions in which the object of a verb is the missing constituent and has been replaced by a preposed *what*. If one looks at the set of what-object questions, which the mother asks the child in the course of the samples of speech, one finds that at stage 1 the child generally does not respond or responds inappropriately, as in:

Mother: *Well, did you hit?*
Child: *Hit.*

Mother: *What did you do?*
Child: *Head.*

Mother: *What do you want me to do with his shoe?*
Child: *Cromer shoe.*

Mother: *What are you doing?*
Child: *No.*

At this stage, then, the children are not producing questions that even superficially resemble what-object questions, and they do not understand this construction when they hear it.

The child's interrogative system at stage 1 may be summarized as:

S→(Q(*yes/no*))Nucleus
  →Q*what* NP (*doing*)
  →Q*where* NP (*go*)

Stage 2. Some of the questions to consider are:

See my doggie?
Dat black too?
Mom pinch finger?
You want eat?
I have it?

Where my mitten?
Where baby Sarah rattle?
Where me sleep?

What book name?
What me think?
What the dollie have?
What soldier marching?

Why?
Why you smiling?
Why you waking me up?

Why not?
Why not he eat?
Why not me sleeping?
Why not...me can't dance?
Why not me drink it?

You can't fix it?
This can't write a flower?

There is some development in the superficial structure of the sentences since stage 1. Notably, pronouns have developed, articles and modifiers are more often present, some inflections (present progressive and plurals) occur, and the verb phrase may include a prepositional phrase or preverb. There are no modal auxiliaries in affirmative sentences, and only two negative modal forms (*don't* and *can't*). There are few indeterminates or indefinites.

There seems to be a gradual development of rules and not necessarily the wholesale replacement of one set by another. The same form of constituent questioning is continued as in stage 1. Although the interrogative word *what* appears in sentences which have a missing object, there are frequent occurrences of that interrogative without those conditions. It is perhaps premature to associate this word with a particular deleted element; here, as in other structures in the child's sentences, there is an indication that certain elements have been too closely linked. Certainly there is already an association of what will be referred to as an interrogative constituent with zero form and the interrogative introducer *what*. In the next stage it is quite clear that the association is made. Let us begin with the nounphrase:

$$\text{NP} \rightarrow (\text{Det}) \ \text{N}$$
$$\text{N} \rightarrow \text{interrog}$$

where *interrog* may represent any N in a question which is not a *yes/no* question (i.e. in an s of the form Q – Nucleus). The ultimate form of interrog is ϕ:

$$\text{S} \rightarrow (\text{Q}(yes/no)) \ \text{Nucleus}$$
$$\rightarrow what - \text{Nucleus}$$
$$\rightarrow where - \text{Nucleus}$$

where the nucleus has some interrogative (i.e. a ϕ) in an N – constituent. For example:

What [*the dollie have* [interrog]N]Nucleus
What [*soldier marching*] Nucleus

In the *wh*-question, all *wh*-interrogative words are in initial position; the auxiliaries are missing in all questions. The set of *why* and *why not* questions relates this stage to stage 1:

$$\rightarrow why \ (not \ (\text{V}^{neg})) \ \text{Nucleus}$$

203

where the negative *not* is related to the negation in stage 1 and some of the children's sentences still are produced in this way, and the V^{neg} is related to the negation in stage 2. A transformational rule gives the appropriate order:

why not – V^{neg} – Nominal – M V $\Rightarrow$ *why not* – Nominal – V^{neg} – M V

Notice that at no other place in the grammar at this stage do we find multiple negation, and this form is no longer produced by the next stage but may be replaced by complex multiple negation.

By this stage there are appropriate answers to most questions. The responses reflect that the child understands that the object of a verb or preposition is being questioned:

Mother: *What d'you need?*
Child: *Need some chocolate.*

Mother: *Who are you peeking at?*
Child: *Peeking at Ursula.*

Mother: *Who were you playing with?*
Child: *Robin.*

Mother: *What d'you hear?*
Child: *Hear a duck.*

The system which we have hesitantly suggested for stage 2 is:

N P $\rightarrow$ (Det) N
N $\rightarrow$ interrog (where interrog may represent any N in a question which is not a *yes/no* question. The ultimate form of interrog is ϕ.)
S $\rightarrow$ (Q(*yes/no*))Nucleus
$\rightarrow$ *what* – Nucleus
$\rightarrow$ *where* – Nucleus
$\rightarrow$ *why* (*not* (V^{neg})) – Nucleus

Transformation

why not – V^{neg} – Nominal – M V $\Rightarrow$ *why not* – Nominal – V^{neg} – M V

Stage 3. The questions to consider are:

Does the kitty stand up?
Does lions walk?
Is Mommy talking to Robin's grandmother?
Did I saw that in my book?
Oh, did I caught it?
Are you going to make it with me?

Will you help me?
Can I have a piece of paper?
Where small trailer he should pull?
Where the other Joe will drive?
Where I should put it when I make it up?
Where's his other eye?
Where my spoon goed?
What I did yesterday?
What he can ride in?
What you had?
What did you doed?
Sue, what you have in you mouth?
Why the Christmas tree going?
Why he don't know how to pretend?
Why kitty can't stand up?
Why Paul caught it?
Which way they should go?
How he can be a doctor?
How they can't talk?
How that opened?
Can't it be a bigger truck?
Can't you work this thing?
Can't you get it?

Between the previous stage and this one there is an impressive and sweeping set of developments in the children's grammar. There is now a class of verbal forms that inverts with the subject in certain interrogatives (*yes/no* questions) and may take the negative particle with it. One particular verb, *do*, occurs only in its function as a helping-verb in inverted questions and negatives, seldom in *wh*-questions. At this point, the system that has been developed bears striking similarities to the adult pattern. Notice, however, that the auxiliary verbs are not inverted with the subject nounphrase in *wh*-questions. There are other aspects that set this child's system apart from the adult language, namely the child does not produce the full set of sequences of the adult auxiliary system. In the adult system, the possible sequences are (M) (*have*-pp) (*be*-prp); that is, any combination of these, but always in that order, where tense appears always on the first, or if none of these are present, then with the main verb. The children, at this stage, do not produce any combinations of auxiliaries.

Considerable development is found in the children's grammar by this

205

stage. In addition to the noun and verb inflections appearing in the previous stage, one finds possessive markers, third person singular present indicative, and the regular past indicator. The sentences are no longer limited to simple English sentences. There is considerable development in complexity, and we find relative clauses and other embeddings present for the first time: *You have two things that turn around*; *I told you I know how to put the train together*; *I gon' get my chopper for chopping down cows and trees*; *They don't turn when I get on the floor*; *Let's go upstairs and take it from him because it's mine*;

Let us begin with the same basic structure as for negatives at stage 3:

$$S \rightarrow (Q) - \text{Nominal} - \text{Aux} - \begin{Bmatrix} \text{Predicate} \\ \text{MV} \end{Bmatrix}$$

$$\text{Aux} \rightarrow T - V^{aux} - (\text{Neg})$$

$$V^{aux} \rightarrow \begin{Bmatrix} can \\ do \\ will \\ be \end{Bmatrix}$$

$$NP \rightarrow wh + \text{indet}$$

Transformations

I. Interrogative Preposing

$$Q - X^1 - wh + \text{indet} - X^2 \Rightarrow Q - wh + \text{indet} - X^1 - X^2$$

II. Interrogative Inversion (for *yes/no* questions only)

$$Q - NP - V^{aux} - X \Rightarrow Q - V^{aux} - NP - X \text{ (provided NP is not } wh + \text{indet)}$$

III. *D* deletion

$$do - V \Rightarrow V$$

In *yes/no* questions, we have noted that the children invert the auxiliary component with the subject noun phrase appropriately. Affirmative sentences generally have an auxiliary. In *wh* questions, however, the auxiliary is generally not inverted. The auxiliary form of *be* is optional at this stage, and the auxiliary *do* is not present in the final shape of most of the wh questions.

RULES FOR QUESTIONS IN CHILDREN'S SPEECH

Stage 1.

$$S \rightarrow (Q(yes/no)) - \text{Nucleus}$$
$$\rightarrow Q^{what} - NP - (doing)$$
$$\rightarrow Q^{where} - NP - (go)$$

Stage 2.

$NP \rightarrow (Det) N$

$N \rightarrow interrog$ (where interrog may represent any N in an S of the form Q – Nucleus. The ultimate form of interrog is ϕ.)

$S \rightarrow (Q(yes/no))$ Nucleus

$\rightarrow what$ – Nucleus

$\rightarrow where$ – Nucleus

$\rightarrow why \, (not \, (V^{neg}))$ – Nucleus

why not – V^{neg} – Nominal – MV $\Rightarrow$ *why not* – Nominal – V^{neg} – MV

Stage 3.

$S \rightarrow (Q)$ – Nominal – Aux – $\begin{Bmatrix} \text{Predicate} \\ \text{Main Verb} \end{Bmatrix}$

$Aux \rightarrow T - V^{aux} - (Neg)$

$V^{aux} \rightarrow \begin{Bmatrix} can \\ do \\ will \\ be \end{Bmatrix}$

$NP \rightarrow wh + indet$

Transformations

I. Interrogative Proposing

$Q - X^1 - wh + indet - X^2 \Rightarrow Q - wh + indet - X^1 - X^2$

II. Interrogative Inversion (for *yes/no* questions)

$Q - NP - V^{aux} - X \Rightarrow Q - V^{aux} - NP - X$ (provided NP is not *wh* + indet)

III. *Do* deletion

$do - V \Rightarrow V$

SUMMARY

The speech of the three children consists primarily of a small set of words strung together at the earliest stage we have investigated in two and three word sentences. Among the early systematic aspects of child speech in its step-by-step approximation to the adult system are the following: in the early period the negatives and an ever-growing class of interrogative introducers occur first in the sentence, as sentence modifiers in the basic framework. The association of the interrogative word with other constituents of the sentence is very limited at first, restricted at the beginning to a complement of one or two particular verbs (e.g., *go*

207

in *Where NP go*). Only later does the association apply to whole categories, such that the proposing of *wh* + prefixed elements can be spoken of with any generality. The auxiliary verb emerges first (anticipated perhaps by the optional occurrence of the copula *be*) always associated with negatives (as *can't, don't*). Not until afterwards do the modal auxiliary verbs and *do* appear inverted with the subject, and then only in the *yes/no* questions (i.e the question not introduced by an interrogative word). At the same time, the modal auxiliary verbs, but not *do*, finally emerge independent of interrogatives and negatives. Not until the next stage does the inversion of auxiliary verbs extend to questions introduced by an interrogative word. Negation is embedded in the auxiliary verbs by this third stage, but the complex relation of negative and indefinite is not established yet. We have attempted to capture the regularities which we found in the speech of the three children in the rules which we have suggested for negatives and interrogatives.

Discussion

RENIRA HUXLEY

Our main topic at this conference is the nature of the relationship between competence models and performance in language. The competence model is really an abstraction; yet it is difficult to characterize the linguistic competence of children.[1] In many, by the age of about two and a half, a large number of utterances can be described in the same theoretical terms as simple adult utterances; that is, in terms of a single phrase marker with a restricted set of sub-categorizations of the verb and slightly different low-level rules. At ages younger than two and a half, however, almost none of the language of children can be described in this way, and yet it contains obvious regularities. There is here a difficult problem: both stages have somehow to be described in terms of the child's competence, and his linguistic knowledge. Chomsky has commented on this problem (in Brown & Bellugi, 1964:36):

> ...it seems to me that if anything far-reaching and real is to be
> discovered about the actual grammar of the child, then rather
> devious kinds of observation of this performance, his abilities and
> his comprehension in many different kinds of circumstances will

---

1. The author is currently engaged upon the research into children's language being carried out at Edinburgh University with the support of the Nuffield Foundation (Principal investigator: T. T.S. Ingram). It is this research which is referred to below as 'the Edinburgh survey'.

have to be obtained so that a variety of evidence may be brought to bear on the attempt to determine what is in fact his underlying linguistic competence at each stage of development. Direct description of the child's actual output is no more likely to provide an account of the really underlying competence in the case of child language than in the case of adult language, ability to multiply or any other non-trivial rule governed behaviour.

Lees (in Brown & Bellugi, 1964) and Weksel (1965), and others have made similar observations. On reading K & B's paper, it is apparent that such suggestions have influenced work in child language. The paper begins by stating that the 'immediate goal' is the 'general linguistic competence' of children, although collected data cannot give the whole answer in terms of a subject's performance at any age, child or adult. The authors also make the point that the only real way to gain insight into competence is by careful experiment. Roger Brown's group have made such experiments; K & B quote those with the passive in their introductory section. But once the discussion of negatives starts, the 'immediate goal' of characterising competence weakens to becoming what the authors want to achieve 'eventually', and they conclude their work thus: 'We have attempted to capture the regularities which we found in the speech of these children in the rules which we have suggested for negatives and interrogatives'. Capturing regularities is very different from studying grammatical capacity! K & B have produced a data-reduction scheme of a type criticized by Chomsky, Lees and Weksel. Certainly it is superior to some of these earlier studies, because the paper under discussion includes a careful examination of English negation made by Klima. Careful studies of child language need such a rigorous background of an adult competence model, if they are to be at all revealing.

Early in the paper, the authors describe the actual scope of the grammatical rules written for the three children examined: 'It should be understood that when we write rules for the children's grammar it is just a rough attempt to give substance to our feelings about, and general observations demonstrating, the regularity in the syntax of children's speech'. Their main concern in dealing with these utterances is with 'lower level syntactic phenomena like position, permutability and the like'. Thus the paper deals with the surface-structure of the utterances. There are many objections to this approach. At the earliest stages of grammatical development many utterances have the same first morpheme, for instance *no*, followed by a noun or verb. Such utterances abound with ambiguities: the formula NO + (Nucl) could be expanded in a variety of ways by an adult familiar with a particular child's language. Let me give you an example of two two-word utterances produced by a child of eighteen months, who would, I think, be considered to be at Bellugi's stage I. The child was looking for her toy which her elder sister had removed from the room. After searching for a bit she said *No Dolly*. Some such expansion as *Dolly isn't here, Dolly's gone* or *Where's Dolly* could be supplied. A few minutes later, after I had been playing with her on the sofa, bumping her up and down, she said *No bumps*. The meaning was clear enough; she had tired of the game and was requesting me to stop. The sentence was imperative in this case and quite different from the earlier *No Dolly*. K & B would have expressed both these sentences by the same rule, s[NO + Nucl]. By doing so they would have obscured the underlying difference between the two and forced the data to appear more homogeneous than it really is. Although they have one imperative similar to this in the data (*no fall*), it is not accounted for in the rules (it is mentioned in the text of the paper).

For reasons such as ambiguity, it is questionable whether the writing of grammatical rules is the real answer to studying the competence of the very young child. Rules elevate the status of the data on which they are based. Moreover, this speech does not have the same order of appearance of classes as the speech of a child in the Edinburgh survey, who appears to use both possessives and prepositions frequently to express relationships between objects and their environment, neither of these classes appearing in Bellugi's data at this stage. In our Edinburgh study we have recorded utterances like *baby up, Helen down, Mummy's rings*. The fact that two different sets of data could produce different types of rule is another reason why data-based grammatical rules are not the best way to characterize linguistic competence in children. It is certainly true that writing such schemes for children's linguistic data is essential as a first step towards characterizing linguistic competence. It is a tedious and time-consuming job, but it is only one stage in the whole process and merely enables us to attempt the answers to more interesting questions. For instance, although it is certain that comprehension of language is in advance of linguistic performance, one is not sure what is meant by this statement, since it is not known how much structure needs to be comprehended for an utterance to be understood by a child. To say, as do K & B, that a child possesses a limited grammar coupled with a liberal perceptual device is a little unclear. The grammar is certainly limited but what is the liberal perceptual device? If it means an ability to make use of situational clues in interpreting utterances whose structure is too complex for children, this makes sense. If on the other hand, some means of analysing grammatical structure is intended outside the child's range of competence, this is more difficult to accept.

Very little seems to have been done in spite of the claims made, to test the relationship between produced sentences and the child's grammatical competence. There are several possible ways of testing a child's competence which make use of obtained data to see how the child behaves with sentences. At the stage when a child has forms of utterance with and without *be* as a verb, rather than an auxiliary (for instance, *that hot, that's hot*), we can ask what this alternation means in terms of the child's competence. In order to make some assessment of what his competence with the verb *be* is, the linguist tries to elicit responses to see if these are really free variants. Giving a deliberately wrong sentence, the experimenter says to the child *Tell Dolly she naughty*.[1] The child in this case replied *she not*—a frustrating answer in the circumstances, but certainly a form without *be*. Later she was told *Tell Dolly she's naughty* and then produced the form *she's*. In other words the child accepts both forms and reproduces each in turn; for it appears that both are well established in her speech at this time.

Although K & B say that 'approaching the grammar of child language from the other direction answers some of the problems', they appear to have made very little use of this approach, either to verify the rules which they write, or to test the child's competence beyond the data available. One further remark made by K & B is, I think, revealing: they say that they supplemented the data by performing small experiments to begin investigation of the children's grammatical comprehension and competence. The word 'supplemented' gives away the weakness of the approach. They appear to regard the analysis of data as their main concern and look upon experiment as a way of corroborating data. A much sounder approach would be to regard the gathering of data as a way of getting ideas which could then be tested with the child by ingenious manipulation of the grammar obtained in the first data reduction scheme. Consider, for instance, their discussion of the question with *what + doing*, which K & B regard as a bound form. They suggest this is the case because *what* in their corpus occurs with *doing*. They support this by quoting the following exchanges between the mother and child in which the child fails to answer the question:

Mother: *Well, what did you hit?*
Child: *Hit*

---

1. This example is given by kind permission of Antony Traill, Department of Linguistics, University of Witwatersrand, Johannesburg.

Mother: *What did you do?*
Child: *Head*
Mother: *What are you doing?*
Child: *No*

It would certainly appear from this that *what* in an adult sentence form does not get much of an answer. The fact that the child could not even cope with *What are you doing*, however, makes me suspect that it was his attention perhaps that was lacking and not his grammar. That is of course a difficult problem. What it was that the child found easy about his sentence *what cowboy doing* is more readily testable and should perhaps have been tested in this situation. It is not enough to say that *what doing* is a bound form. Is it the actual structure *what + do + ing* that has been formed, or could any verb from his repertoire occur in that sentence frame? If K & B have tested for this they do not say so. From once-fortnightly visits it would be quite possible to have missed days on which other verbs occur in the same frame. The way to test whether it was the *do* or the *ing* or both together, would have been to go through the data at that period picking out other verbs and then substituting these in the frame, saying things like: *what cowboy pushing, what Dolly making*. One must be very precise in saying with what part of linguistic structure a child can or cannot cope.

Once a basic regularity had been observed in the data from which tentative rules could be written, it would be interesting to have attempted to elicit negatives from the child; for instance, in discussing the negative at stage 2 K & B remark that the child used a negative to negate a proposition. Had they examined a little further they might have found that if the negative was based on a NOUN rather than a VERB they could have included this in stage 1. In the Edinburgh survey we have deliberately used a sentence based on the wrong word to see if the child was aware of the mistake. *What pretty Wellingtons you have*, we would say. If we were lucky, and we often were, the child would answer *no is shoes*. This was repeated several times and we observed that the child had a correct series of names for several articles of clothing. It then became clear that the child could form negatives to negate a noun at this stage, but not a verb. Asking a laughing child why he was crying, I got the short answer *no* (this was with a child at Bellugi's first stage.) This is interesting and reflects the child's competence with negatives at stage 1. —not easy to write in the form of a grammatical rule, but nevertheless worth observing.

K & B also discuss the question of how child language should be

212

regarded in relation to adult language. 'Not very much is known about how people understand a particular sentence, or what goes into producing one; but something is known about the systematicity of adult language. It has seemed to us that the language of children has its own systematicity and that the sentences of children are not just an imperfect copy of those of an adult'. This statement is not in dispute; we also are interested in this systematicity; but there is perhaps a danger here of treating child language as too self-sufficient. Another linguist has suggested that the study of child language be treated as if it were the study of an exotic language. This has perhaps contributed to a concentration on obtained data in some work in child language and is further confused in the minds of some by a misunderstanding of the term 'generate'. On the contrary, it is only by keeping a really explicit version of an adult competence model in mind that progress will be made. K & B partly succeeded here, since they had an adult model; but they did not remain faithful to their stated aims.

Other speakers have mentioned the importance of studying developing language beside the other features of developing behaviour. This is so important that I would like to return to it again. We know that children perceive visual patterns differently from adults. Asked to copy a picture of two overlapping geometrical figures, the child frequently separates them and produces them side by side. The child had abstracted something different from the pattern as being mainly important. In other cases the child's comprehension of pattern appears greatly at variance with his reproduction of it. Shown a picture of a square, a child may draw a circle (his only way of producing an enclosing pattern) and substitute four diverging lines for where the corner of the square should have been. In this way we see reflected both his different perception and his differing ability to produce. His speech can show parallel tendencies: a child asked to produce sentences with several degrees of embedding may break them down into separate units; on the other hand, essential features such as a negative morpheme are first crudely attached to an utterance preceding the verb phrase, before being incorporated in the verb phrase.

If these observations have seemed over-critical of certain stages in K & B's argument, it must be remembered that they and their colleagues at Harvard and MIT have produced work considerably in advance of similar studies on this side of the Atlantic. It is indeed a mark of respect for any work if it can stimulate others, even if along rather different lines.

213

General Discussion

Ruth Clark, L. J. Cohen, C. Fraser, Julie Greene, M.P. Haggard, Renira Huxley, T. T. S. Ingram, P. N. Johnson-Laird, Sheila Jones, W. Lawrence, D. McNeill, J. C. Marshall, J. P. Thorne, P. Van Buren, and R. J. Wales.

The main points raised had to do with: (i) research strategies and procedures; (ii) memory limitations; (iii) the relative priority of syntax and phonology in the development of language.

Sheila Jones suggested that children were perhaps more competent than adults in handling certain kinds of negatives, especially negative imperatives and contradictory negatives, because these are the forms they hear most commonly in their earliest years, and such forms have the greatest 'survival value'; adults, on the other hand, have greater difficulty with negative imperatives than with the other negatives (cf. Eifermann, 1961). This could be the result of an adolescent reaction to prohibition. When the child hears the mother say *I'm not sure*, he might understand this negative form less readily because it is 'nebulous' in information content.

There followed an extensive discussion of systems, research strategies, stages, and related topics (Van Buren, Renira Huxley, McNeill, Fraser, Ruth Clark, Wales, Ingram, Marshall, Julie Greene). The paper by K & B resulted from finding sufficient identity among the progression of grammars written for the three children in question for it to be possible to collapse them into one summary statement (McNeill). Some speakers felt that, since one was compelled in writing grammars for children to rely exclusively on the speech they actually produced, it was in principle impossible to investigate the linguistic competence of children; others considered that the task was more difficult, not inherently impossible. McNeill argued that what K & B were trying to do was to give a description in some standard form, namely that of generative grammars, in order then to be able to trace the child's development towards what we know he will in fact have acquired in the final stage, adult English. There was some argument as to whether it was necessary to supplement descriptive approaches of the kind followed by K & B with (immediate) experimental tests of the hypotheses being entertained as descriptions: everyone seemed to agree that this would be highly desirable, if practicable; but it was suggested that, because of the increase in the complexity of the problems involved in an experimental situation, the K & B approach was a necessary preliminary which

214

yielded rigorously-formulated information upon which further experimental hypotheses could be based (cf. also Ingram's comments below).

Susan Ervin's work (1964) was mentioned as evidence of the usefulness of considering other individual identities across children's grammars than those investigated by K & B. McNeill pointed out, in this connection, that the correct inflection of strong English verbs in the past tense appears earlier than the correct inflection of the weak verbs; this is a strong counter-example to any explanation of language-acquisition in terms of frequency of occurrence. McNeill also indicated that in Stage 3, there seems to be a limit on the number of transformations the child can perform at one time. This might relate to the findings of Savin & Perchonock (1965) that transformations take up computation storage space. There was some discussion of the claim that speech-production in particular was dependent upon finite memory restrictions. Haggard stressed the importance of distinguishing between rote memory and immediate memory. He also pointed out that children slightly older than those discussed in the paper by K & B are sometimes reported as beginning sentences for the completion of which they have the necessary syntactic competence but as 'losing the drift' (as adults do in anacolouthon) for reasons of semantic complexity. Wales suggested that a further clarification of the notion of 'memory' was necessary: in particular it should be made clear how one should conceptualize the structuring of memory and the ordering of information in memory—the apparent increase in memory with age, might be a function of the increase in the ability to sructure information; on the other hand, there might be some way in which biological memory capacity increased.

The role of phonology in language development came up for discussion (Lawrence's comments are printed in full below). McNeill pointed out that in the case of 'Adam' (in K & B's work) the regular plural form of nouns occurred about eight months before the third person verbal inflection (e.g. *walls*); the phonological rule was, however, identical in both instances. McNeill also mentioned that Irvin had transcribed the vocalization of some eighty children from birth to about thirty months and had found that in the rank order of frequency of phone types at every age, there seems to be a stable rank order which changes with age. If one looked at the first point at which these changes in frequency begin to converge toward the characteristic frequency of adult English, one found that out of the thirty-five phone types in the table produced from the data, only four or five began to converge at thirty months and the rest had not begun to change. This suggested that the frequency of occurrence rests upon the production of gram-

215

matical speech rather than the converse. On the other hand, it had often been claimed that the intonation of adult speech appears even during babbling (cf. Jakobson's 'public speech without words'). If such intonation-contours (presumably defined over the surface structure of sentences) were present at an extremely early age, this would seem to imply that children had learned the surface structure of sentences even before they had acquired the words to go with them. Marshall believed that there was evidence to suggest that the child can produce *cats* as a plural noun before *cats* as a possessive: once again this would imply that it was the grammar that determines the phonology. Some observations made in Oxford would suggest that there might also be three stages in the development of preposition phrases. In the first stage, the child uses no preposition at all; in the second, he uses the same vowel sound (some kind of [i] sound) to 'stand for' all prepositions—merely 'marking', as it were, the place in the structure; and, finally, the prepositions are differentiated, and given a distinct meaning and the correct phonological interpretation. Marshall felt that those facts again pointed to the priority of grammar over phonology in the development of language in children.

The question was raised whether the occurrence of the negative early in the sentence might have the status of a psychological universal for language performance; but a number of speakers pointed out that, in this respect, there is considerable variation across languages.

LAWRENCE: I am, by training, a communication engineer and aspire to become a phonetician. My acquaintance with the subject of general linguistics is, as may appear, very slight. My excuse for joining in this discussion is that I believe that the human infant, in acquiring language competence, follows a somewhat similar progression. He feels the need to communicate first, and he achieves this (since he has no other competence) by gesture and by non-verbal cries. Later, when he has progressed through general phonetics (babbling) and the phonology of English (imitating and recognizing his mother's speech sounds) to the lexical use of words, he will still be largely dependent on gesture to give his utterances shape. Exclusive use of gesture is then supplemented by rhythm and intonation, to give more elaborate patterning and rudimentary sentence structure to his communications. Rhythm and intonation may, perhaps, be regarded as gesture made audible. In some speakers the rise and fall of the vocal pitch follows the up and down movements of the head, and the isochronous chest pulses that produce salient syllables may be synchronized with hand and arm movements.

At this stage the child (no longer *infans*) will be signalling negation by head-shaking and indifference by shrugging his shoulders. Questions will be given a final rise in the intonation pattern. Stress and timing may be used to identify sentence structure with the equivalent parts of a simple prototype as:

|*Jóhn*|*nó go*|*hóme*
|*Jóhn don'*|*wánna go silly*|*býe bye*

said with the same timing. The imperative mood (significantly so called!) is clearly differentiated from the indicative by tone of voice, long before the grammatical forms appropriate to the literary language are mastered or understood.

All this becomes clearer when we consider the allegedly ambiguous phrases quoted by Thorne and by Morton. The *playing card* sentences would normally be distinguished by rhythm. If we add a few semantically neutral syllables to the sentence, to ensure that the isochronous beat of the foot structure is not lost, we hear at once that:

I *dis-*|*líke*|*pláying*|*cárds said*|*Hénry*

has four feet, and that

I *dis-*|*líke*|*pláying cards said*|*Hénry*

has only three. With this addition (adapting a device proposed by Halliday) we find that ambiguity is almost impossible. As for *ask the way to the station* and *ask the waiter the time*, this is a variant of that well-known text book pair: *Take Grey to London* and *Take Greater London*. In spoken English the existence of a word boundary after *Grey* is signalled by lengthening this syllable and preserving the isochronous beat by shortening the following syllable. The distinction, though inconspicuous, is perfectly specific, and is part of the structure of the (spoken) language. The same analysis can be used for the *matador* sentences.

I suggest, therefore, with some diffidence, that psycholinguistics may be led seriously astray if it neglects to study the use and comprehension of intonation, rhythm and gesture. Those who seek to trace the emergence of linguistic competence in children's speech, should not omit to record and interpret such feature in the utterances they observe. Might it not be found that those children who show the greatest mastery of these 'pre-grammatical' structural markers, are the slowest to exhibit a competence in the use of 'literary' grammatical forms? Should not Thorne's paper have been entitled 'On reading sentences' rather than

217

'On hearing sentences'? A good test of whether a reader has comprehended the structure of a sentence is to find out whether he can speak it out loud, employing rhythms and pitch patterns that at once make its meaning clear. Speech is more transparent than literature.

INGRAM: Wales seems to suggest that the responses of a child may be altered by the presence of an experimenter but not by an observer. It is important to recognise that the presence of any interloper will modify the environment in which the child finds himself and this is likely to have a significant influence upon what he says.

Perhaps insufficient attention is being paid to the effects of environment in current studies of child speech. How much a child says and what he says are likely to differ considerably according to whether he is in the company of other children or is performing for an attentive adult. Motor performance and 'play' are likely to be much more important media of communication for the two-to four-year-old child when he is with his contemporaries than when he is in the company of adults. Differences in the grammatical structure of his utterances must be expected. It is even necessary to consider the unlikely possibility that he uses different grammars in these situations.

It is also important to remember that what the child comprehends of child speech is not necessarily what the adult comprehends. Preliminary studies suggest that children aged between three and five years may comprehend many more utterances of very young children than do adults even when the utterances of children are played to them in the form of tape recordings and without environmental clues.

Possibly different features of spoken language are important in determining the intelligibility of particular utterances to the child and to the adult listener. It is likely for example that non-segmental features are more important to the child than to adults, for it is known that children can imitate the intonation and stress pattern of adult utterances months before they can produce the appropriate strings of phonemes.

It should be remembered that most studies of the speech of children to date have relied upon adults' criteria of intelligibility; these are not necessarily the same as those of the child.

THORNE: The important point in this paper is that, for the first time in the study of the development of children's language, an attempt has been made to do more than just set up grammars representing the child's competence at certain stages—an attempt has also been made to relate these grammars. In an earlier paper (1965), Klima has shown that

218

a correct analysis of the verb phrase (more particularly of the auxiliary elements in the verb phrase) is crucial for a correct account of the grammar of negative sentences. What this present paper shows is that as the child develops an increasingly more complex analysis of the verb phrase, so the number of types of negative sentences he can produce also increases. At the earliest stage the child can produce negative sentences only by adding a negative morpheme to a nucleus. He cannot, so to speak, place the negative morpheme anywhere inside the nucleus, because at this stage the nucleus has no structure. However, as it becomes more structured, so there arise more positions where the negative morpheme can be inserted, and hence more types of negative sentences can be produced.

In short, this paper actually provides an account of what it is that develops in the speech of the child—his language becomes more highly structured. To my knowledge this is the first time that this point has been clearly made.

BIBLIOGRAPHY

INDEX OF NAMES

Bibliography

ALEXANDER, C. (1964) *Notes on the Synthesis of Form*. Cambridge Mass., Harvard University Press.

ANDERSON, B. (1963) *The Short-Term Retention of Active and Passive Sentences* (Unpublished doctoral dissertation. The Johns Hopkins University).

AUSUBEL, D.P. (1964) A cognitive structure view of word and concept meaning. In R.C. Anderson & D.P. Ausubel (eds.) *Readings in the Psychology of Cognition*, 58–77. New York, Holt.

BAR-HILLEL, Y. (1960) A demonstration of the nonfeasibility of fully automatic high quality translation. In F.L. Alt (ed.) *Advances in Computers*, vol. 1. New York, Academic Press.

BARTLETT, F.C. (1932) *Remembering: A Study in Experimental and Social Psychology*. New York, Cambridge University Press.

BASSETT, M.F. & WARNE, C.J. (1919) On the lapse of verbal meaning with repetition. *American Journal of Psychology* 30, 415–18.

BATESON, G., JACKSON, D.D., HALEY, J. & WEAKLAND, J. (1956) Towards a theory of schizophrenia. *Behavioral Science* 1, 251–64.

BELLUGI, U. (1964) The emergence of inflections and negation systems in the speech of two children. (Paper read at New England Psychol. Assn.)

(1965) The development of interrogative structures in children's speech. In *The Development of Language Functions*. Center for Human Growth and Development, The University of Michigan, Rept. No. 8.

BELLUGI, U. & BROWN, R. (1964) eds. *The Acquisition of Language* (Monographs of the Society for Research in Child Development, 92.) Lafayette, Ind., Child Development Publications.

BERKELEY, G. (1843) *An Essay towards a New Theory of Vision* (*Works*, vol. 1.) London, Thomas Tegg.

BEVER, T.G., FODOR, J.A. & WEKSEL, W. (1965a) The acquisition of syntax: a critique of contextual generalization. *Psychological Review* 72, 467–82.

(1965b) Is linguistics empirical? *Psychological Review* 72, 493–500.

BEVER, T.G. & MEHLER, J. (1966a) The Coding Hypothesis and Short-Term Memory. (Unpublished, M.I.T.)

BEVER, T.G., FODOR, J.A., GARRETT, M. & MEHLER, J. (1966b) Transformational Operations and Stimulus Complexity. (Unpublished, M.I.T.)

223

BLUMENTHAL, A.L. (1965) *Prompted Recall of Sentences* (forthcoming).

BOOMER, D. (1965) Hesitation and grammatical encoding. *Language and Speech* 8, 148–58.

BOUSEFIELD, W.A. (1953) The occurrence of clustering in the recall of randomly arranged associates. *Journal of General Psychology* 49, 229–40.

BOUSEFIELD, W.A., WHITMARSH, G.A. & BERKOWITZ, H. (1960) Partial response identities in associative clustering. *Journal of General Psychology* 63, 233–8.

BRAINE, M.D.S. (1963a) On learning the grammatical order of words. *Psychological Review* 70, 323–48.

(1963b) The ontogeny of English phrase structure: the first phase. *Language* 39, 1–13.

(1965a) The insufficiency of a finite state model for verbal reconstructive memory. *Psychonomic Science* 2, 291–2.

(1965b) On the basis of phrase structure: a reply to Bever, Fodor & Weksel. *Psychological Review* 72, 483–92.

(1965c) A reply to Bever *et al*. *Psychological Review* 72, 490-1.

BRANCA, A.A. (1957) Semantic generalizations at the level of the conditioning experiment. *American Journal of Psychology* 70, 541–9.

BROADBENT, D. (1958) *Perception and Communication*. New York, Pergamon.

BROADBENT, D. & LADEFOGED, P. (1960) Perception of sequence in auditory events. *Quarterly Journal of Experimental Psychology* 12, 162–70.

BROWN, R. & BELLUGI, U. (1964) Three processes in the child's acquisition of syntax. In E.H. Lenneberg (ed.), *New Directions in the Study of Language*. Cambridge Mass., M.I.T. Press.

BROWN, R. & BERKO J. (1960) Word association and the acquisition of grammar. *Child Development* 31, 1–14.

BROWN, R. & FRASER, C. (1964) The Acquisition of Syntax. In Bellugi & Brown (1964).

BRUCE, D. (1956) Effects of context upon the intelligibility of heard speech. In. C. Cherry (ed.) *Information Theory*, 245–52. London, Butterworth.

BRUNER, J.S. (1951) Personality dynamics and the process of perceiving. In J.R. Blake & G.V. Ramsey (eds.) *Perception : An Approach to Personality*. New York, The Roland Press.

BRUNER, J.S., GOODNOW, J.J. & AUSTIN, G.A. (1956) *A Study of Thinking*. New York, Wiley.

BRUNER, J. S. & OLVER, R. (1966) eds. *Studies of Cognitive Growth*. New York, Wiley.

CAREY, S. E. (1964) The Syntactic and Referential Aspects of Linguistic Encoding. (Unpublished bachelor's thesis. Radcliffe College)

CARROLL, J. B. (1964) *Language and Thought*. Englewood Cliffs, N.J., Prentice-Hall.

CARROLL, J. B., KJELDERGAARD, P. M. & CARTON, A. S. (1962) Number of opposites versus number of primaries as a response measure in free-association tests. *Journal of Verbal Learning and Verbal Behavior* 1, 22–30.

CHATTERJEE, B. B. & ERIKSEN, C. W. (1960) Conditioning and generalization of G. S. R. as a function of awareness. *Journal of Abnormal and Social Psychology* 60, 396–403.

CHRISTOVICH, A., ALIAKRINSKII, V. V. & ABULIAM, V. A. (1960) Time delays in speech repetition. *Problems of Psychology* 1, 64–70.

CHOMSKY, N. (1955) *The Logical Structure of Linguistic Theory*. Mimeographed, M.I.T. Library, Cambridge Mass.

(1956) Three models for the description of language. *I.R.E. Transactions on Information Theory* vol. IT-2, 113–24.

(1957) *Syntactic Structures* (Janua Linguarum, Series Minor, 4.) The Hague, Mouton.

(1959a) On certain formal properties of grammars. *Information and Control* 1, 91–112.

(1959b) Review of *Verbal Behavior* by B. F. Skinner. *Language* 35, 26–58.

(1961) On the notion 'Rule of Grammar'. In R. Jakobson (ed.) *Structure of Language and its Mathematical Aspects*, Proc. *12th Symposium in Applied Math*. Providence, R.I., American Mathematical Society, 6–24.

(1963) Formal properties of grammars. In R. Luce, R. Bush & E. Galanter (eds.) *Handbook of Mathematical Psychology*, vol. 2, 323–418. New York, Wiley.

(1964a) *Current Issues in Linguistic Theory* (Janua Linguarum, Series Minor, 34) The Hague, Mouton.

(1964b) Degrees of grammaticalness. In Fodor & Katz (1964).

(1965) *Aspects of the Theory of Syntax*. Cambridge, Mass., M.I.T. Press.

CHOMSKY, N. & HALLE, M. (1965) Some controversial questions in phonological theory. *Journal of Linguistics* 1, 97–138.

225

CHOMSKY, N. & MILLER, G.A. (1959) Finite state languages. *Information and Control* 1, 91–112.
   (1963) Introduction to the formal analysis of natural languages. In R. Luce, R. Bush & E. Galanter (eds.) *Handbook of Mathematical Psychology*, vol. 2. 269–322. New York, Wiley.

CLARK, H.H. (1965) Some structural properties of simple active and passive sentences. *Journal of Verbal Learning and Verbal Behavior* 4, 365–70.

CLOWES, M. (1966) Perception, picture processing and computers. In D. Michie (ed.) *Machine Intelligence* 65. Edinburgh, Oliver and Boyd.

COFER, C.N. (1957) Associative commonality and rated similarity of certain words from Haagen's list. *Psychological Reports* 3, 603–6.
   (1965) On some factors in the organizational characteristics of free recall. *American Psychologist* 20, 261–72.

COHEN, L. JONATHAN (1965) On a concept of degree of grammaticalness. *Logique et Analyse* 8, 141–53.
   (1966) Critical study (Review of *The Structure of Language* edited by Fodor, J.A. & Katz, J.J.) *The Philosophical Quarterly* 16, (forthcoming).

COLEMAN, E.B. (1964a) The comprehensibility of several grammatical transformations. *Journal of Applied Psychology* 48, 186–90.
   (1964b) Learning of prose written in four grammatical transformations. *Journal of Applied Psychology* 49, 332–41.
   (1965) Responses to a scale of grammaticalness. *Journal of Verbal Learning and Verbal Behavior* 4, 521–7.

CONRAD, R. (1964) Acoustic confusions in immediate memory. *British Journal of Psychology* 55, 75–84.

CRAIK, K. (1952) *The Nature of Explanation*. Cambridge, Cambridge University Press.

DEESE, J. (1959) On the predictions of occurrence of particular verbal intrusions in immediate recall. *Journal of Experimental Psychology* 58, 17–22.
   (1962) On the structure of associative meaning. *Psychological Review* 69, 161–75.

DONALDSON, M. (1959) Positive and negative information in matching problems. *British Journal of Psychology* 50, 253–62.

EIFERMANN, R.R. (1961) Negation: a linguistic variable. *Acta Psychologica* 18, 258–73.

EMPSON, W. (1955) *Seven Types of Ambiguity*. New York, New Directions.

226

EPSTEIN, W. (1961) The influence of syntactical structure on learning. *American Journal of Psychology* 74, 80–5.
(1962) A further study of the influence of syntactical structure on learning. *American Journal of Psychology* 75, 121–6.

ERVIN, S. (1961) Changes with age in the verbal determinants of word association. *American Journal of Psychology* 74, 361–72.
(1964) Imitations and structural change in children's language. In E.H. Lenneberg (ed.) *New Directions in the Study of Language.* Cambridge Mass., M.I.T. Press.

ESPER, E.H. (1918) A contribution to the experimental study of analogy. *Psychological Review* 25, 468–87.

FEATHER, B.W. (1965) Semantic generalization of classically conditioned responses: a review. *Psychological Bulletin* 63, 425–41.

FEIGENBAUM, E. (1959) *An Information Processing Theory of Verbal Learning* (Paper No. 1817.) Santa Monica, California, Rand Corporation.
(1962) The Simulation of verbal learning behavior. In E. Feigenbaum & J. Feldman (eds.) *Computers and Thought*, 297–309. New York, MacMillan.

FILLENBAUM, S. (1964) Semantic satiation and decision latency. *Journal of Experimental Psychology* 68, 240–4.

FILLMORE, C.J. (1963) The position of embedding transformations in a grammar. *Word* 19, 208–31.

FODOR, J.A. (1964a) The ontogenesis of the problem of reference. M.I.T. (mimeo).
(1964b) Explanation in psychology. In M. Black (ed.) *Philosophy in America*, 161–79. London, Allen & Unwin.
(1965) Could meaning be an r_m? *Journal of Verbal Learning and Verbal Behavior* 4, 73–81.
(1966) Review of Carroll (1964) *The Journal of Modern Languages* (forthcoming).

FODOR, J.A. & BEVER, T.G. (1965) The psychological reality of linguistic segments. *Journal of Verbal Learning and Verbal Behavior* 4, 414–20.

FODOR, J.A. & KATZ, J.J. (1964) eds. *The Structure of Language. Readings in the Philosophy of Language.* Englewood Cliffs, New Jersey, Prentice Hall.

FODOR, J.A., JENKINS, J. & SAPORTA, S. Some Tests on Implications from Transformational Grammar (Unpublished. Center for Advanced Study, Palo Alto, California.)

FORREST, D.V. (1965) Poiesis and the Language of Schizophrenia. *Psychiatry* 28, 1–18.

FRASER, C., BELLUGI, U. & BROWN, R. (1963) Control of grammar in imitation, comprehension and production. *Journal of Verbal Learning and Verbal Behavior* 2, 121–35.

FRIES, C. (1952) *The Structure of English*. London, Longmans.

GARRETT, M., BEVER, T.A. & FODOR, J.A. (1966) The active use of grammar in speech perception. *Perception and Psychophysics* 1, 30–2.

GARNER, W.R. (1962) *Uncertainty and Structure as Psychological Concepts*. New York, Wiley.

GLANZER, M. (1962) Grammatical category: a rote learning and word association analysis. *Journal of Verbal Learning and Verbal Behavior* 1, 31–41.

GOLDMAN-EISLER, F. (1958) Speech production and the predictability of words in context. *Quarterly Journal of Experimental Psychology* 10, 96–106.

(1964) Discussion and further comments. In E. Lenneberg (ed.) *New Directions in the Study of Language*, 109–30. Cambridge Mass., M.I.T. Press.

GOMULICKI, B.R. (1956) Recall as an abstractive process. *Acta Psychologica* 12, 77–94.

GONZALEZ, R.C. & COFER, C.N. (1959) Exploratory studies of verbal context by means of clustering in free recall. *Journal of Genetic Psychology* 95, 293–320.

HALE, H. (1886) *The Origin of Languages, and Antiquity of Speaking Man*. Cambridge, John Wilson & Son.

HALLE, M. & CHOMSKY, N. (1966) *The Sound Pattern of English*. New York, Harper & Row (forthcoming).

HALLE, M. & STEVENS, K.N. (1964) Speech recognition: A model and a program for research. *IRE Transactions on Information Theory*, 1962, IT-8, 155–9. (Reprinted in revised form in Fodor & Katz, 1964.)

HANSON, N.R. (1965) *Patterns of Discovery*. 2nd ed. Cambridge, Cambridge University Press.

HARTLEY, D. (1749) *Observations on Man, His Fame, His Duty and His Expectations*. London & Bath.

HATTORI, S. (1965) The sound and meaning of language. *Foundations of Language* 1, 95–111.

HEMMING, I. (1966) Honours Project, Department of Psychology, University of Edinburgh.

228

HIGA, M. (1962) *An Experimental Comparison of Six Bases for Assessing Intralist Similarity in Verbal Learning*. (Unpublished doctoral dissertation. Harvard University.)

HOBBES, T. (1839) *Human Nature*. London, Bohn.

HÖFFDING, H. (1891) *Outlines of Psychology*. London & New York, MacMillan.

HOVLAND, C.L. & WEISS, W. (1953) Transmission of information concerning concepts through positive and negative instances. *Journal of Experimental Psychology* 45, 175–82.

HULL, C. (1943) *Principles of Behavior*. New York, Appleton-Century-Crofts.

JAKOBSON, R., FANT, C. & HALLE, M. (1952) *Preliminaries to Speech Analysis*. (M.I.T. Acoustics Laboratory, Technical Report, No. 13.) Cambridge Mass., M.I.T. Press.

JAKOBSON, R. & HALLE, M. (1956) *Fundamentals of Language*. The Hague, Mouton.

JAMES, W. (1890) *The Principles of Psychology*. New York, Holt.

JARRETT, R.F. & SCHEIBE, K.E. (1963) Association chains and paired-associate learning. *Journal of Verbal Learning and Verbal Behavior* 1, 264–8.

JENKINS, J. (1963) Mediated associations: paradigms and situations. In C.N. Cofer & B. Musgrave (eds.) *Verbal Behavior and Learning: Problems and Processes*, 210–44. New York, McGraw-Hill.
    (1965) Mediation theory and grammatical behavior. In S. Rosenberg (1965: 66–97).

JENKINS, J. & PALERMO, D. (1964) Mediation processes and the acquisition of linguistic structure. In Bellugi & Brown (1964: 141–69).

JENKINS, J.J., MINK, W.D. & RUSSELL, W.A. (1958) Associative clustering as a function of verbal associative strength. *Psychological Reports* 4, 127–36.

JENKINS, J.J. & RUSSELL, W.A. (1952) Associative clustering during recall. *Journal of Abnormal and Social Psychology* 47, 818–21.

JESPERSEN, O. (1917) *Negation in English and Other Languages*. London, Allen & Unwin.

JOHNSON, N.F. (1965) Linguistic models and functional units of language behavior. In S. Rosenberg (ed.) *Directions in Psycholinguistics*, 29–65. New York, Macmillan.

JOOS, M. (1954) *Readings in Linguistics*. New York, American Council of Learned Societies.

JUNG, C.G. (1919) *Studies in Word-Association*. New York, Moffat.

229

KAPLAN, R.J. (1959) A study of semantic generalization through the use of established conceptual mediations. *Journal of Experimental Psychology* 57, 288–93.

KATZ, J.J. (1964a) Mentalism in linguistics. *Language* 40, 124–37.

(1964b) Semi-sentences. In Fodor & Katz (1964).

(1964c) Semantic theory and the meaning of 'Good'. *The Journal of Philosophy* 61, 739–66.

(1964d) Analyticity and contradiction in natural language. In Fodor & Katz (1964).

(1966) *Philosophy of Language*. New York, Harper & Row.

KATZ, J.J. & FODOR, J.A. (1963) The structure of a semantic theory. *Languge* 39, 170–210.

KATZ, J.J. & POSTAL, P.M. (1964) *An Integrated Theory of Linguistic Description*. Cambridge, Mass., M.I.T. Press.

KELLER, F.S. & SCHOENFELD, W.N. (1950) *Principles of Psychology*. New York, Appleton-Century-Crofts.

KENT, G.H. & ROSANOFF, A.J. (1910) A study of association in insanity. *American Journal of Insanity* 67, 37–96, 317–90.

KIRSCH, R.A. (1964) Computer interpretation of English text and picture patterns. *I.E.E.E. Transactions on Electronic Computers*, vol. E.C.-13, No. 4, 363–76.

KISS, G.R. (1965) *Computer Simulation of Word Association Processes*. (Report No. 3 of the D.S.I.R. Project on computer simulation of cognitive processes.)

KLIMA, E.S. (1964) Negation in English. In Fodor & Katz (1964: 246–323).

KOCH, S. (1963) ed. *Psychology : A Study of a Science*, vol. 6:2. New York, McGraw-Hill.

KÖHLER, W. (1938) Physical Gestalten. In W. Ellis (ed.) *A Source Book of Gestalt Psychology*. London, Kegan Paul.

KOEN, F. (1965) An intra-verbal explication of the nature of metaphor *Journal of Verbal Learning and Verbal Behavior* 4, 129–33.

KRULEE, G.K., KUCK, D.J., LANDI, D.M. & MANELSKI, D.M. (1964) Natural language inputs for a problem-solving system. *Behavioral Science* 9, 281–7.

KURODA, S.Y. (1965) Generative Grammatical Studies in Japanese (Doctoral Dissertation, M.I.T.)

LACEY, J.I. & SMITH, R.L. (1954) Conditioning and generalization of unconscious anxiety. *Science* 120, 1045–52.

LAFFAL, J., LENKOSKI, L.D. & AMEEN, L. (1956) 'Opposite speech' in a schizophrenic patient. *Journal of Abnormal and Social Psychology* 52, 409–13.

LAIRD, P.J. (1966) Does the passive mean the same as the active? (Paper read to the Experimental Psychology Society, London meeting, 5–7 January.)

LAMBERT, W.E. & JAKOBOVITS, L.A. (1960) Verbal satiation and changes in intensity of meaning. *Journal of Experimental Psychology* 60, 376–83.

LAMBERT, W.E. & PAIVO, J. (1956) The influence of noun-adjective order on learing. *Canadian Journal of Psychology* 10, 9–12.

LASHLEY, K.S. (1951) The problem of serial order in behaviour. In L.A. Jeffress (ed.) *Cerebral Mechanisms in Behavior*, 112–36. New York, Wiley. (Reprinted in Saporta (1963).)

LEES, R.B. (1957) Review of Chomsky (1957). *Language* 33, 375–407.
(1960) *The Grammar of English Nominalizations*. The Hague, Mouton.
(1964) On the so-called 'substitution in frames' technique. *General Linguistics* 6, 11–20.

LEES, R.B. & KLIMA, E.S. (1963) Rules for English pronominalization. *Language* 39, 17–28.

LENNEBERG, E.H. (1963) A biological perspective of language. (Unpublished paper.)
(1964) The capacity for language acquisition. In Fodor & Katz (1964: 579–603).

LEVIN, S. (1962) *Linguistic Structures in Poetry* (Janua Linguarum, Series Minor, 23.) The Hague, Mouton.

LIBERMAN, A.M. (1957) Some results of research on speech perception. *Journal of the Acoustical Society of America* 29, 117–23.

LIBERMAN, A.M., COOPER, F.S., HARRIS, K.S., & MACNEILAGE, P.F. (1963) A motor theory of speech perception. In C.G.M. Fant (ed.) *Proceedings of the Speech Communications Seminar*. Speech Transmission Laboratories. Royal Institute of Technology, Stockholm.

LIEBERMAN, P. (1965) On the acoustic basis of perception of stress by linguists. *Word* 21, 40–55.

LORENZ, M. (1961) Problems posed by schizophrenic language. *Archives of General Psychiatry* 4, 603–10.
(1963) Criticism as approach to schizophrenic language. *Archives of General Psychiatry* 9, 235–45.

LOUNSBURY, F.G. (1963) Linguistics and Psychology. In Koch (1963: 552–82).

LURIA, A.R. & VINOGRADOVA, O.S. (1959) An objective investigation of the dynamics of semantic systems. *British Journal of Psychology* 50, 89–105.

LYONS, J. (1966) Towards a 'notional' theory of the 'parts of speech'. *Journal of Linguistics* 2.

MACKAY, D.M. (1960) On the logical indeterminacy of a free choice. *Mind* 63, 31–40.

MACLAY, H. & OSGOOD, C.E. (1959) Hesitation phenomena in spontaneous English speech. *Word* 15, 19.

MACLAY, H. & SLEATOR, M. (1959) Responses to language: judgements of grammaticalness. *International Journal of American Linguistics* 26, 275–82.

McMAHON, E. (1963) *Grammatical Analysis as Part of Understanding* (Unpublished doctoral dissertation. Harvard University.)

McNEILL, D. (1963) The origin of association within the same grammatical class. *Journal of Verbal Learning and Verbal Behavior* 2, 250–62.

(1966) Developmental psycholinguistics. In F. Smith & G.A. Miller (eds.) *The Genesis of Language : in children and animals.* Cambridge Mass., M.I.T. Press.

MALMBERG, B. (1963) *Structural Linguistics and Human Communication.* Berlin, Springer-Verlag.

MALTZMAN, I. & BELLONI, M. (1964) Three studies of semantic generalization. *Journal of Verbal Learning and Verbal Behavior* 3, 231–5.

MARKS, L. (1965) *Psychological Investigations of Semigrammaticalness in English* (Unpublished doctoral dissertation. Harvard University.)

MARKS, L. & MILLER, G.A. (1964) The role of semantic and syntactic constraints in the memorization of English sentences. *Journal of Verbal Learning and Verbal Behavior* 3, 1–5.

MARSHALL, G.R. & COFER, C.N. (1961) *Associative Category and Set Factors in Clustering among Word Pairs and Triads* (Technical Report, No. 4.) New York University.

MARSHALL, J.C. (1964) *Behavioural Concomitants of Linguistic Complexity* (M.R.C. Psycholinguistics Unit, Oxford Report, PLU/64/7.)

(1965) Syntactic analysis as part of understanding. *Bulletin of the British Psychological Society* 18, 2A.

(1966) The syntax of reproductive behaviour in the male pigeon. *British Journal of Mathematical and Statistical Psychology* (forthcoming).

232

MARSHALL, J.C. & NEWCOMBE, F. (1966) Syntactic and semantic errors in paralexia. *Neuropsychologia* 4, 169–76.

MARSHALL, J.C. & WALES, R.J. (1966) Which syntax: a consumer's guide. *Journal of Linguistics* 2.

(in preparation) The probabilities of error scores and grammatical encoding.

MARTIN, C.J., BOERSNA, F.J. & COX, D.L. (1965) A classification of associative strategies in paired-associate learning. *Psychonomic Science* 3, 455–6.

MATTHEWS, G.H. (1962) Analysis by synthesis of sentences in natural languages. In *Proceedings of International Congress on Machine Translation and Applied Language Analysis*. London, H.M.S.O.

MEEHL, P. (1950) On the circularity of the law of effect. *Psychological Bulletin* 47, 52–75.

MEHLER, J. (1963) Some effects of grammatical transformations on the recall of English sentences. *Journal of Verbal Learning and Verbal Behavior* 2, 346–51.

(1964) *How Some Sentences are Remembered* (Unpublished Ph.D. Harvard University.)

(1965) Personal Communication.

MENYUK, PAULA (1963) Syntactic structures in the language of children. *Child Development* 34, 407–22.

MILL, J. (1829) *Analysis of the Phenomena of the Human Mind*. London.

MILLER, G.A. (1951) *Language and Communication*. New York, McGraw-Hill.

(1956a) The magical number seven, plus or minus two: Some limits on our capacity for processing information. *Psychological Review* 63, 81–97.

(1956b) The perception of speech. In M. Halle (ed.) *For Roman Jakobson*. The Hague, Mouton.

(1962a) Decision units in the perception of speech. *IRE Transactions on Information Theory*. IT-8, 81-3.

(1962b) Some psychological studies of grammar. *American Psychologist* 17, 748–62.

MILLER, G.A. & CHOMSKY, N. (1963) Finitary models of language users. In R.D. Luce, R. Bush & E. Galanter (eds.) *Handbook of Mathematical Psychology*, vol. 2; Ch. 13. New York, Wiley.

MILLER, G.A., GALANTER, E. & PRIBRAM, K. (1960) *Plans and the Structure of Behavior*. New York, Holt.

MILLER, G.A., HEISE, G. & LICHTEN, W. (1951) The intelligibility of speech as a function of the context of the test materials. *Journal of Experimental Psychology* 41, 329–35.

MILLER, G.A. & ISARD, S. (1963) Some perceptual consequences of linguistic rules. *Journal of Verbal Learning and Behavior* 2, 217–28. (1964) Free recall of self-embedded English sentences. *Information and Control* 7, 292–303.

MILLER, G.A. & McKEAN, K. (1964) A chronometric study of some relations between sentences. *Quarterly Journal of Experimental Psychology* 16, 297–308.

MILLER, G.A., McKEAN, K. & SLOBIN, D. (1962) The exploration of transformations by sentence matching. In G.A. Miller, Some psychological studies of grammar. *American Psychologist* 17, 748–62.

MILLER, G.A. & SELFRIDGE, J. (1951) Verbal context and the recall of meaningful material. *American Journal of Psychology* 63, 176–85.

MILLER, G.A. & STEIN, M. (1963) *Grammarama*. Center for Cognitive Studies, (Scientific Report No. cs-2.) Cambridge Mass., Harvard University.

MILLER, W. & ERVIN, S. (1964) The development of grammar in child language. In U. Bellugi & R. Brown (1964).

MINK, W.D. (1957) *Semantic Generalization as Related to Word Association* (Unpublished doctoral dissertation. University of Minnesota.)

MINSKY, M. (1965) Matter, minds and models. In *Proceedings of I.I.F.P.S. Congress*. New York, Spartan.

MORAN, L.J., MEFFERD, R.B. & KIMBLE, J.P. (1964) Idiodynamic sets in word association. *Psychological Monographs* 78, (Whole No. 579)

MORTON, J. (1964a) A model for continuous language behaviour. *Language and Speech* 7, 40–70. (1964b) A preliminary functional model for language behaviour. *International Audiology* 3, 1–10. (1964c) The effects of context on the visual duration threshold for words. *British Journal of Psychology* 55, 165–80.

MORTON, J. & BROADBENT, D.E. (1964) Passive *vs.* active recognition models or is your homunculus really necessary?. To appear in Proc. AFCRL Symp. on *Models for Perception of Speech and visual form*. Boston.

MOWRER, O.H. (1954) The psychologist looks at language. *American Psychologist* 9, 660–94.

234

MOWRER, O. H. (1960) *Learning Theory and the Symbolic Process*. New York, Wiley.

NEWCOMBE, F. & MARSHALL, J. C. (1966) Immediate recall of sentences by dysphasics (forthcoming).

NEWELL, A. & .SIMON, H. (1963) Computers in psychology. R. Luce, R. Bush & E. Galanter (eds.) in *Handbook of Mathematical Psychology*, vol. 1, 361–428.

OLDFIELD, R. C. & ZANGWILL, O. (1938) The acquisition of verbal repetition habits. *British Journal of Psychology* 29, 12–26.

OSGOOD, C. (1949) The similarity paradox in human learning: a resolution. *Psychological Review* 56, 132–43.

(1953) *Method and Theory in Experimental Psychology*. New York, Oxford University Press.

(1963a) On understanding and creating sentences. *American Psychologist* 18, 735–51.

(1963b) Psycholinguistics. In Koch (1963: 244–316).

OSGOOD, C. & SEBEOCK, T. A. (1954) eds. *Psycholinguistics: A Survey of Theory and Research Problems*. Indiana University Publications in Anthropology & Linguistics, Memoir 10. (Reprinted with 'A Survey of Psycholinguistical Research, 1954–1964', by A. Richard Diebold Jr. Bloomington Indiana, Indiana University Press, 1965.)

PARSONS, D. (1965) *Funny Ha Ha and Funny Peculiar*. London, Pan.

PETERS, R. S. (1951) Observationalism in Psychology, *Mind* 60, 43–61.

PETERSON, L. R. (1963) Immediate memory: data and theory. In C. Cofer and R. Musgrove (eds.) *Verbal behavior and learning: problems and processes*, 336–52. New York, McGraw-Hill.

PETRICK, S. R. (1965) *A Recognition Procedure for Transformational Grammars* (Unpublished Ph.D. dissertation. M.I.T.)

PIAGET, J. (1952) *The Origins of Intelligence in Children*. New York, International University Press.

(1954) *The Construction of Reality in the Child*. New York, Basic Books.

POSTAL, P. (1964a) *Constituent Structure: A Study of Contemporary Models*. The Hague, Mouton.

(1964b) Limitations of phase structure grammars. In Fodor & Katz (1964).

(1964c) Underlying and superficial linguistic structure. *Harvard Educational Review* 34, 246–66.

POSTMAN, L. (1951) Toward a general theory of cognition. In J. Rohrer & M. Sherif (eds.) *Social Psychology at the crossroads*. New York, Harper & Brothers.

RAZRAN, G. (1961) The observable unconscious and the inferable conscious in current Soviet psychophysiology. *Psychological Review* 68, 81–140.

RICHARDS, I.A. (1929) *Practical Criticism.* New York, Harcourt, Brace.

RICHARDSON, J. (1962) The learning of concept names mediated by concept examples. *Journal of Verbal Learning and Verbal Behavior* 1, 281–8.

RIESS, B.F. (1940) Semantic conditioning involving the galvanic skin reflex. *Journal of Experimental Psychology* 26, 238–40.

ROBERTS, R. & MARSHALL, J.C. (1966) Psychological studies of semi-sentences (forthcoming).

ROCK, I. (1962) A neglected aspect of the problem of recall: the Höffding function. In J. Scher (ed.) *Theories of Mind,* 645–59. New York, Free Press.

ROSENBERG, S. (1965) ed., *Directions in Psycholinguistics.* New York, Macmillan.

ROZEBOOM, W.W. (1960) Do stimuli elicit behavior? A study in the logical foundations of behavioristics. *Philosophy of Science* 27, 159–70.

RUBENSTEIN, H. & ABORN, M. (1960) Psycholinguistics. *Annual Review of Psychology* 11, 291–322.

RUSSELL, W.A. & JENKINS, J.J. (1954) The complete Minnesota norms for responses to 100 words from the Kent-Rosanoff word association test. (Tech. Ref. No. 11, contract N8–ONR–66216.)

RUSSELL, W.A. & STORMS, L.H. (1955) Implicit verbal chaining in paired-associate learning. *Journal of Experimental Psychology* 49, 267–93.

SANDMANN, M. (1954) *Subject and Predicate : A Contribution to the Theory of Syntax.* (Edinburgh University Publications, Language & Literature, 5.) Edinburgh, Edinburgh University Press.

SAPORTA, S. (1961) ed. *Psycholinguistics : A Book of Readings.* New York, Holt.

SAPORTA, S., BLUMENTHAL, A., LACKOWSKI, P. & REIFF, D, (1965) Grammatical models and language learning. In S. Rosenberg (1965: 15–28).

SAVIN, H. (1966) Grammatical structure and the immediate recall of English sentences: 2. Embedded clauses (forthcoming).

SAVIN, H.B. & PERCHONOCK, E. (1965) Grammatical structure and the immediate recall of English sentences. *Journal of Verbal Learning and Verbal Behavior* 4, 348–53.

SCHEFFLER, I. (1964) *The Anatomy of Inquiry*. London, Routledge & Kegan Paul.

SCHLESINGER, I. (1966) *Sentence Structure and the Reading Process*. The Hague, Mouton.

SHANNON, C.E. (1948) A mathematical theory of communication. *Bell System Technical Journal* 27, 379–423.

SHANNON, C. (1951) Prediction and entropy of printed English. *Bell System Technical Journal* 30, 50–64.

SKINNER, B.F. (1938) *The Behavior of Organisms : An Experimental Analysis*. New York, Appleton-Century-Crofts.

(1950) Are theories of learning necessary? *Psychological Review* 57, 193–216.

(1957) *Verbal Behavior*. New York, Appleton-Century-Crofts.

SLAMENCA, N. (1959) Studies of retention of connected discourse. *American Journal of Psychology* 72, 409–16.

(1960) Retroactive inhibition of connected discourse of similarity of topic. *Journal of Experimental Psychology* 60, 245–9.

SLOBIN, D.I. (1963) *Grammatical Transformations in Childhood and Adulthood* (Unpublished doctoral dissertation. Harvard University.)

(1965) *Grammatical Development in Russian-speaking Children*. Center for Human Growth and Development. The University of Michigan, Rept. No. 8, 1965.

(1966) The acquisition of Russian as a native language. In Smith & Miller (1966).

SMITH, D.E.P. & RAYGOR, A.L. (1956) Verbal satiation and personality. *Journal of Abnormal and Social Psychology* 52, 323–6.

SMITH F. & MILLER, G.A. (1966) eds., *The Genesis of Language : In Children and Animals*. Cambridge Mass., M.I.T. Press.

SPERLING, G. (1963) A model for visual memory tasks. *Human Factors* 5, 19–32.

SPIELBERGER, C.D. (1965) Theoretical and epistemological issues in verbal conditioning. In Rosenberg (1965).

STAAL, J.F. (1965) Review of Katz & Postal (1964). *Foundations of Language* 1, 133–54.

STOCKWELL, R.P. (1963) The transformational model of generative or predicative grammar. In P. Garvin (ed.) *Natural Language and the Computer*, 23–46. New York, McGraw-Hill.

STOLZ, W. (1965) A probabilistic procedure for grouping words into phrases. *Language and Speech* 8, 219–35.

THORNE, J.P. (1965) Stylistics and generative grammars. *Journal of Linguistics* 1, 49–59.

237

THORNE, J.P., DEWAR, H., WHITFIELD, H., BRATLEY, P. (1965) *A model for the perception of syntactic structure.* University of Edinburgh, English Language Research Unit (mimeo).

THUMB, A. & MARBE, K. (1901) *Experimentelle Untersuchungen über die Psychologischen Grundlagen der Sprachlichen Analogiebildung.* Leipzig, Engelmann.

TREISMAN, A. (1961) *Attention and Speech.* (Unpublished D. Phil. dissertation. Oxford University.)

(1964a) Selective attention in man. *British Medical Bulletin* 20, 12–16.

(1964b) Monitoring and storage of irrelevant messages in selective attention. *Journal of Verbal Learning and Verbal Behavior* 3, 449–59.

UNDERWOOD, B.J. (1965) The language repertoire and some problems in verbal learning. In Rosenberg (1965: 99–120).

UNDERWOOD, B.J. & RICHARDSON, J. (1956) Verbal concept learning as a function of instructions and dominance level. *Journal of Experimental Psychology* 51, 229–38.

VERPLANCK, W. (1954) Burrhus F. Skinner. In W. Estes *et al. Modern Learning Theory.* New York, Appleton-Century-Crofts.

WALES, R.J. (1964) Problems of repetition in verbal learning. (Paper read at the meeting of the British Psychological Society, London, December.)

(forthcoming) Some influence of grammatical structure on encoding English sentences.

WALES, R.J. & GRANT, N. (1966) Contextual generalization with adults (forthcoming).

WASON, P.C. (1961) Response to affirmative and negative binary statements. *British Journal of Psychology* 52, 133–42.

(1965) The contexts of plausible denial. *Journal of Verbal Learning and Verbal Behavior* 4, 7–11.

WASON, P.C. & JONES, S. (1963) Negatives: denotation and connotation. *British Journal of Psychology* 54, 299–307.

WEINREICH, U. (1963) On the semantic structure of language. In J. Greenberg (ed.) *Universals of Language.* Cambridge Mass., M.I.T. Press.

WEKSEL, W. (1965) Review of Bellugi & Brown (1964). *Language* 41, 692–709.

WELLEK, R. & WARREN, A. (1949) *Theory of Literature.* New York, Harcourt, Brace.

WHITEHORN, J.C. (1959) Problems of communication between

physicians and schizophrenic patients. In P. H. Hoch & J. Zubin (eds.) *Psychopathology of Communication*. New York, Grune & Stratton.

WICKELGREN, W. (1965) Acoustic similarity and retroactive interference in short-term memory. *Journal of Verbal Learning and Verbal Behavior* 4, 53–61.

WITTGENSTEIN, L. (1953) *Philosophical Investigations*. Oxford, Basil Blackwell.

WOODWORTH, R. S. (1938) *Experimental Psychology*. New York, Holt.

YELEN, D. R. & SCHULZ, R. W. (1963) Verbal satiation? *Journal of Verbal Learning and Verbal Behavior* 1, 372–7.

YNGVE, V. (1960) A model and a hypothesis for language structure. *Proceedings of the American Philosophical Society* 104, 444–66.

ZWICKY, FRIEDMAN, HALL & WALKER (1965) The MITRE Syntactic Analysis Routine for Transformational Grammars. (Information System Language Studies No. 9, August 1965, MTP–9.)

Index of Names

241